Getting Started with

Microsoft®
Excel 3
for Windows™

Getting Started with

Microsoft® Excel 3

for Windows™

Ralph Soucie

PUBLISHED BY
Microsoft Press
A Division of Microsoft Corporation
One Microsoft Way
Redmond, Washington 98052-6399

Library of Congress Cataloging-in-Publication Data

Soucie, Ralph, 1952–
    Getting started with Microsoft Excel / Ralph Soucie.
        p.   cm.   -- (Getting started right)
    Includes index.
    ISBN 1-55615-322-8
    1. Microsoft Excel (Computer program)   2. Business--Computer
programs. I. Title. II. Series.
    HF5548.4.M523S675   1991
    650'.0285'5369--dc20   91-10778
                                            CIP

Printed and bound in the United States of America.

   3 4 5 6 7 8 9 MLML 6 5 4 3 2 1

Distributed to the book trade in Canada by Macmillan of Canada, a division of
Canada Publishing Corporation.

Distributed to the book trade outside the United States and Canada by Penguin Books Ltd.

Penguin Books Ltd., Harmondsworth, Middlesex, England
Penguin Books Australia Ltd., Ringwood, Victoria, Australia
Penguin Books N.Z. Ltd., 182-190 Wairau Road, Auckland 10, New Zealand

British Cataloging-in-Publication Data available.

Acquisitions Editor: Marjorie Schlaikjer
Project Editor: Online Press Inc.
Technical Editor: Online Press Inc.

To the memory of Leonard and Maria Soucie

Contents

Acknowledgments

I would like to thank the following people for contributing to this book:

Marjorie Schlaikjer, Microsoft Press, for shepherding the project through its many phases; Joyce Cox and her team at Online Press for their strong editorial contribution; Sally Brunsman, Microsoft Press, for her timely comments; Mary DeJong, Microsoft Press, for her prompt technical assistance; and Lucinda Rowley, Microsoft Press, for helping out in many little ways.

I would also like to thank Jim Beley, Fog Press, for developing the idea that eventually became this book.

Finally, thanks to the product development team at Microsoft Corporation for their outstanding work on version 3 of Microsoft Excel.

Introduction

When Microsoft Excel was first introduced, it was a new phenomenon in the MS-DOS world. However, the graphical, mouse-driven interface spearheaded by Excel in the 1980s has now become the standard by which other spreadsheet programs are judged. Microsoft Excel version 3 builds on that standard. Numerous added features and functions make it more powerful than earlier versions. New visual elements and mouse capability make it an effective thinking tool, freeing you from procedural concerns so that you can concentrate on the task at hand. Improved linking capabilities reflect the generally accepted principle that spreadsheet programs of the 1990s must include a variety of gateways to other data sources.

WHAT'S NEW WITH VERSION 3

With Microsoft Excel version 3, you'll spend more time solving problems and less time sweating the details. Excel's new tool bar sports an impressive array of icons, many of which represent features that automate mundane tasks. The tool bar also allows you to draw lines, boxes, and curves. Colors, patterns, and graphic images can now be added to worksheets. A worksheet-outlining capability allows you to organize your work in a new way. A number of smaller improvements have also been made to all areas of the program to eliminate drudgery and enhance productivity.

In addition, Excel is now on friendlier terms with the outside world, particularly with Lotus 1-2-3. Linking Excel worksheets is also easier, and the new Consolidate command allows you to summarize several identically formatted worksheets in a separate worksheet.

HARDWARE REQUIREMENTS

To use Microsoft Excel, you need the following equipment:

- An Industry Standard Architecture (ISA) computer, such as an IBM PC/AT or compatible, or Micro Channel Architecture (MCA) computer, such as an IBM Personal System/2 or compatible.

- At least 1 MB of memory (2.5 MB if you use OS/2).

- One floppy-disk drive and a hard disk with at least 2.5 MB of available space.

■ A VGA, EGA, or compatible display, or a Hercules Graphics card or compatible display.

Technically, a mouse is optional equipment, but we regard it as a requirement, and we assume that you have a mouse installed. However, in Chapter 1, "Getting Acquainted," we include instructions for keyboard users so that they can start learning Excel right away.

You must have installed DOS version 3.1 or later and Microsoft Windows version 3. (For more information on Microsoft Windows, see Appendix B, "Using Excel with Other Windows Applications.")

USING THIS BOOK

This book is a complete introduction to Microsoft Excel for Windows. It is designed to get you up and running in the shortest possible time. Working through all the chapters and experimenting on your own is the quickest way to become a near-expert Excel user. A few advanced topics, such as auditing tools and the Solver, are not covered. Completing the book, however, will give you a very solid foundation for further exploration.

Getting Started with Microsoft Excel is divided into five sections, one each for worksheets, charts, databases, and macros, and one for appendixes.

Section I (Chapters 1 through 6) is devoted to worksheets. Chapter 1 is a general introduction. You learn how to move around the worksheet, carry out commands, enter data, and save your work. Chapter 2 discusses formulas and functions. The chapter also shows you how to assign names to ranges within the worksheet and how to perform date and time computations. Chapter 3 shows you how to revise worksheets with cut-and-paste commands. You also learn how to attach notes to cells and create worksheet outlines. In Chapter 4 you learn how to format worksheets to display data the way you want it. Chapter 5 teaches how to link worksheets and consolidate data. Finally, Chapter 6 covers printing Microsoft Excel documents. You learn how to print titles, create headers and footers, and position page breaks.

Section II (Chapters 7 and 8) shows you how to produce charts from Microsoft Excel worksheet data and how to format them for maximum impact.

Section III (Chapters 9 and 10) covers Microsoft Excel database operations. Chapter 9 tells you how to define a database, how to use Excel's data form to examine and edit records in the database, and how to sort the database. Chapter 10 covers the use of criteria to extract selected data from the database.

Section IV (Chapters 11 and 12) discusses Microsoft Excel macros. Chapter 11 teaches how to use the macro recorder to automate worksheet operations, and Chapter 12 introduces Excel's macro language.

Section V contains three appendixes. Appendix A helps you with the installation of Microsoft Excel on your hard disk, Appendix B offers helpful information about using Excel with other Microsoft Windows applications, and Appendix C gives Lotus 1-2-3 users guidance in transferring their spreadsheet data files to Microsoft Excel.

How to Get the Most from This Book

You will get the best results from this book if you read the first six chapters in sequence. You can cover Sections II and III in any order. Section IV, Macros, should generally be left for last. However, if you have an immediate need to automate worksheet tasks, you can skip from Section I to Section IV without any significant problems.

Naturally, you can stop working at any time and pick up later where you left off. Before ending a Microsoft Excel session, however, be sure to save your work first. (Consult Chapter 1 for instructions on saving files.)

TYPOGRAPHIC CONVENTIONS

Getting Started with Microsoft Excel uses certain typographic conventions for clarity. When the text instructs you to enter data, either the data is printed on a line by itself in special type, as in the following phrase:

```
March 1992
```

or, when an instruction is embedded in a paragraph, the data to be entered is printed in italic—for example, "Type *alsports* and press Enter."

Keystroke combinations requiring you to hold down one key while pressing another are represented in two ways. Sometimes, especially in the earlier chapters, the combinations are described in detail: "Hold down the Ctrl key while pressing the Enter key." At other times, the combinations are abbreviated: "Press Ctrl-Enter."

Special symbols draw your attention to Tips and Cautions throughout the text to alert you to techniques for saving time and avoiding errors.

A FINAL WORD

Mastering the many powerful features of Microsoft Excel is an easy and enjoyable experience. Simply place *Getting Started with Microsoft Excel* next to your keyboard, turn to Chapter 1, and have fun!

SECTION I

Worksheets

Chapter 1

Getting Acquainted

In this chapter, we introduce Microsoft Excel version 3 and lay the groundwork for the rest of the book. Because you need Microsoft Windows version 3 to run Excel, we first discuss some Windows basics. Then we start Excel and take a look at the components of a worksheet. After showing you a few fundamentals, such as how to move around the screen, select cells, choose commands from menus, and work with dialog boxes, we pull the pieces together by creating a simple worksheet that summarizes the retail sales of a sporting goods store.

WINDOWS BASICS

In this section, we assume that you've already installed Microsoft Windows version 3 using the Windows Setup program. If you haven't, take a moment to do that now. Appendix A, ''Installing Microsoft Excel,'' summarizes the installation procedure. You can also consult the Microsoft Excel documentation. Because both Windows and Excel are easier to use with a mouse, we also assume that you have installed a mouse and that you know how to carry out basic mouse operations, such as clicking, double-clicking, and dragging. For those of you who have not yet purchased a mouse, this chapter describes how to perform tasks both using the mouse and using the keyboard, but from Chapter 2 on, we mention keyboard methods only when they provide handy shortcuts.

 Clicking means moving the mouse pointer to an object and pressing and releasing the mouse button. Double-clicking means moving the mouse pointer to an object and pressing and releasing the mouse button twice in rapid succession. Dragging means moving the mouse pointer to an onscreen object, pressing the mouse button, and then moving the mouse while holding down the button.

 Unless you specify otherwise, Excel responds only if you use the left mouse button. If you prefer to use the right button, you can make that button active by using the Mouse option on the Windows Control Panel.

You start the Windows program by typing *win* at the DOS prompt. Assuming that you have not customized Windows in any way, the Program Manager window is now displayed on your screen.

 This book assumes that your computer is not connected to a network. If you are working on a network, Microsoft Excel will operate exactly as we describe here, but the procedure for starting Windows may be different.

Windows arranges pictorial representations, called *icons*, of the programs you have installed in Windows into categories, called *groups*. These groups also have icons. When you install Microsoft Excel, Windows puts the Excel icon in the Microsoft Excel 3.0 group. This group's window is now displayed on your screen, as it is in Figure 1-1. If the group appears instead as an icon at the bottom of the Program Manager window, double-click the icon to open the

Microsoft Excel 3.0 group window. (With the keyboard, hold down the Alt key and press W to display the Window menu, and then type the number to the left of *Microsoft Excel 3.0*.)

The Microsoft Excel 3.0 group window also displays icons for the particular Windows application programs you have installed on your computer.

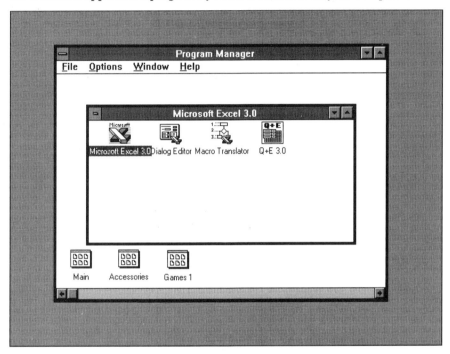

FIGURE 1-1. *The Microsoft Excel 3.0 group window before you start Microsoft Excel.*

STARTING MICROSOFT EXCEL

Starting Microsoft Excel is easy. Simply point to the icon labeled *Microsoft Excel 3.0*, and double-click the mouse button. (With the keyboard, press the direction keys to move the highlight to the Excel icon, and then press Enter.) After a few seconds, you see the screen shown in Figure 1-2 on the next page.

 You can start Microsoft Excel directly from the DOS prompt by typing win excel. *This command first loads Windows and then automatically runs Excel.*

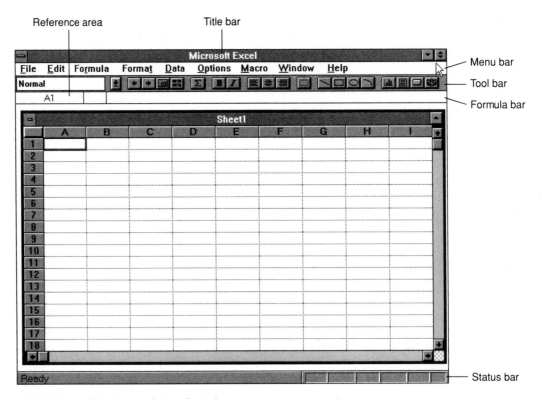

FIGURE 1-2. *The Microsoft Excel window.*

A TOUR OF THE MICROSOFT EXCEL WINDOW

When you first start the Excel program, its window, labeled *Microsoft Excel*, takes up most of the screen. The Microsoft Excel window has many components that you use to size and move the window, and to perform Excel operations. We'll discuss some of these components now, and you'll learn about others later in this chapter.

A *title bar* appears at the top of the Microsoft Excel window. At the left end of the title bar is a box with a minus-sign icon. This icon represents the Application Control menu (discussed later in this chapter). At the right end of the title bar are two boxes, one with a down arrowhead icon and the other with stacked up and down arrowhead icons. These boxes are the Minimize and Restore buttons, which allow you to shrink and expand the Microsoft Excel window.

Unless you are familiar with the Minimize, Maximize, and Restore buttons, which are standard features of all Windows applications, we recommend that you experiment with them on your own, with a practice document on your screen, so that you know what to expect when you click these buttons. Clicking the Minimize button, for example, "minimizes" the Excel program to an icon behind the Program Manager screen. To "maximize" the program back into a window, hold down the Alt key and press Esc until the Microsoft Excel icon is visible, and then double-click the icon.

Below the Microsoft Excel window title bar is the *menu bar*, which lists the names of nine menus, each containing commands that you use to give instructions to Excel. Below the menu bar is the *tool bar*. This new Excel 3 feature consists of 16 icons; some represent common program operations, and some allow you to create simple shapes. You can use the tool bar only if you have a mouse. (You'll learn how to use the tool-bar icons and you'll see the drawing tools in action in Chapter 4, "Enhancing Your Worksheets.")

 *If you don't have a mouse, Excel does not display the tool bar. To see the tool bar, turn it on by pressing Ctrl-7. Press Ctrl-7 again to turn it off.*

Below the tool bar is the *formula bar*, which has three parts. The *reference area* at the left end shows the address of the active cell. (You'll learn about the active cell in a moment.) The middle and right areas of the formula bar are now blank. You use them when you enter or change data.

A *status bar* appears at the bottom of the Microsoft Excel window. The left part of the bar displays helpful messages. You now see the message *Ready*, indicating that the program is ready to accept data or to carry out commands. The right part of the status bar contains *keyboard-status indicators*. Right now, this part is blank; but if you press the Caps Lock and Num Lock keys, two indicators appear on the screen. Figure 1-3 shows these indicators, which tell you that any text you enter will appear in capital letters and that pressing the keys on the numeric keypad will enter numbers rather than move the active cell. (We discuss the active cell shortly.)

FIGURE 1-3. *The status bar, displaying the Caps Lock and Num Lock indicators.*

A TOUR OF THE DOCUMENT WINDOW

Within the Microsoft Excel window is a *document window.* The document window currently contains *Sheet1*, a blank *worksheet*. A worksheet is like a gigantic piece of columnar paper in which data is organized by location. Only a small portion of the worksheet, which can potentially have 256 columns and 16,834 rows, is shown in the document window.

A *title bar* at the top of the document window displays the title of the worksheet that appears in the window. (The worksheet is named *Sheet1* in this example.) As with the Microsoft Excel window title bar, at the left end of the document window title bar is a box with a minus-sign icon. This icon represents the Document Control menu (discussed later in this chapter). At the right end of the title bar is a box with an up arrowhead icon. You can use this Maximize button to quickly expand the document window to fill the whole screen.

 The Document Control-menu icon also serves as a close box. Double-clicking the close box is a quick way of closing the document window.

The document window is surrounded by a narrow *border.* Down the right side and across the bottom of the window are *scroll bars.* If you create a worksheet that is too large to be displayed in its entirety in the document window, you use the scroll bars to move different parts of the worksheet into view. (You'll see how in a moment.)

THE MOUSE POINTER

When you move the mouse pointer around the Microsoft Excel window, the pointer often changes shape to signal what will happen if you click the mouse in that area of the window. While the mouse pointer is over the worksheet in the document window, the pointer resembles a plus sign. Within the formula bar, the pointer is shaped like an I-beam, which is tailor-made for positioning an insertion point accurately between two characters. Within the menu bar, the pointer is shaped like an arrow. Table 1-1 illustrates the pointer shapes you are most likely to see.

Shape	Location
✛	Over the worksheet cells
↖	Over the title bar, tool bar (except as noted below), icons, and menu bar
I	In the formula bar and in the text box at the left end of the tool bar
↔ ↕	Over a column or row header (for sizing)
⇔ ⇕	Over the document-window borders
⬉	At the bottom-right and top-left corners of the window border
⬀	At the top-right and bottom-left corners of window border
⇕ ⬌	Over the window split bars

TABLE 1-1. *The most common shapes of the Microsoft Excel mouse pointer.*

UNDERSTANDING CELLS

Every Microsoft Excel worksheet is divided into a grid of 256 columns and 16,384 rows. Across the top of the worksheet are the *column headers*, labeled A, B, C, and so on. Down the left side are the *row headers*, labeled 1, 2, 3, and so on. The intersection of a column and a row is a *cell*. Right now, each cell is surrounded by dotted lines known as *gridlines*.

Each item of data—text, a number, or a formula—resides in a cell. Each cell has an *address* that consists of the column letter followed by the row number; for example, the address C5 refers to the cell at the intersection of column C and row 5.

Notice that cell A1 in *Sheet1* is surrounded by a heavy border. This border indicates that cell A1 is the *active cell*—the cell that will be affected by the commands you choose and that will receive any data you enter. Only one cell can be active at a time. As we mentioned earlier, the reference area of the formula bar displays the address of the active cell.

Many Microsoft Excel commands operate on particular cells within the document. To tell Excel which cells the command should affect, you *select* individual cells or groups of cells before issuing the command.

Selecting Individual Cells

To select a cell with the mouse, simply move the mouse pointer over the cell, and click. The heavy border then surrounds the new active cell, indicating that it is selected.

Selecting cells with the keyboard

To select a cell with the keyboard, press a direction key. (Be sure that Num Lock is turned off; otherwise, you'll enter numbers in the worksheet instead of selecting cells.) Starting from cell A1, press the Right (→) direction key once to move to cell B1. Hold down the Right direction key to move the active cell steadily to the right. If you continue pressing the Right direction key after the cell at the far right of the window is active, the window scrolls to the right so that you can select the cell in the next column. Similarly, you can select cells to the left, above, and below the currently active cell by pressing the Left (←), Up (↑), and Down (↓) direction keys.

Pressing the Home key moves the active cell to column A *within the current row.* For example, if cell I14 is active, pressing Home selects cell A14. To select cell A1, regardless of which row currently contains the active cell, hold down the Ctrl key, and press the Home key.

To select the cell in the top-left corner of the *current window* (the part of the worksheet now displayed on the screen), press the Scroll Lock key to prevent the worksheet from scrolling (*SCRL* appears toward the right end of the status bar), and then press the Home key. To select the cell in the bottom-right corner of the current window, with Scroll Lock turned on, press the End key. (If you are following along on your computer, turn off Scroll Lock before proceeding.)

Pressing the PgUp and PgDn keys moves the window up and down one windowful and selects the cell in the current column of the row at the top of the document window.

 Although we haven't yet discussed menus and commands, this section would be incomplete if we did not mention that you can select a specific cell by using the Goto command on the Formula menu. If you know the exact address of the cell you want to make active, you can either choose the Goto command (we'll tell you how later) or press the F5 key. Type the cell address in the box that appears, and then press Enter to complete the command. For example, to make cell K7 the active cell, press F5, type K7, and then press Enter.

Selecting Groups of Cells

Often you'll want a command to act on more than one cell, so you need to learn how to select *ranges*. A range is a rectangular block of cells. Figure 1-4 shows some examples of ranges. The entire worksheet can also be a range.

To select a range of cells with the mouse, move the mouse pointer to one corner of the range, hold down the mouse button, and drag the pointer to the opposite corner of the range. Excel highlights all the cells in the selected range, except the active cell (the one at which you started). For example, if you point to cell B4, hold down the mouse button, and drag to cell C5, Excel highlights cells C4, B5, and C5, and leaves the active cell, B4, unhighlighted but surrounded by a dotted line.

To select an entire column, click its column header. To select an entire row, click its row header. To select multiple rows or columns, drag the mouse pointer through their headers.

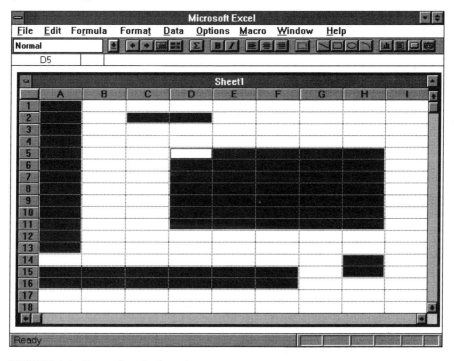

FIGURE 1-4. *Examples of selected ranges.*

Selecting a range with the keyboard

To select a range of cells with the keyboard, select the cell in any corner of the range, and then hold down the Shift key while you press the direction keys. To select an entire row, select any cell in that row, hold down the Shift key, and press the Spacebar. To select an entire column, select any cell in that column, hold down the Ctrl key, and press the Spacebar.

 To remember which Spacebar combination to use, keep in mind that Ctrl *and* column *both begin with* C. *Then you can associate* Shift *with* row *by a process of elimination.*

You can refer to the selected range by a composite name made up of the references for top-left and bottom-right cells, separated by a colon. For example, you can refer to the range that consists of cells B4, B5, C4, and C5 as the range B4:C5.

MOVING AROUND THE WORKSHEET

If the cell you want to select isn't visible, you can use the scroll bars on the right and bottom sides of the document window to bring the cell into view. Within each bar is a small rectangle called the *scroll box*, shown in Figure 1-5. To move up or down in the worksheet, drag the scroll box in the right scroll bar up or down; to move from side to side in the worksheet, drag the scroll box in the bottom scroll bar to the right or left.

To move an entire window at a time, simply click the scroll bar. In the vertical scroll bar, clicking above or below the scroll box moves the window up or down one windowful; in the bottom scroll bar, clicking to the left or right of the scroll box moves the window left or right one windowful.

To scroll more gradually, you can click one of the four *scroll arrows*. In the vertical scroll bar, clicking the up or down arrow moves the window up or down one row; in the bottom scroll bar, clicking the left or right arrow moves the window left or right one column.

When you move around the worksheet using the scroll bars, you don't change the active cell. However, you can't move around the worksheet using the keyboard without changing the active cell. For example, pressing the PgUp and PgDn keys moves the window up and down one windowful but also moves the active cell to the row at the top of the window.

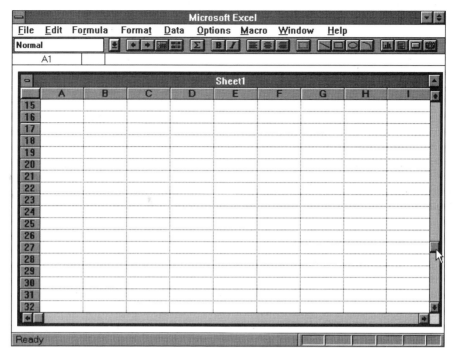

FIGURE 1-5. *Dragging the scroll box.*

WORKING WITH MENUS

As we mentioned earlier, you usually tell Microsoft Excel what you want it to do by choosing commands. The easiest way to choose commands is from menus—lists of items and actions—that are located on the menu bar.

Choosing Commands from Menus

You can choose commands from a menu with the mouse or with the keyboard.

Choosing commands with the mouse

To display a menu with the mouse (called *pulling down a menu*), point to the menu name, and click the mouse button. To close a pulled-down menu, click the menu name again, and then click anywhere outside the menu or press Esc.

To choose a command from the pulled-down menu, point to the command, and then click the mouse button. The menu disappears, and Microsoft Excel carries out the command. If you hold down the mouse button instead of click-ing, Excel displays the command in light type on a dark background (called *highlighting the command*) and displays a brief explanation of the command's action in the status bar. When you release the mouse button, Excel carries out the command as usual. (If you highlight a command with the mouse and then decide not to carry it out, simply move the pointer off the menu before releasing the mouse button.)

Choosing commands with the keyboard

One letter in each menu name on the menu bar is underlined. To pull down a menu with the keyboard, hold down the Alt key, and press the key that corre-sponds to the underlined letter in the menu you want. Alternatively, press the Alt key to activate the menu bar, use the Right or Left direction keys to move to the menu you want, and then press Enter or the Up or Down direction key. If you select a menu and then decide not to use it, press the Esc key to remove the menu from the screen.

Each of the commands on the menus also has an underlined letter. After you pull down a menu, you can choose a command by pressing the key that cor-responds to its underlined letter. Alternatively, you can use the Up and Down direction keys to move to the command name, and then press Enter.

Using Keyboard Shortcuts

Keyboard shortcuts allow you to choose commands without going through the menus, by pressing one or more keys simultaneously. After you become famil-iar with Microsoft Excel, you'll probably find keyboard shortcuts very conve-nient, even if you usually use a mouse.

 If you want to see a complete list of keyboard shortcuts, choose the Keyboard command from the Help menu. As you can see from the display in the Help window, Microsoft Excel offers extensive support for those who prefer to use the keyboard rather than a mouse.

For example, instead of pulling down the Help menu and choosing the In-dex command, you can simply press F1, the shortcut key for accessing Excel's Help feature. Press F1 now. Your screen displays the Help window shown in Figure 1-6. To remove the Help window from the screen, double-click the close box (the box with the minus-sign icon) at the left end of the title bar, or choose the Close command from the Control menu that appears when you click the close box.

14

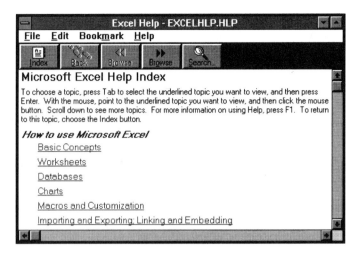

FIGURE 1-6. *The Microsoft Excel Help window.*

 If you have chosen a command or selected an option in a dialog box, pressing F1 displays a Help screen with information about that particular command or option.

Short Menus vs. Full Menus

The specific commands displayed on each menu depend on whether the Short Menus or Full Menus option is active. A short menu contains only the most frequently used commands for that menu; a full menu contains all the commands available for that menu. When you start Microsoft Excel for the first time, the screen displays short menus. If you change the option to Full Menus and then quit Excel, when you start the program again full menus will be in effect.

Let's look at a short menu. Click the Options menu in the menu bar (or hold down the Alt key and press O—the letter *o* key). As shown in Figure 1-7, the short Options menu has 5 commands.

FIGURE 1-7. *The short Options menu.*

One of the commands on the short Options menu is Full Menus. Choose this command by clicking it (or by pressing M). The Options menu disappears from your screen. Now click the Options menu again (or hold down Alt and press O). As shown in Figure 1-8, the full Options menu has 6 additional commands, for a total of 11. Leave Full Menus in effect, because the rest of the book covers commands that are not available with the Short Menus option.

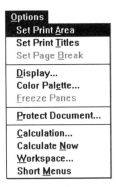

FIGURE 1-8. *The full Options menu.*

Touring the Menus

To get an idea of the commands at your disposal, let's take a look at each menu on the menu bar. Some of the command names are self-explanatory; others may seem a bit obscure. Don't worry for now if you can't figure out what all the commands do; we'll explain them all as we use them.

The File menu

Click File in the menu bar (or hold down Alt and press F) to see the File menu, shown in Figure 1-9. You use the commands on the File menu to open, close, save, and delete files. You also use this menu to print worksheets and exit from Microsoft Excel. Notice that some of the commands are followed by three dots (...), meaning that you must give Microsoft Excel more information before it can carry out these commands.

FIGURE 1-9. *The File menu.*

The Edit menu

Click Edit in the menu bar (or hold down Alt and press E) to see the Edit menu, shown in Figure 1-10. You use the commands on the Edit menu to copy, rearrange, and revise data. Notice that some of the commands are dimmed, indicating that you cannot use them now. Some of the commands have keyboard shortcuts, which are indicated next to the commands. For example, Shift+Del is the keyboard shortcut for the Cut command.

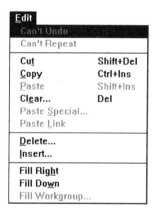

FIGURE 1-10. *The Edit menu.*

The Formula menu

Click Formula in the menu bar (or hold down Alt and press R) to see the Formula menu, shown in Figure 1-11. You use the commands on the Formula menu to build and revise formulas and to attach names and notes to cells.

FIGURE 1-11. *The Formula menu.*

The Format menu

Click Format in the menu bar (or hold down Alt and press T) to see the Format menu, shown in Figure 1-12. You use the commands on the Format menu to

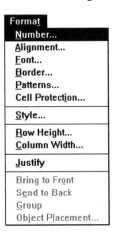

FIGURE 1-12. *The Format menu.*

alter the appearance of data in your worksheets. For example, you can change font sizes and styles. You also use commands on this menu to protect data from inadvertent changes.

The Data menu

Click Data in the menu bar (or hold down Alt and press D) to see the Data menu, shown in Figure 1-13. You use the commands on this menu to manage Microsoft Excel databases and to summarize data from multiple worksheets. (A database is a convenient way to organiz~~e~~ and retrieve infor~~mation~~ arranged in a table. We give you infor~~mation~~ ''Using Databases,'' and Chapter 10, ''M~~anaging~~

FIGURE 1-13. *The Data menu.*

The Options menu

Earlier in this chapter, you pulled down the Options menu by clicking Options in the menu bar (or by holding down Alt and pressing O). You use the commands on the Options menu to set display options (to show or hide gridlines, for example), to protect data, to choose when and how to calculate formulas, and to set certain printing options.

The Macro menu

Click Macro in the menu bar (or hold down the Alt key and press M) to see the Macro menu, shown in Figure 1-14 on the next page. You use the commands on the Macro menu to ''record'' keystrokes and store them as macros (small programs), which you can ''play back'' later. Most of the commands are dimmed because they aren't available right now. (We discuss macros in Chapter 11, ''Creating Macros,'' and Chapter 12, ''More Advanced Macro Techniques.'')

FIGURE 1-14. *The Macro menu.*

The Window menu

Click Window in the menu bar (or hold down Alt and press W) to see the Window menu, shown in Figure 1-15. You use the commands on the Window menu to move quickly between windows and to hide and reveal windows. You can also use this menu to open new windows, to arrange multiple windows on the screen, and to modify several worksheets as a group.

FIGURE 1-15. *The Window menu.*

The Help menu

Click Help in the menu bar (or hold down Alt and press H) to see the Help menu, shown in Figure 1-16. You use the commands on the Help menu to get information about the various features of Microsoft Excel. You can also start the Excel tutorial from this menu.

FIGURE 1-16. *The Help menu.*

The Control menus

Microsoft Excel has two menus that are not on the menu bar: the Document Control menu and the Application Control menu.

The Document Control menu: To see the Document Control menu, shown in Figure 1-17, click the minus-sign icon in the top-left corner of the document window, or hold down Alt and press the hyphen (-) key. You use the commands on the Document Control menu as an alternative to using the mouse to move, size, or close the document window, and to split the window into subwindows, called *panes*.

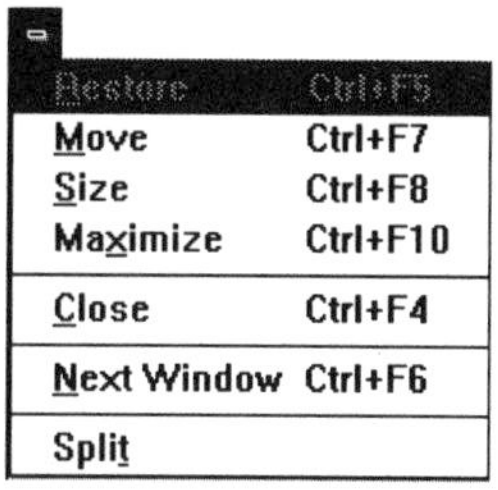

FIGURE 1-17. *The Document Control menu.*

The Application Control menu: To see the Application Control menu, shown in Figure 1-18, click the bar icon in the top-left corner of the screen—the one *above* the Document Control icon—or hold down Alt and press the Spacebar. You use the commands on the Application Control menu to control the size and position of the Microsoft Excel window and to switch to other currently running Windows applications.

FIGURE 1-18. *The Application Control menu.*

WORKING WITH DIALOG BOXES

Before Microsoft Excel can carry out some commands, you will need to supply more information. Excel uses *dialog boxes* to prompt you to supply the information it needs. As mentioned earlier, the names of commands that require additional information are followed by three dots (...) on the menu.

To display a typical dialog box, choose the Display command from the Options menu. The Display dialog box, shown in Figure 1-19, allows you to control the appearance of Microsoft Excel worksheets on the screen, by means of buttons, check boxes, and a drop-down list.

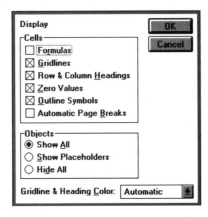

FIGURE 1-19. *The Display dialog box.*

The rectangular buttons, called *command buttons*, in the top-right corner of the dialog box carry out actions. For example, clicking the OK button instructs Excel to carry out the Display command using the options you have specified in the dialog box.

The square buttons, called *check boxes*, that are grouped within the Cells box at the top of the dialog box offer options that can be selected independently of each other. Simply click the appropriate check box to turn on a desired option (reflected by an *X* in the box). If an option is already turned on, clicking its check box turns it off (removes the *X*). For example, click the Gridlines check box to turn off this option, and then click the OK button to carry out the Display command. The gridlines vanish from the worksheet. To restore the gridlines, choose the Display command from the Options menu again, and click the Gridlines check box to turn the option back on. Leave the Display dialog box displayed for now.

The round buttons, called *radio buttons*, that are grouped within the Objects box are mutually exclusive; that is, only one of these buttons can be selected at a time. For example, click the Hide All button, and notice that Excel moves the large dot that indicates the selection from the Show All option to the Hide All option. Click Show All again to restore the original selection.

If you simply want to change the setting of one radio button in a dialog box, you can double-click the button instead of clicking the button and then clicking OK. This shortcut usually carries out the command in one step.

Now try using a different dialog box. Click the OK button in the Display dialog box to restore gridlines and return to the worksheet. Then choose the Font command from the Format menu. The dialog box in Figure 1-20 appears.

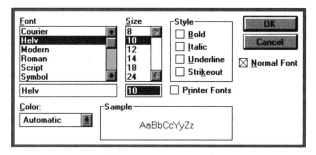

FIGURE 1-20. *The Font dialog box.*

The Font and Size *list boxes* each present a list of several selections. You can select only one item from each list box. List boxes that contain more items than can be displayed at one time have a scroll bar on the right. You use the scroll bar to bring other items into view.

The Color box in the bottom-left corner of the dialog box is a *drop-down list box.* Only one option appears on the screen right now, but if you click the arrow at the right end of the box, a list box drops down to display all the available color options.

Selecting Options with the Keyboard

You can select a dialog-box option with the keyboard in two ways. First, you can select individual options by holding down Alt and pressing the underlined letter in the name of the option. Second, you can press the Tab key to cycle through the options one by one. (Holding down the Shift key while pressing the Tab key moves you backward through the options.)

Exiting from a Dialog Box

When you're satisfied with all your selections, you can close the dialog box and tell Microsoft Excel to carry out the command in two ways. First, as you've already seen, you can click the OK button. Second, you can press Enter. To close a dialog box without carrying out the command, click the Cancel button, or press Esc.

UNDOING ACTIONS

One of the most important Microsoft Excel commands is Undo on the Edit menu—it reverses your last action. Even experienced users slip up occasionally, and it's nice to be able to undo the mistake and start over.

You can undo any change you've made in the formula bar, even after you've entered the change, but not after you've moved on and made an entry in another cell. To see how Undo works, follow these steps:

1. Select cell A1.

2. Type your first name, and press Enter.

3. Select the Edit menu. The first menu command is now Undo Entry. (Excel changes the name of this command to let you know exactly what action it will reverse when you choose Undo.)

4. Choose the Undo Entry command. Your name disappears from the worksheet.

5. Enter your first name in cell A1 again.

6. Select cell B1, type your last name, and then press Enter.

7. Choose Undo Entry from the Edit menu. Your last name disappears, but your first name remains in cell A1. Because you carried out a subsequent action, the entry in cell A1 cannot be undone.

The Undo command not only removes data you've entered, but it can also undo most worksheet commands. If a command cannot be undone, a dimmed Can't Undo appears on the Edit menu instead of the Undo command.

Three Microsoft Excel commands cannot be undone: Delete on the File menu, Delete on the Data menu, and Extract on the Data menu. To avoid accidentally destroying your valuable data, think twice before deleting files, and be sure to save your files before choosing Delete or Extract from the Data menu.

ENTERING DATA

Let's enter some data in *Sheet1*. We'll start by entering some text; you'll learn about entering numbers later.

Entering Text

The best way to describe entering text is by example. Suppose you've been asked to analyze some sales figures for a chain of sporting goods stores and you want to use a Microsoft Excel worksheet to do the job. To begin, give the worksheet a title:

1. Select cell A1, and type the store's complete name:

   `Allen's Sporting Goods Emporium`

   Notice that the characters you type appear in the formula bar. A blinking vertical line, called the *insertion point*, moves to the right of the characters as you type them. Also notice that two symbols in boxes are now displayed in the middle section of the formula bar; we'll discuss these symbols later in the chapter.

2. Press Enter. Excel displays the name of the store in cell A1, and the insertion point disappears, indicating that the formula bar is no longer active.

Suppose you realize you've made an error; the name should be *Alan's* instead of *Allen's*. To correct the entry, follow these steps:

1. Reactivate the formula bar by selecting cell A1 and pressing F2—the Edit key. Use this key when you want to edit the contents of the active cell. The insertion point reappears at the end of the entry in the formula bar.

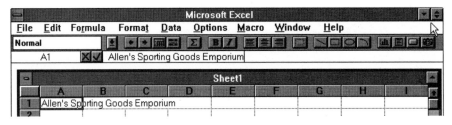

2. Move the insertion point between the two *l*'s in *Allen's*, either by positioning the pointer and clicking, or by pressing the Left direction key.

3. Press the Del key twice to remove *le*.

4. Type *a*.

5. Press Enter to enter the correction in the worksheet.

Now try making the same correction in a different way. To undo the edit you just made, choose the Undo Entry command from the Edit menu. Then follow these steps:

1. Position the pointer between the *e* and the *n*, and click to activate the insertion point.

2. Press the Backspace key twice.

3. Type *a*.

4. Press Enter to enter the correction in the worksheet.

As you can see, the Backspace key removes characters to the left of the insertion point; the Del key removes characters to the right of the insertion point.

You can use other keys to move quickly through an entry you are editing. To move to the beginning of the entry, press Home while the formula bar is active. To move to the end of the line that contains the insertion point, press End. To move to the end of a multiple-line entry, hold down the Ctrl key, and press End. To move one word at a time, hold down Ctrl, and press the Right or Left direction key.

Try making changes and reversing them with the Undo command. You can reverse an Undo command by choosing Redo, which appears on the Edit menu after you choose Undo. Figure 1-21 shows the Redo Entry command.

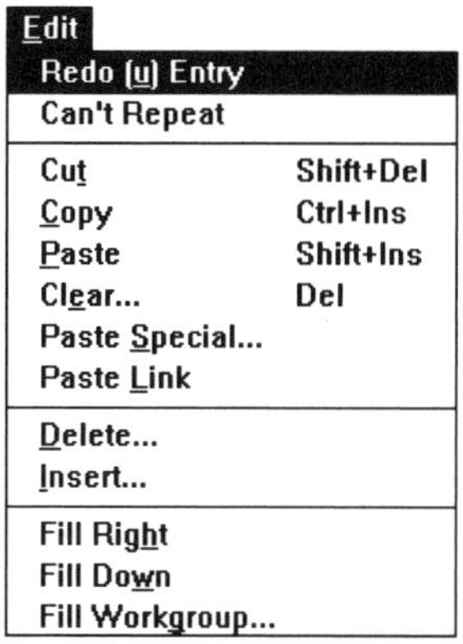

```
 Edit
  Redo [u] Entry
  Can't Repeat

  Cut            Shift+Del
  Copy           Ctrl+Ins
  Paste          Shift+Ins
  Clear...       Del
  Paste Special...
  Paste Link

  Delete...
  Insert...

  Fill Right
  Fill Down
  Fill Workgroup...
```

FIGURE 1-21. *The Redo command.*

The Enter and Cancel Boxes

The two symbols that appear in the middle section of the formula bar when you make an entry represent the *enter box* (the checkmark) and the *cancel box* (the *X*). Clicking the enter box enters the data you type in the formula bar in the worksheet, in the same way that pressing Enter does. If you have not yet entered the data by pressing Enter or clicking the enter box, clicking the cancel box cancels the entry.

Entering Numbers

Numeric data in Microsoft Excel can take one of two forms: It can be a *constant* or a *formula*. Constants are simply numeric values; you enter them in the same way you enter text. Formulas are *numeric expressions* or *logical expressions* that result in different values depending on the values of their components. Don't worry about formulas for now; you'll learn more about them in Chapter 2, "Using Formulas and Functions."

Excel treats numbers differently from text, so it must have a way of distinguishing between the two. Excel treats an entry as a constant if the entry consists only of numeric characters (the numbers 0 through 9) and any of these special characters:

$$= + - ( ) . E e , \$ \%$$

You must use these special characters in certain ways for Excel to recognize the entry as a constant. Excel ignores an equal sign (=) or plus sign (+) at the beginning of a numeric constant, as well as embedded commas. When you enter a negative value, you can precede the value with a minus sign (−) or enclose it in parentheses. Excel treats a single period (.) in a numeric constant as a decimal point. A capital or lowercase *E* embedded in a series of numeric characters denotes scientific notation. You can use a dollar sign ($) in front of a number or a percent sign (%) after a number.

If an entry contains anything other than numbers and the special characters, Excel treats the entry as text. For example, the address *1000 Wilshire Boulevard* is a text entry. If you want to enter a number but have Microsoft Excel treat it as text, simply precede the number with an equal sign (=) and enclose it in quotation marks, as in this example:

="1991"

Again, let's use the worksheet for Alan's Sporting Goods Emporium to demonstrate entering data. Suppose you need to enter sales results for July 1991, broken out by department. You've been given the following sales figures:

Dept.	Sales
Skiing	15,600
Hunting	27,280
Camping	13,750
Apparel	15,920
Other	22,600

To enter this information in the worksheet, you could select cell A3 and type *Dept.*, select cell B3 and type *Sales*, and so on. But there's a faster way of accomplishing this task.

Entering data the quick way

You can save time by selecting the data-entry area before you type the data. To enter the data this way, follow these steps:

1. Point to cell A3, hold down the mouse button, and then drag down and to the right to select the range A3 through B8 (or select cell A3, and hold down the Shift key while pressing the Down and then the Right direction keys). Your worksheet now looks like the following one.

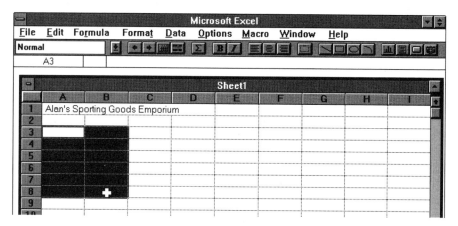

2. Type the first heading, *Dept.*, and press the Tab key. Notice that the range you selected remains highlighted, but the active cell is now B3.

3. Type the second heading, *Sales*, and press the Tab key. Cell A4 is now the active cell.

4. Continue entering the department names and the July sales data from the table, pressing the Tab key after each entry. Each time you press the Tab key, the active cell moves one cell to the right. If the active cell is the last selected cell in that row, the first selected cell in the next row becomes the active cell. (To move backward, hold down the Shift key while you press Tab.)

To move through the range column by column instead of row by row, press Enter after each entry. For example, if cell A3 is active when you press Enter, cell A4 becomes the active cell. If the active cell is the last selected cell in that column, the first selected cell in the next column becomes the active cell.

Correcting Errors

Now that you know how to make entries in a worksheet, we can give you a few tricks for formula-bar editing.

Suppose the sporting goods company shortens its name to *Alan's Sports*. To correct the title of the worksheet, you could use the Del key or the Backspace key to revise the entry, but there's an easier way: You can select a group of characters and delete them all at one time.

To delete a group of characters, follow these steps:

1. Start by selecting cell A1, which contains the name *Alan's Sporting Goods Emporium.*

2. Drag through the characters in the formula bar to select them. In this case, position the I-beam pointer after the *t* in *Sports*, and drag just past the *d* in *Goods*. Be sure you've selected only the characters you want to remove, and then release the mouse button. (With the keyboard, press the direction keys until the insertion point is between the *t* and the *i*, hold down the Shift key, and then press the Right direction key until all the characters from *i* through the *d* in *Goods* are highlighted.) Your worksheet looks like this:

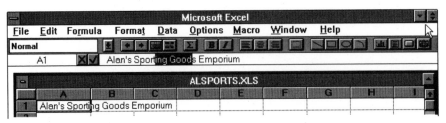

3. Now press the Del key. The name becomes *Alan's Sports Emporium.*

Let's use a different method to delete the word *Emporium.*

1. Point to the word *Emporium*, and double-click. This selects the entire word. (With the keyboard, position the insertion point before the *E* in *Emporium*, hold down both Shift and Ctrl, and then press the Right direction key. The Shift-Ctrl-Right direction key combination extends the selection one word at a time.)

2. Press the Del key to remove the selected word.

3. Examine the entry for errors, and make any necessary corrections before pressing the Enter key to enter the change in the worksheet.

MANAGING DISK FILES

We'll come back to the Alan's Sports worksheet in the next chapter. First, however, you need to learn how to save and retrieve worksheets, delete obsolete worksheets, create new worksheets, and close worksheets without saving any changes you may have made.

Saving Your Work

If you want to exit from Microsoft Excel and pick up later where you left off, you must save your work on a disk. While you're working in Excel, you should save your work at least once every 10 or 15 minutes, to avoid losing data if a power failure or other problem requires you to restart the computer.

Naming a worksheet

Excel has assigned the name *Sheet1* to the Alan's Sports worksheet. Because *Sheet1* isn't a very meaningful name, you will want to change it. To save the worksheet with the name *ALSPORTS*, follow these steps:

1. Choose the Save As command from the File menu. Excel displays this dialog box:

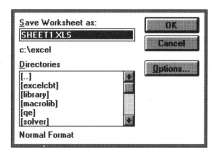

2. Type *ALSPORTS* in the Save Worksheet As text box. As you type, *ALSPORTS* replaces *SHEET1.XLS* in the text box. (Excel adds the XLS extension to all worksheet names, unless you specify a different extension in the Save Worksheet As box.)

3. Click the OK button, or press Enter, to save the worksheet under its new name.

You can edit an existing name in the Save Worksheet As text box just as you would edit an entry in the formula bar.

Saving a worksheet on a different drive or in a different directory

When you installed Microsoft Excel, the program created an EXCEL directory for storing Excel programs and worksheets. Unless you tell Excel to do otherwise, when you save a worksheet, Excel stores it in the EXCEL directory. You can tell Excel to store the worksheet on a different drive or in a different directory, by editing the name of the worksheet in the Save Worksheet As text box.

For example, to save the *ALSPORTS* worksheet on a floppy disk in drive A, follow these steps:

1. Insert the floppy disk in drive A of your computer.

2. Choose the Save As command from the File menu.

3. Scroll to the bottom of the Directories list box, where you will see letters representing the drives installed in your computer.

4. Double-click [-a-] to select drive A. Click OK, or press Enter, to save the worksheet on the disk in drive A.

To reset the drive and directory to its original setting, choose the Save As command again, scroll to the bottom of the Directories list box, select [-c-], and then click OK or press Enter.

Now suppose you want to save *ALSPORTS* on drive C but in the LIBRARY directory, a subdirectory of the EXCEL directory. Follow these steps:

1. Choose the Save As command from the File menu to display the Save As dialog box.

2. Click [LIBRARY] in the Directories list box. Excel inserts *library* in front of *ALSPORTS.XLS* in the Save Worksheet As text box.

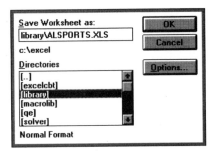

3. If you want to save the worksheet under a different filename, edit or replace *ALSPORTS* in the Save Worksheet As text box, being careful not to change the directory specification.

4. Click OK, or press Enter.

Excel then saves the worksheet in the EXCEL\LIBRARY directory.

Saving a worksheet without changing its name

After you have assigned a name to the worksheet, you can choose the Save command from the File menu to save the latest version with the same name.

Microsoft Excel does not display a dialog box when you choose the Save command; it simply overwrites the old version of the file with the new version. Even though you have not made any changes to the *ALSPORTS* worksheet, try choosing the Save command now.

If you type the name of an existing worksheet in the Save Worksheet As text box, Microsoft Excel displays a message asking whether you want to replace the existing worksheet with the current one. However, this message does not *appear when you choose the Save command from the File menu. If you want to make changes to a worksheet but still retain the original version, use the Save As command to change the worksheet's name immediately after opening it.*

Saving a worksheet in a "foreign" format

If you want to save your worksheet in a format that can be read by other applications (for example, by Microsoft Word), choose the Save As command, and click the Options button in the Save As dialog box. The dialog box shown in Figure 1-22 appears. Select the file format you want, and then click the OK button or press Enter. Table 1-2 explains the available format options.

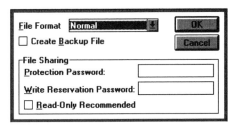

FIGURE 1-22. *The Save As Options dialog box.*

Option	Format
Normal	Microsoft Excel standard format
Template	Microsoft Excel template (explained in Chapter 4, "Enhancing Your Worksheets")
Excel 2.x	Microsoft Excel version 2.0/2.1 standard format
SYLK	Format used to transfer data among different applications

TABLE 1-2. *The formats in which you can save Microsoft Excel worksheets.*   *(continued)*

TABLE 1-2. *continued*

Option	*Format*
Text	Tab-separated ASCII format, useful for moving Microsoft Excel data into word-processing programs
Text (OS/2 or DOS) and Text (Macintosh)	Text-only formats for programs running under these operating systems
WKS, WK1, and WK3	Formats for Lotus 1-2-3 Release 1A, Release 2, and Release 3, respectively
DIF	Data Interchange Format for Visicalc
DBF 2, DBF 3, and DBF 4	Formats for dBASE II, III, and IV, respectively
CSV (OS/2 or DOS) and CSV (Macintosh)	Comma-separated format, useful for moving Microsoft Excel data to other applications

Creating a New Worksheet

To open a new, blank file, choose New from the File menu. The dialog box shown in Figure 1-23 appears, asking what type of file you want to open. (You'll learn how to create chart and macro files later.) The Worksheet option is already selected, so click the OK button, or press Enter, to open a new worksheet.

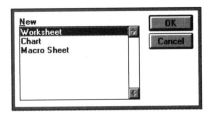

FIGURE 1-23. *The New dialog box.*

Microsoft Excel gives the new worksheet the title *Sheet2* and displays it in a new document window in front of the *ALSPORTS* worksheet. You'll need the new worksheet in a minute, so save it now with the name *Sheet2* by choosing the Save command from the File menu. Excel displays the Save As dialog box, just as if you had chosen the Save As command instead of Save. Why? Because Excel assumes you want to give the worksheet a name of your own choosing instead of the name Excel assigned. In this case, though, simply click the OK button to save the worksheet as *Sheet2*.

Closing a Worksheet

You close the current worksheet by choosing the Close command from the File menu. Close the *Sheet2* worksheet now. Because you haven't made any changes to the worksheet since you last saved it, the program closes the file without first asking whether you want to save it.

If you make changes to a worksheet without saving them, when you choose Close, the dialog box shown in Figure 1-24 appears, asking whether you want to save the revised worksheet before closing it. To save the worksheet, click the Yes button, or press Y or Enter. To close the file without saving the changes, click the No button, or press N. To cancel the Close command, click the Cancel button, or press Esc.

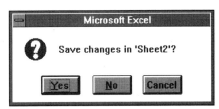

FIGURE 1-24. *The message that appears when you try to close a worksheet without saving changes.*

After you close the *Sheet2* worksheet, its document window disappears from the screen, uncovering the *ALSPORTS* worksheet. Choose the Close command again to close *ALSPORTS*.

Most of the Microsoft Excel window is now blank. With no worksheets open, only the File and Help menus are available. To bring back the full menu bar, simply create a new worksheet, or open one that you have previously saved on a disk.

Opening an Existing Worksheet

The method you use to open an existing worksheet depends on how recently you used the worksheet.

Opening a recently used worksheet with the File command

Microsoft Excel ''remembers'' the four worksheets you most recently worked with and displays them as options on the File menu. To open the *ALSPORTS* worksheet, follow the steps on the next page.

1. Pull down the File menu. Near the bottom, you'll see the filenames
   SHEET2.XLS and *ALSPORTS.XLS*—the files for the two worksheets
   you have worked with so far.

2. Choose the *ALSPORTS* worksheet to tell Excel to open it.

Now close the worksheet so that you can see how to open it another way.

Opening a worksheet with the Open command

Whether the worksheet you want appears on the File menu or not, you can
choose the Open command from the File menu to open an existing file. When
you choose this command, Excel displays a dialog box similar to the one shown
in Figure 1-25. To open the *ALSPORTS* worksheet from this dialog box, select
the worksheet in the Files list box, and then click the OK button, or press Enter,
to carry out the command.

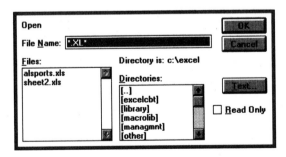

FIGURE 1-25. *The Open dialog box.*

Opening a worksheet that is stored in another directory

When you choose Open from the File menu, Excel displays in the Files list box the names of the worksheets stored in the current directory. Right now, the current directory is *c:\excel*, as indicated by the message just above the Directories list box. If the worksheet you want to open is not in the current directory, you can display the worksheets stored in other directories on the current disk by selecting from the list of directory names shown in the Directories list box.

Suppose you need to retrieve a document that is stored in the *root*, or main, directory (C:\), which is one level higher in the directory hierarchy than the EXCEL directory. To move to the C:\root directory from the EXCEL directory, follow these steps:

1. Choose the Open command from the File menu to display the Open dialog box.

2. Double-click [..] (the first option) in the Directories list box. The Files list box now displays the Excel files on the root directory. (If the list box is blank, no files with extensions beginning with XL are currently stored on the C:\root directory.)

3. Click the name of the worksheet you want to open, and click OK or press Enter.

No matter where you are in the directory hierarchy, double-clicking [..] always moves you up one level. For example, if you are currently working in the EXCEL\LIBRARY directory, double-clicking [..] moves you to the EXCEL directory.

Deleting Worksheets

After a while, you'll find that you've created many files that are no longer useful. You can clean up your disk from within Microsoft Excel by choosing the Delete command from the File menu.

Let's delete *Sheet2* now. Follow these steps:

1. Choose the Delete command from the File menu. The Delete dialog box appears. This dialog box is similar to the Open dialog box, except that the specification in the File Name text box is *.*, and all the files in the current directory are listed in the Files list box.

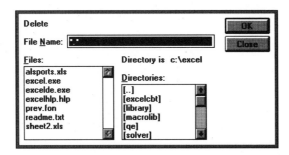

2. To avoid deleting any of the Microsoft Excel program files, change the specification in the File Name text box to *.*XLS*. Only two files, *ALSPORTS.XLS* and *SHEET2.XLS*, are now listed.

3. Select *SHEET2.XLS*.

4. Click the OK button, or press Enter. Because you can't undo the Delete command, Excel always displays a dialog box asking you to confirm the deletion.

5. Click the Yes button, or press Y or Enter, to delete the file.

6. Click the Close button, or press Esc, to close the dialog box.

EXITING FROM MICROSOFT EXCEL

To exit from Microsoft Excel, choose the Exit command from the File menu. If any open worksheet has unsaved changes, Excel displays a dialog box like the one shown in Figure 1-24 on page 35.

After you respond to this dialog box for each worksheet that has unsaved changes, Excel simply returns you to the Windows screen.

CONCLUSION

We've covered a lot of territory in this first chapter. You now know how to select cells and make entries in them, and you know the basics of saving and retrieving files. In the next chapter, we introduce formulas and functions so that you can start doing useful work with Microsoft Excel.

Chapter 2

Using Formulas and Functions

By now, you should be comfortable entering text and numbers in worksheets and making corrections to your entries. But if this were all you could do using Microsoft Excel, you could just as easily use a word-processing application. The power of Microsoft Excel lies in its ability to work with the information you enter—to calculate, to analyze, and to predict. In this chapter, you will begin harnessing this power by learning how to use Microsoft Excel formulas and functions.

UNDERSTANDING MICROSOFT EXCEL FORMULAS

You enter a formula in a cell in the same way you enter text—through the formula bar. Excel calculates the result (value) of the formula and displays that result (sometimes referred to as *returning a value*) in the cell that contains the formula.

If you quit the Microsoft Excel program at the end of Chapter 1, start Excel again now. (Type *win excel* at the DOS prompt.) Then try entering a simple formula in a blank worksheet. (If you need to open a new worksheet, choose New from the File menu, and click OK in the New dialog box to accept the Worksheet option.) As mentioned in Chapter 1, in a new worksheet, cell A1 is the active cell. Now type

    =40+27

As you type, notice that your keystrokes appear both in the formula bar and in cell A1. Press Enter. The formula you typed is still displayed in the formula bar, but the result of the formula, 67, is displayed in cell A1.

Every formula must begin with an equal sign (=). If you omit the equal sign, Excel interprets the entry as text and displays the "text" in cell A1, instead of calculating its value.

Now try selecting each of the cells listed in the first column of the following table, one by one, and entering the corresponding formula shown in the second column. (Remember, to select a cell, you simply click it.) The result of each formula is shown in the third column of the table.

Cell	Formula	Value
A2	=3*16	48
A3	=53/20	2.65
A4	=100−36.83	63.17

Using Numeric Operators in Formulas

The formulas you just typed included *numeric operators*: plus (+) for addition, minus (−) for subtraction, asterisk (*) for multiplication, and slash (/) for division. Other kinds of numeric operators include percent (%), which divides the preceding value by 100, and caret (^), which multiplies the preceding value by itself the number of times specified by the following value (exponentiation).

For example, select cell A5, type

    =23^3

and then press Enter. Microsoft Excel multiplies 23 by itself three times and displays the result: 12167.

Using more than one operator

Each cell in Microsoft Excel can contain as many as 255 characters. As long as you don't exceed this limit, you can create long formulas that include as many operators as you need. The longer the formula, however, the greater the risk of error. Consider the following formula:

    =84*0.7^2/24*3.26-29

Excel has to make five different computations—one for each operator—to calculate this formula. The result depends on the sequence in which Excel performs the computations. Excel follows a rigid set of rules when performing multiple computations in a single formula. For formulas to work the way you want them to, you need to be familiar with these rules, known as the *order of precedence*. Table 2-1 lists the Microsoft Excel numeric operators in order of precedence (from first to last). When two operators have equal precedence (for example, division and multiplication), Excel performs the computations from left to right.

Operator	*Action*
–	Negation
%	Percentage
^	Exponentiation
/, *	Division, multiplication
+, –	Addition, subtraction

TABLE 2-1. *The order of precedence of numeric operators.*

Order of precedence is best shown by example. Let's look again at the previous formula:

    =84*0.7^2/24*3.26-29

The following table shows, step-by-step, the procedure Microsoft Excel goes through as it calculates the formula. In the third column, the computation made at each step appears in bold.

Step	Operation	Formula
1	Exponentiation	**=84*0.7^2/24*3.26−29**
2	Multiplication	**=84*0.49/24*3.26−29**
3	Division	**=41.16/24*3.26−29**
4	Multiplication	**=1.715*3.26−29**
5	Subtraction	**=5.5909−29**
6	Result	−23.4091

You can override Excel's order of precedence by enclosing parts of the formula in parentheses. Excel performs the enclosed computations before proceeding with the usual order of precedence. So, if you enter the formula

```
=84*0.7^2/24*(3.26-29)
```

Excel performs the subtraction operation as the first step instead of the fifth step. The result is −44.1441.

 Be careful: If you don't consider the order of precedence when you create complex formulas, the formulas might yield unexpected results.

Using Cell Addresses in Formulas

So far, the formulas we've shown you have consisted solely of values and operators. But formulas can also refer to other cells. For example, the formula =C3+C4+C5 returns the sum of the values in cells C3, C4, and C5.

Try using a formula that uses cell addresses in the *ALSPORTS* worksheet you created in Chapter 1. To open the *ALSPORTS* worksheet, choose the Open command from the File menu, and double-click *ALSPORTS.XLS* in the Files list box. Cells B4 through B8 of the worksheet contain sales amounts. To total these amounts, select cell B10, type

```
=B4+B5+B6+B7+B8
```

and then press Enter. Your screen looks like Figure 2-1. Cell B10 displays the value 95150, the sum of all the departments' sales. (If your result is different, look for typographical errors in your formula or in the sales amounts.)

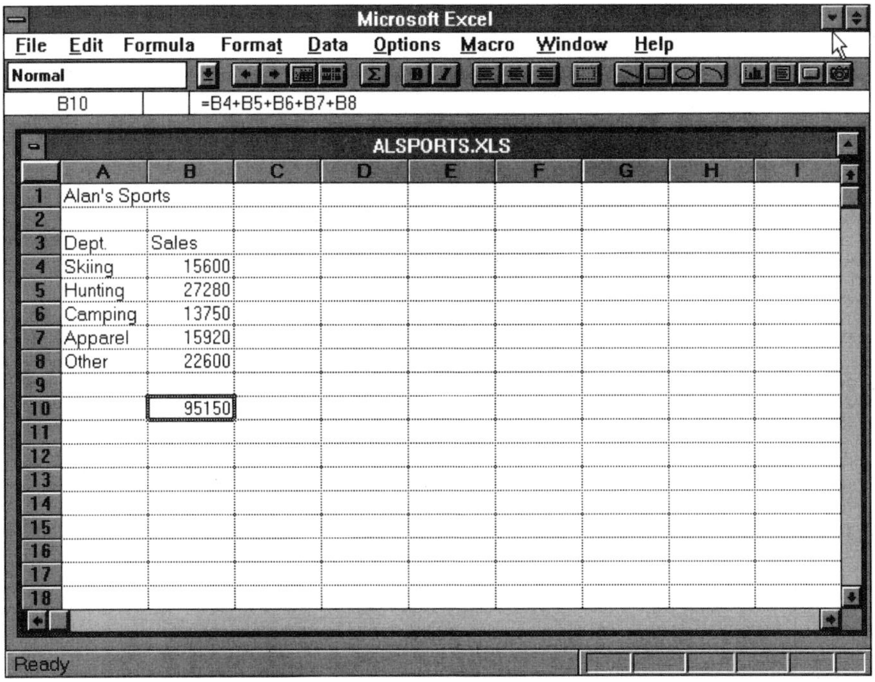

FIGURE 2-1. *A simple addition formula using cell addresses.*

Typing cell addresses can be tedious. Fortunately, you can enter cell addresses in a formula simply by clicking the cell you want the formula to reference. For example, you can enter the formula

    =B4+B5+B6+B7+B8

by selecting cell B10, typing =, clicking cell B4, typing +, clicking cell B5, typing +, clicking cell B6, typing +, clicking cell B7, typing +, and finally clicking cell B8. When you click the enter box or press Enter, Excel enters the result, 95150, in cell B10.

UNDERSTANDING MICROSOFT EXCEL FUNCTIONS

Some formulas—for example, those for calculating financial transactions involving compound interest and variable payments over long periods of time—can be extremely complex. Microsoft Excel offers a battery of *functions* that take a lot of the hard work out of entering formulas. For example, to calculate the monthly payment necessary to amortize a five-year loan of $15,000 at an interest rate of 11.5 percent, you can simply tell Excel that you want to use the PMT function with a principal of 15000, an interest rate of 0.9583% (11.5%/12 equals monthly interest), and a term of 60 months. Behind the scenes, Excel calculates the correct formula and gives you the result: $329.89 per month.

Functions are merely a shorthand method of entering complex formulas. You use functions to save keystrokes and because they are easier to enter and read than long formulas. Excel has functions for common mathematical, financial, and statistical calculations.

Every Excel function consists of a *name* followed by opening and closing parentheses. Within the parentheses, most functions have at least one *argument*. Arguments are values that you supply. For example, in the function

    =SUM(B4,B5,B6,B7,B8)

SUM is the function name and B4, B5, B6, B7, and B8 are the arguments. As you might have guessed, the SUM function adds the values of all the cells listed within the parentheses. As you can see in Figure 2-2, this particular SUM function performs the same calculation as the formula

    =B4+B5+B6+B7+B8

which you entered earlier in cell B10 of the worksheet.

 Although all function names are shown in capital letters in this book, you don't have to enter them in capital letters; Microsoft Excel converts them for you. So if you enter =sum(A1+A2), when you press Enter you'll see =SUM(A1+A2) in the formula bar.

Using Ranges in Functions

As Figure 2-2 shows, entering the function

    =SUM(B4,B5,B6,B7,B8)

in cell B10 requires more keystrokes than the addition formula you started out with. However, the SUM function can be a real timesaver when you use cell ranges as arguments.

Try using a cell range now, by typing the following function in cell B10 of the *ALSPORTS* worksheet:

    =SUM(B4:B8)

You get the same sales total, but you've saved quite a few keystrokes.

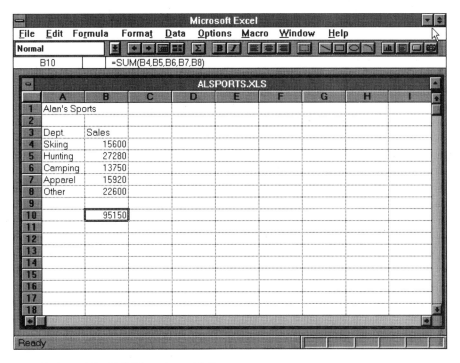

FIGURE 2-2. *The SUM function with five arguments.*

 To minimize keystrokes, use this rule of thumb when deciding whether to use a simple formula or the SUM function to total cell values: For two or three cells, use a formula; for four or more cells, use the SUM function.

In the example we have been using, all the cells in the range are in one column (B) of the worksheet. However, you can also specify rectangular ranges. For example, the function

```
=SUM(F6:K10)
```

returns the sum of all the values in a rectangular block of cells that has cell F6 in the top-left corner and cell K10 in the bottom-right corner.

You learned earlier that you can enter individual cell addresses in formulas by clicking the cells with the mouse. You can also enter a cell range in a function using the mouse.

To enter a cell range in a function:

1. Select cell B10.

2. Type the first part of the function:

   =SUM(

3. Drag through the range B4:B8 to select it. The range appears in the formula bar and is surrounded by a marquee (a dotted rectangle) in the worksheet.

4. Type the right parenthesis. The marquee disappears.

5. Press Enter to complete the function.

Cell B10 again displays the total of all departments' sales.

 You can use the keyboard to enter a range in a function by pressing the direction keys until the cell in one corner of the range is selected (surrounded by a marquee), and then holding down the Shift key and pressing the direction keys until the entire range is surrounded by the marquee.

You can include more than one range as arguments for the SUM function by simply separating the items with commas, and you can mix single cells and ranges, as in the following example:

   =SUM(F6:K10,K12,L6:M10)

You can include as many as 14 arguments in a Microsoft Excel function, but because Excel treats a range as one argument, you can actually include the addresses of many more than 14 cells.

Using Functions in Formulas

You can use functions as part of formulas. For example, suppose the management at Alan's Sports wants to compare the performance of individual departments with the average performance of all departments. Enter the following formula in cell B12 of the *ALSPORTS* worksheet:

   =SUM(B4:B8)/5

This formula determines the total of all department sales and then divides the total by 5, to give the average sales per department (19030).

Now enter the following formula in cell C4:

   =B4/SUM(B4:B8)

This formula results in a decimal fraction that represents the portion of total sales made by the Skiing department.

 You enter only one equal sign at the beginning of each formula; you don't enter an equal sign before a function that is embedded in a formula.

Other Ways of Entering Functions

So far, you've entered functions by typing them in the formula bar, but you can enter them in other ways.

Using the Autosum button

You can enter SUM functions quickly by using the Autosum button in the tool bar, shown here:

The Autosum button is the one labeled with the Greek summation symbol ($\sum$), to the left of the button labeled with the large capital *B*.

When you click the Autosum button, Microsoft Excel enters a SUM function in the formula bar, along with its guess as to the range you want to sum. This guess is based on the contents of the surrounding cells and is usually a good starting point. For example, select cell B10 again, and click the Autosum button. Excel highlights the range B4:B9 in the formula bar. You can press Enter to accept the formula, or you can edit the formula. Here, you need to change B9 to B8 to create the same formula we entered previously. Because cell B9 is empty, however, the result remains the same.

Pasting functions in cells

Microsoft Excel provides another shortcut for entering functions: pasting, or copying, them from a list. Pasting functions is a convenient way of promoting accuracy in your worksheets.

As shown in Figure 2-3 on the next page, the Paste Function command on the Formula menu displays a list of all Excel functions. You can select a function from this list, paste it into the formula bar, and then fill in the function's arguments. If you select the Paste Arguments option, Excel puts *placeholders* for the arguments between the parentheses that follow the pasted function's name. (These placeholders are also displayed below the list of functions in the Paste Function dialog box.)

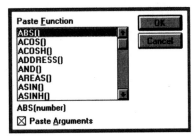

FIGURE 2-3. *The Paste Function dialog box.*

To use the Paste Function command on the Function menu to enter a SUM function, follow these steps:

1. Select cell B10 in the *ALSPORTS* worksheet.

2. Choose the Paste Function command from the Formula menu.

3. If the Paste Arguments option is not already selected, click its check box to turn it on.

4. Scroll through the Paste Function list by pointing to the down scroll arrow and holding down the mouse button. Release the button when the SUM function comes into view.

 You can press the S key to move directly to the part of the Paste Function list that contains the functions whose names begin with the letter S.

5. Click SUM() to select it.

6. Click the OK button, or press Enter. The following screen shows how the formula bar in your worksheet now looks.

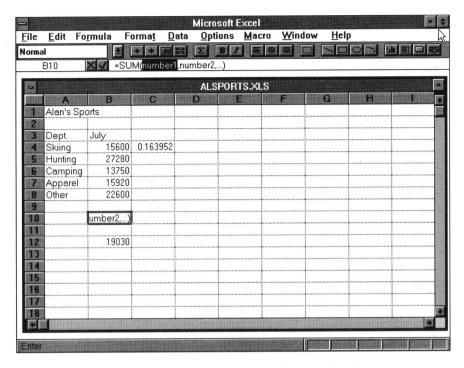

Now you need to replace the placeholders with actual values:

6. Drag through the entire SUM argument (everything inside the parentheses) to highlight it.

7. Select the range B4:B8.

You can select one of several arguments by moving the I-beam pointer anywhere in the argument and double-clicking. Excel highlights the entire argument.

8. Press Enter.

If you have entered everything correctly, the formula results in the usual value: 95150.

Some functions have optional arguments. If you don't replace the placeholders for these arguments with values, Excel displays a #NAME? error value in the cell containing the formula. (Error values are discussed later in this chapter.) If you don't use a particular optional argument, delete the corresponding placeholder.

Entering a Formula in a Cell Range

Let's put functions and formulas together using the *ALSPORTS* worksheet, and at the same time demonstrate a shortcut for entering the same formula in a range of cells.

Suppose you want to create a report that shows how the various departments are performing. Assume that it's now September 1991, and you need to add more data to update the *ALSPORTS* worksheet. Follow these steps to set up the worksheet:

1. Change the label in cell B3 from *Sales* to *July*, and enter *August* in cell C3.

2. In column C, select cells C4:C8, and enter the following sales figures for August 1991, pressing Enter to move from cell to cell:

Cell	Dept.	August
C4	Skiing	21270
C5	Hunting	25900
C6	Camping	11085
C7	Apparel	23540
C8	Other	23635

3. Click the Autosum button to enter the total of cells C4:C8 into cell C10.

In your analysis, you want to display the percentage gain in sales for each department from July to August. For example, to calculate the percentage gain for the Skiing department, you need to subtract the July figure (B4) from the August figure (C4) and divide by the July figure (B4). Proceed as follows:

1. Select cell D3, and enter the label *Gain(%)*.

2. Select the range D4:D8, starting your selection with cell D4 so that D4 is the active cell within the range.

3. Type

   ```
   =(C4-B4)/B4
   ```

   but don't press Enter. Instead, hold down Ctrl, and press Enter. You now see the following screen.

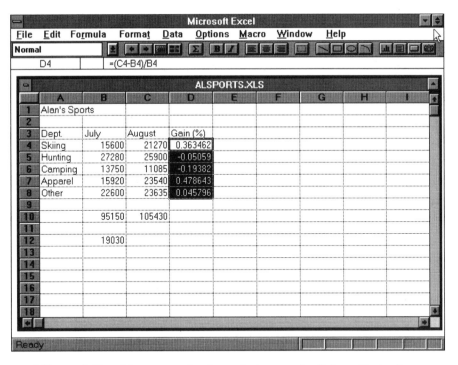

Microsoft Excel has entered a formula into each of the cells in the range you selected. Use the Up and Down direction keys to select each cell in the range D4:D8, and as you move from cell to cell, look at the formulas in the formula bar. Notice that they're not identical. The formula in cell D4 refers to cells B4 and C4, the formula in cell D5 refers to cells B5 and C5, and so on. By entering one formula into a range of cells, you have entered formulas for the entire range, leaving Excel to adjust the cell references as needed.

Right now, the gains and losses in column D appear as decimal fractions rather than as percentages. You'll learn how to change the values to percentages later on, in Chapter 4, "Enhancing Your Worksheets."

UNDERSTANDING MICROSOFT EXCEL MESSAGES

As you're learning Microsoft Excel, you're bound to make mistakes from time to time when entering formulas. When this happens, Excel gives you a clue about where you went astray, by displaying an *error value* in a cell or an *alert message* in a dialog box.

Error Values

An error value is one of a set of "codes" that Microsoft Excel uses when it cannot make sense of a formula. An error value in a cell doesn't necessarily mean the entry in that particular cell is causing the problem. The problem may lie somewhere else in the worksheet. When the formula in one cell refers to another cell's value, which is itself the result of a formula that refers to yet another cell, and so on, errors tend to ripple through the worksheet and produce multiple error values.

Table 2-2 shows all the Excel error values you might encounter, and gives brief explanations of probable causes of the errors.

Error value	Cause
#DIV/0!	You've entered a formula that asks Excel to divide an amount by 0. You may have done this indirectly by entering a reference to a cell that is currently blank.
#N/A	You've probably omitted one or more arguments from a function, although other errors also produce this value.
#NAME?	You've entered a formula containing text that Excel does not recognize. You've made a typographical error or used a name that hasn't yet been defined. (You'll learn about names in the next chapter.)
#NULL!	You've specified an intersection between two ranges that don't intersect. (This error value occurs only with certain advanced Excel features, which are beyond the scope of this book.)
#NUM!	You've used an inappropriate argument in a mathematical function (for example, you've asked Excel to calculate the square root of a negative number).

TABLE 2-2. *Error values and their causes.* *(continued)*

TABLE 2-2. *continued*

Error value	Cause
#REF!	You've probably deleted from the worksheet a cell that is referenced by another cell.
#VALUE!	You've entered text where a number or logical value is expected, or you've entered a range as an argument where a single value is required. (The logical values TRUE and FALSE are returned by logical functions, such as the IF function, which is discussed later in this chapter.)

Of course, the absence of error values doesn't guarantee that a worksheet contains no errors. It simply means that nothing in the worksheet prevents Microsoft Excel from calculating a result.

Alert Messages

Some types of errors cause Microsoft Excel to display the alert message shown in Figure 2-4 immediately after you enter a formula. Excel also highlights the part of the formula that is causing the problem and will not enter the formula until you correct the error.

FIGURE 2-4. *The alert message displayed for certain types of formula errors.*

Excel displays other alert messages in response to procedural errors. When you see an alert message, click OK, or press Enter, to close the dialog box. You can also press F1 to display a Help screen that provides an explanation of that particular message. The Help screen associated with the *Error in formula* message is shown in Figure 2-5 on the next page.

To close the Help screen and return to your worksheet, choose Exit from the File menu in the Excel Help window. When the alert message reappears, click the OK button, or press Enter.

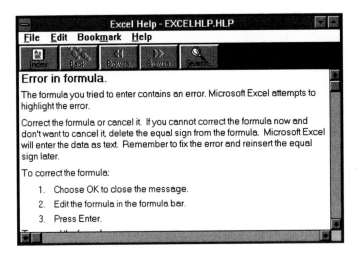

FIGURE 2-5. *The Help screen for the* Error in formula *alert message.*

EXPLORING MICROSOFT EXCEL'S FUNCTIONS

As we mentioned earlier, Microsoft Excel offers functions for most common formulas and also for many not-so-common ones. As you have seen, you can display the Paste Function dialog box to see the names of all of Excel's built-in functions.

Other Basic Functions

You will use some of Microsoft Excel's functions often, and others rarely. In this section, we take a look at a few functions you might use frequently.

The AVERAGE function

The AVERAGE function calculates the average of a set of values. The function has the form

    =AVERAGE(*number1,number2*...)

where *number1*, *number2*, and so on are placeholders for the actual values you want to average.

For example, if you enter the following function in cell B14:

    =AVERAGE(B4:B8)

the result is the same as that of the formula in cell B12:

```
=SUM(B4:B8)/5
```

which also calculates the average sales per department for the month. In this example, the argument of AVERAGE was one range of cells, but like other functions, the AVERAGE function can include up to 14 arguments. This function is quicker to enter than its mathematical equivalent, and you don't need to know the exact number of cells to be included in the computation.

The MIN and MAX functions

At times you may need to know the lowest or highest value in a range of cells. The MIN function returns the minimum value in its arguments, and the MAX function returns the maximum value in its arguments. These functions have the form

=MIN(*number1,number2*...)

and

=MAX(*number1,number2*...)

where *number1, number2*, and so on are placeholders for the actual values from which you want Microsoft Excel to determine the highest or lowest value.

To see how these functions work, enter the following function in cell B16:

```
=MAX(B4:B8)
```

This function returns a value of 27280, the highest sales value in the specified range. The function

```
=MIN(B4:B8)
```

returns a value of 13750, the lowest sales value in the same range.

The ROUND function

Microsoft Excel computes all values to 15 digits. You may not want to calculate your values that precisely, however. In calculating prices, for example, tracking fractions of pennies is sometimes more trouble than it's worth. To round off a value, you can simply use the value as the first argument of the ROUND function. This function has the following form:

=ROUND(*value,number of decimal places*)

The *number of decimal places* argument indicates how many decimal places you want in the result.

To experiment with rounding, move to a blank cell in your worksheet, and enter the following function:

```
=ROUND(6123.77889,2)
```

The result, 6123.78, is rounded to two decimal places. Now replace the second argument (2) with 0:

```
=ROUND(6123.77889,0)
```

to round the value to the nearest whole number.

To round the value to the *left* of the decimal point, you use a negative number for the second argument. For example, to round the value in the cell to the nearest thousand, change the 0 to –3.

The IF Function

The IF function is the most important of Microsoft Excel's *logical functions*— functions that return one value if a condition is true and another if it is false. The IF function has the following form:

=IF(*logical test,value if true,value if false*)

The *logical test* argument is usually a comparison of two items. The items can be values, cell references, formulas, functions, or text. You indicate the kind of comparison you want by using one of the *comparison operators* listed in Table 2-3.

Operator	Meaning
<	Less than
>	Greater than
=	Equal to
<>	Not equal to
<=	Less than or equal to
>=	Greater than or equal to

TABLE 2-3. *Comparison operators for use in logical tests.*

The concept of the IF function is easier to demonstrate than explain, so let's look at an example. Suppose that cell K6 contains the function

```
=IF(J6="APPROVED",50,"N/A")
```

The *logical test* argument specifies that if cell J6 contains the text *APPROVED*, the result in cell K6 will be the value 50 (the *value if true* argument). If cell J6 doesn't contain *APPROVED*, the result in cell K6 will be the text *N/A* (the *value if false* argument).

Now let's see how we can put the IF function to work at Alan's Sports. Suppose that, in an effort to boost sales, Alan's Sports has decided to allocate money for bonuses based on total sales for July and August. The total amount made available for bonuses is to be 25 percent of the amount by which sales for each month exceeded $100,000.

To compute the bonus totals, enter the following functions in the cells indicated (if necessary, replace any practice entries you may have made):

Cell	Function
B12	=IF(B10>100000,25%*(B10−100000),0)
C12	=IF(C10>100000,25%*(C10−100000),0)

Because total sales in August (the value in cell C10) exceeds $100,000, the logical test of the function in cell C12 is true, and Excel enters the *value if true* argument, 1357.5, in cell C12. Because July sales were less than $100,000, the function in cell B12 returns the *value if false* argument, 0.

The arguments of the IF function can themselves be IF functions. In fact, you can nest IF functions up to seven levels deep. Here's a formula with three nested IF functions (entered as one long formula, but broken into two lines here for readability). See if you can figure out what the function does:

```
=IF(A1=100,"Bravo",IF(A1=85,"Well done",
   IF(A1=70,"You can do better","See me after class")))
```

Excel's Financial Functions

If you frequently perform financial calculations, Microsoft Excel's financial functions may save you more calculation time than any other type of worksheet function. They are perfect for computing compound interest, and they're also convenient for determining the wisdom of an investment. In this section, we'll give you a few examples of ways you might use these functions.

As we discuss the Microsoft Excel financial functions in this section, remember that a plus or minus sign attached to an argument indicates the direction in which the money flows. For both the arguments you enter and the values Excel returns as results, a negative (–) number means a payment (money that you must spend) and a positive (+) number means money that you receive.

The FV function

The FV function determines the future value of an investment. It answers the question, ''How much money will I accumulate if I put away a given amount regularly for a given time at a given interest rate?'' The FV function has the following form:

=FV(*rate,nper,pmt,pv,type*)

The *rate* argument is the annual interest rate; if you make periodic payments during the year, divide this rate by the number of payments per year to get the periodic interest rate. Include the percent sign (%) after this number when you enter it in the formula. The *nper* (number of periods) argument is the number of actual payments you will make over the term of the investment. The *pmt* (payment) argument is the periodic payment you will make. The *pv* (present value) argument and the *type* argument, both of which are optional, specify whether the investment has an initial value and whether the payments will be made at the beginning (0) or at the end (1) of each period.

Suppose you're interested in saving money to send your child to college ten years from now. You estimate that you will be able to put away $100 per month for this purpose at a 5 percent after-tax rate of return. You want to know if this will be enough. To find out, open a blank worksheet by choosing New from the File menu, and clicking OK or pressing Enter. Then enter the following information in the cells indicated:

Cell	Entry
A1	Rate
B1	5%
A2	Years
B2	10
A3	Amount
B3	100
A5	Total

Now enter the following function in cell B5:

```
=FV(B1/12,B2*12,-B3)
```

(The minus sign in front of the third argument, B3, is necessary because the savings amount represents money that you pay out.) Excel returns the value 15528.23. Now all you have to do is figure out how much four years of college will cost ten years from now. If it's more than $15,528.23, you'll need to save more than $100 per month.

> *Notice that cell B1 gives the* annual *rate of return and that the period in cell B2 is also expressed in years. The amount of savings in cell B3, however, is a monthly amount. To adjust for the different time periods, you must divide cell B1 by 12 and multiply cell B2 by 12. Failure to coordinate the rate of return with the time period is a common error in this type of function.*

The PV function

The PV function determines the present value of an investment. It answers the question, "How much is it worth to me to receive a given amount at regular intervals for a given time at a given rate of return?" The PV function has the following form:

=PV(*rate,nper,pmt,fv,type*)

The arguments for this function are the same as those for the FV function, except that you use the *fv* (future value) argument instead of the *pv* (present value) argument when you want to calculate the present value of a series of lump-sum payments that will be made in the future.

For example, suppose your retired parents have decided to sell their home. They will realize $100,000 from the sale. They've been told that the $100,000 can purchase an annuity that will pay them $600 per month for 20 years, and they want to know whether you think the annuity is a good investment. You estimate that they could earn 5 percent annually after taxes on the money in conservative investments. To evaluate the annuity, enter these values in the cells indicated, overwriting the values you entered for the FV calculation:

Cell	Entry
B1	5%
B2	20
B3	600

Now enter the following function in cell B5:

```
=PV(B1/12,B2*12,B3)
```

Microsoft Excel returns the value –90915.2. This means your parents could achieve the same $600 monthly income by simply investing about $91,000, leaving them more than $9,000 to spend or to save as they pleased. Assuming they're willing to bear whatever risks are involved in alternative investments, purchasing the annuity is not advisable.

The PMT function

The PMT function determines the periodic payment needed to amortize a loan. It answers the question, "What periodic payment must I make to pay off a loan of a given amount over a given number of periods at a given interest rate?" The PMT function has the following form:

=PMT(*rate,nper,amount of loan,fv,type*)

where the arguments are the same as those described for the FV and PV functions, except for *amount of loan*, which is the principal amount.

Suppose you're considering buying a house with a 30-year mortgage loan of $72,000 and an annual mortgage interest rate of 10.5 percent. To calculate your monthly payments, enter the following function in an empty cell:

```
=PMT(10.5%/12,360,72000)
```

The result is –658.612, meaning your monthly payment would be $658.61.

 Be sure to include the percent sign in the interest rate. If you omit it, the payment returned will be alarming! For example, omitting the percent sign in the previous formula produces a monthly payment of $63,000!

Now suppose a 15-year loan is also available at the lower interest rate of 10 percent. To find the monthly payments on that loan, enter the following function in another cell of your worksheet:

```
=PMT(10%/12,180,72000)
```

The payment for this loan would be $773.72 a month. You can now decide whether the larger monthly payments (approximately $115 more) are acceptable in return for a mortgage that will be fully paid after 15 years, saving you almost $100,000 in interest.

By using the following formula, you can have Excel round the results of the PMT function:

```
=ROUND(PMT(10.5%/12,360,72000),2)
```

DEALING WITH CIRCULAR REFERENCES

Sooner or later, you'll encounter the Microsoft Excel circular-reference alert message, shown in Figure 2-6. Excel displays this message when you enter a formula that refers to its own cell, as cell A2 in Figure 2-7 does. The circular reference can also be indirect, as when cell A3 refers to cell B5, cell B5 refers to cell B10, and cell B10 refers to cell A3.

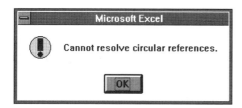

FIGURE 2-6. *The circular-reference alert message.*

FIGURE 2-7. *A worksheet with a circular reference in cell A2.*

The circular-reference alert message means that Excel can't calculate a result because the computation depends on the value of the formula itself. Generally, a circular reference results from a data-entry error or from a flaw in the logical structure of your worksheet. You can usually track down data-entry errors quickly. Look first in the cell listed in the message area of the status bar. Then, if you see no mistake there, look in each of the cells referred to by the formula. If you can't find the error there, you may have made an error that requires a thorough, methodical examination of the interrelationships in the worksheet.

At times, you may intentionally create a circular reference to calculate a value. For example, suppose you want to make a contribution equal to 25 percent of your net income to a retirement plan. By "net income," you mean income after all expenses, *including* the retirement-plan contributions. This computation is expressed algebraically as follows:

$$C = .25 * N$$
$$N = 60000 - C$$

where C is the amount of the contribution, N is net income, and the net income before the contribution is deducted is \$60,000.

To solve this type of equation in Excel, follow these steps:

1. Drag through cells A1:B5, and choose the Clear command from the Edit menu. Click OK, or press Enter, to clear all the entries in your practice worksheet. (You'll learn more about the Clear command in Chapter 3, "Revising and Reviewing Worksheets.")

2. Enter the following formula in cell A1:

    =60000-A2

3. Enter the following formula in cell A2:

    =A1*25%

After you enter the formulas, Excel beeps, displays the alert message shown in Figure 2-6, and stops without performing any calculations. The problem is that to compute the value of cell A1, Excel first has to compute the value of cell A2. But the value of cell A2 is dependent on the value of cell A1. To solve the equations, Excel must temporarily overlook the circular reference. To proceed, follow these steps:

1. Click the OK button, or press Enter, to remove the alert message from your screen.

2. Choose Calculation from the Options menu. The following dialog box appears.

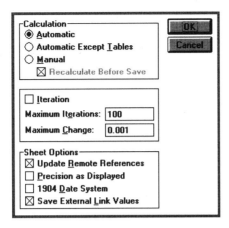

3. Click the Iteration check box to tell Excel you want it to try to resolve the circular reference, and change the entry in the Maximum Iterations box to 1.

4. Click the OK button, or press Enter.

When the dialog box disappears, the value of cell A2 changes to 15000 (25 percent of 60000). Excel has set the initial value of cell A2 to 0 for the purpose of calculating a value for cell A1. After Excel has a value for cell A1 (60000), it uses that value in the formula in cell A2.

Now press F9, the shortcut key for choosing the Calculate Now command from the Options menu. Excel recalculates the formulas based on the current values of cells A1 and A2. The value of cell A1 changes to 45000, and the value of cell A2 changes to 11250.

If you continue pressing F9, the values of cells A1 and A2 continue changing, but by ever-decreasing amounts. Each time you press F9, Excel calculates new values for the two cells, using their current values. Each round of calculations is called an *iteration*. Eventually, the values in the cells change little, if at all, with each iteration. At that point, your problem is solved.

The following table lists the values displayed after each iteration in this example. When the values no longer change, cell A1 equals 60000 less cell A2, and cell A2 equals 25 percent of cell A1.

Iteration number	Cell A1 value	Cell A2 value
1	60000.00	15000.00
2	45000.00	11250.00
3	48750.00	12187.50
4	47812.50	11953.13
5	48046.88	12011.72
6	47988.28	11997.07
7	48002.93	12000.73
8	47999.27	11999.82
9	48000.18	12000.05
10	47999.95	11999.99
11	48000.01	12000.00
12	48000.00	12000.00

When you chose Calculation from the Options menu and changed the Maximum Iterations value to 1, you told Excel to calculate values for the cells once and then stop, so that you could step through the iterations and see how the values of the cells changed. Normally, however, you'll want the program to run through as many iterations as are necessary to find correct values for the formulas, without you having to press F9 for each calculation. Choose the Calculation command from the Options menu again, and change the value in the Maximum Iterations box back to 100. This setting tells Excel to perform up to 100 iterations, but to stop when the maximum change in the computed values is less than or equal to 0.001, the value in the Maximum Change box. (These default entries in the Maximum Iterations and Maximum Change boxes allow Microsoft Excel to return correct values in most cases.) To close the dialog box, click the OK button, or press Enter.

To see the default iteration settings in action, select cell A2 in the worksheet, and change the formula to

```
=A1*20%
```

When you press Enter, the value in cell A1 becomes 50000, and the value in cell A2 becomes 10000. Excel has instantaneously "iterated" its way to the correct values.

When the Iteration option is selected in the Calculation dialog box, you won't see a message if you accidentally create a circular reference, so choose the Calculation command from the Options menu again, and turn off the Iteration option. Turn on iteration only when you've consciously decided to use a circular reference.

 Remember that when Excel displays the circular-reference alert message, it also displays a status-bar message that shows the address of the cell that contains the circular reference.

WORKING WITH DATES AND TIMES

With Microsoft Excel, you can use dates and times in formulas. For example, suppose you will receive payments on a loan, and the exact amount to be allocated to interest depends on the time that has elapsed since the previous payment. Excel represents time intervals as decimal numbers, making short work of this type of calculation.

Entering Dates and Times

You can type dates and times in Microsoft Excel worksheets in a number of formats. For example, all of the following are valid ways to enter *April 15, 1991, at 5:00 PM*:

    4/15/91 5:00 PM
    15 Apr 91 17:00
    April 15, 1991 5 PM
    17:00:00 4-15-1991

To see how Microsoft Excel handles these different formats, select an empty column in your worksheet, and enter each of the dates from the list. As you do so, watch the formula bar after you press Enter. The date value always appears there in the following format:

    4/15/1991 5:00:00 PM

However, Excel has filled the cells with pound signs (#) because the cells weren't wide enough to display the dates. Widen the cells now by pointing to the right border of the header of the column in which you made the entries and dragging the border to the right. As you can now see, Excel displays date/time entries in m/d/yy h:mm format (4/15/1991 17:00) unless you specify a different format. You'll learn how to change the format in Chapter 4, ''Enhancing Your Worksheets.''

▽ *If you enter 4/15 for April 15, omitting the year, Excel supplies the current year from your system clock. However, if you enter April 15, Excel treats the number as a year and displays the date 4/1/2015. Take a minute to enter a variety of dates in m/dd format to become familiar with how Excel handles them.*

Microsoft Excel can use dates and times in formulas and functions because it stores all dates and times as serial numbers in your computer's memory. The numbers from 1 through 65380 represent the dates January 1, 1900, through December 31, 2078. If you try to enter a date outside this range, Excel treats the entry as text. Internally, Excel expresses any date within this span as a number equal to the number of days between December 31, 1899, and the given date. Thus, *April 15, 1991*, is represented as 33343, the number of days that have elapsed since December 31, 1899.

Excel expresses time as a decimal fraction of a whole day. For example, the time 5:00 PM is represented as the value 0.7083333333 (that is, 17 divided by 24). Thus, the complete serial number for *April 15, 1991, at 5:00 PM* is the day number plus the time fraction: 33343.7083333333.

Using Dates and Times in Formulas

Suppose that on March 1, 1991, you purchased a new home and in the process took out a second mortgage for $20,000. You're required to make payments on this second mortgage once a year, and the interest rate is 15 percent. It is now August 10, 1991, and interest rates have dropped. You realize that because of the high interest rate, you should pay off this loan as quickly as possible. You would like to know how much interest has accumulated to date.

To calculate the interest, enter the following data in the cells indicated (overwriting any existing entries):

Cell	Entry
A1	3/1/91
A2	8/10/91
A3	=ROUND(20000*((A2–A1)/365)*15%,2)

The formula in cell A3 returns 1331.51, the amount of interest that has accumulated on the $20,000 balance as of August 10, 1991. To pay off the loan, then, you'll need to come up with a total of $21,331.51.

Using Date and Time Functions

Thanks to some useful Microsoft Excel functions, you have considerable flexibility in using dates and times in worksheets. Let's take a look at a few of these functions.

The NOW function is one of the few Excel functions that do not require any arguments. Open a blank worksheet, and then type the following function in cell A1:

```
=NOW()
```

The NOW function obtains the current date and time from your computer's internal clock and displays the information in the cell as a serial number. To make a readable date, time, or both appear, you must format the cell appropriately (a technique you'll learn in Chapter 3, ''Revising and Reviewing Worksheets''). You'll use this worksheet again in a moment, so keep it on your screen now.

 The date and time displayed in the cell aren't continuously updated. They change only when the worksheet is opened or recalculated.

Table 2-4 lists functions that extract parts of a date or time from the serial number. You can use these functions to determine, for example, what day of the week a particular date falls on. Each of these functions returns an integer. The ranges of possible values are shown in the third column of the table.

Function	Value returned	Range
YEAR()	Year	1900 through 2078
MONTH()	Month of the year	1 through 12
DAY()	Day of the month	1 through 31
WEEKDAY()	Day of the week	1 through 7
HOUR()	Hour of the day	0 through 23
MINUTE()	Minute of the hour	0 through 59
SECOND()	Second of the minute	0 through 59
DATEVALUE()	Serial number corresponding to the specified date	1 through 65380 (for example, =DATEVALUE("11/30/90") produces 33207)

TABLE 2-4. *Date and time functions.* *(continued)*

TABLE 2-4. *continued*

Function	Value returned	Range
TODAY()	Serial number of the current date	1 through 65380
DAYS360()	Number of days between two dates based on a 360-day year	1 through 32559 (for example, =DAYS360("11/1/89","11/1/90") produces 360)

Experiment with these functions using the value returned by the NOW function in cell A1 of your worksheet. For example, to display the year, select cell A2 and enter the function *=YEAR(A1)*. Then close all worksheets except *ALSPORTS*. (You don't need to save them.)

USING NAMES

Microsoft Excel allows you to assign names to individual cells and ranges so that you can refer to the cell or range by name instead of by reference. This capability means that you don't have to worry about remembering the precise locations of the cells you want to use in your formulas, and you don't have to spend time scrolling around the worksheet looking for them.

Naming Individual Cells

To assign a name to a single cell (for example, cell B5 in the *ALSPORTS* worksheet), follow these steps:

1. Select cell B5.

2. Choose the Define Name command from the Formula menu. The following dialog box appears:

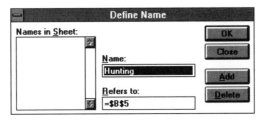

When you select the Define Name command, Microsoft Excel searches adjacent cells for text entries that might provide an appropriate name. Having found the word *Hunting* in cell A5, Excel suggests that name for cell B5. Excel also displays the reference of the active cell. (The reference is displayed in fixed-reference format, which we'll discuss in Chapter 3, "Revising and Reviewing Worksheets.") Now edit the name.

3. Type *JulyHunting* in the text box. The name Excel suggested disappears as you start typing.

4. Click the Add button.

5. Click the Refers To box.

6. Press the Down direction key. The cell reference in the Refers To box changes to $B$6.

7. Type *JulyCamping* in the text box.

8. Click the Add button again.

9. Click the Close button.

Now select a blank cell in the worksheet, and enter the formula:

```
=JulyHunting
```

Microsoft Excel displays the value from cell B5 in the formula bar, just as if you had entered the formula

```
=B5
```

After you define a name, it appears in the Name list box whenever you choose the Define Name command from the Formula menu.

 Microsoft Excel names can contain numeric characters, but names must begin *with a letter. The letters* R *(for* row) *and* C *(for* column) *are valid first letters only if they are immediately followed by an additional letter, not a number.*

Naming Ranges

You can assign a name to a range of cells in the same way you assign a name to a single cell. Simply select the range, and then choose the Define Name command from the Formula menu. In the Define Name dialog box, type the name you want to assign, and then click OK.

Allowing Excel to Assign Names

You can define multiple names with one command. To define multiple names in the *ALSPORTS* worksheet, follow these steps:

1. Select the range A3:C9.

2. Choose the Create Names command from the Formula menu. The following dialog box appears:

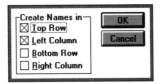

   Microsoft Excel goes to the edge of the specified range to find text entries to use as names.

3. Because you have entered text in column A and row 3, accept the default options (Top Row and Left Column) by pressing Enter.

You can now use any of the words in the top row and left column of the selected range as names for the corresponding cells. For example, to reference a cell in the *ALSPORTS* worksheet by name, all you need to do is enter the department name and month, in any order, separated by a space. To try this for yourself, move to a remote part of the worksheet, and press F5 (the shortcut key for the Goto command). Then type *August Camping* in the dialog box that appears. When you press Enter, the active cell jumps to cell C6, which is the intersection of the *August* column and the *Camping* row.

Using Names in Formulas

One of the most compelling reasons for naming cells and ranges is that you can use the names as arguments in formulas. To see how this works, follow these steps:

1. Select a blank cell, and enter the following formula:

   ```
   =SUM(Hunting:Other)
   ```

2. Select another blank cell, and enter the following formula:

   ```
   =SUM(B5:C8)
   ```

Both formulas return the same value (163710).

Deleting Names

When you select a rectangular range and choose the Create Names command from the Formula menu, Microsoft Excel assigns the label in the top-left corner to *every* cell in the range. The word *Dept.* has therefore been assigned to every cell in the range A3:C9. However, in the *ALSPORTS* worksheet, only the specific departments and the months are useful as names, so you can delete the name *Dept.* and any other names you no longer need.

To delete *Dept.* and *JulyHunting*, follow these steps:

1. Choose the Define Name command from the Formula menu.

2. Select *Dept.* from the list box.

3. Click the Delete button to delete the name.

4. Select *JulyHunting* from the list box.

5. Click the Delete button again.

6. Click OK, or press Enter.

Clean up the worksheet now by deleting the other entries you made in blank cells while learning to use cell names. Then save the *ALSPORTS* worksheet for use in the next chapter.

CONCLUSION

This chapter has introduced formulas, briefly explained some of the most important Microsoft Excel functions, and explained the concept of cell and range names. We will discuss more Microsoft Excel functions later on. Many functions, however, such as the functions that manipulate text, are not covered in this introductory book. For detailed information on these functions, use the Help command, or refer to the Microsoft Excel documentation.

Chapter 3

Revising and Reviewing Worksheets

The real beauty of Microsoft Excel worksheets is the ease with which you can make revisions. In this chapter, you'll learn how to revise worksheets, and you'll see how Excel keeps track of your data changes and recalculates the worksheet. You'll also learn how to use Excel's data protection to prevent other people from making unwanted revisions to your worksheets. Finally, you'll find out how to use outlining to review and revise the structure of your worksheets.

COPYING AND MOVING DATA

The ability to copy and move data and formulas is important when you are constructing large, sophisticated worksheets. In this section, we'll look at the tools Microsoft Excel provides for copying, cutting, and pasting.

 You can display more of your worksheet on the screen by enlarging (maximizing) both the Microsoft Excel window and the document window. Simply click the Maximize button (the up-pointing arrowhead) in the top-right corner of each window.

Copying Data

To demonstrate copying, let's calculate the sales gain from July to August in the *ALSPORTS* worksheet. You could, of course, select cell D10 and enter the appropriate function, but it's much easier to simply copy the formula in cell D8 to cell D10. To copy a formula, follow these steps:

1. Select cell D8.

2. Choose the Copy command from the Edit menu. The marquee surrounds the cell.

3. Select cell D10.

4. Press Enter.

Cell D10 now displays 0.10804—the increase in sales from July to August.

Although it might seem that you carried out only one command, you actually carried out two. Copying in Microsoft Excel requires choosing two successive commands: the Copy command and the Paste command. Because you began this operation with the Copy command, Excel interprets the Enter key to be a shortcut key for the Paste command.

Microsoft Excel copies data to a *paste range* the same size and shape as the *copy range*, with the top-left cell as the active cell. The following example shows how this works.

Suppose you have just received the September sales figures for Alan's Sports. You want to add another section to your worksheet to show the increase in sales, for each department, from August to September. To create the new section, copy the department names, as follows:

1. Select the range A4:A8.

2. Use the keyboard shortcut for the Copy command: Hold down Ctrl, and press Ins.

3. Select cell A13.

4. Press Enter to paste the department names in the range A13:A17.

 The data you copy or move into a given cell replaces any data currently occupying that cell. Remember, though, that if you mistakenly overwrite data with the Paste command, you can recover it with the Undo command from the Edit menu (if you haven't yet carried out any other command).

Now for some more copying practice: First, copy cell D3 to cell D12. Then copy the range C3:C10 to B12:B19, using the same procedure you used a moment ago. Your worksheet now looks like Figure 3-1.

If you need to copy a given range to multiple locations in a worksheet, hold down Shift, and press Ins instead of Enter to complete the copy operation. The marquee remains active, signaling that you can paste the selected data in as many locations as you want, as long as you paste using Shift-Ins. To complete the command, press Enter to paste the data to its final location, or press Esc to remove the marquee when you've finished pasting.

```
─                    Microsoft Excel - ALSPORTS.XLS                    ▼ ▲
─   File   Edit   Formula   Format   Data   Options   Macro   Window   Help        ▶
 Normal              ▪│ ◆ ◆ ▦ ▦ Σ │ B I │ ▤ ▤ ▤ │ ▤ │ ◥ ▢ ◯ ◥ │ ▥ ▣ ▢ ▩
         J1
         A          B          C          D          E      F      G      H      I
 1   Alan's Sports
 2
 3   Dept.       July       August     Gain (%)
 4   Skiing        15600     21270      0.363462
 5   Hunting       27280     25900     -0.05059
 6   Camping       13750     11085     -0.19382
 7   Apparel       15920     23540      0.478643
 8   Other         22600     23635      0.045796
 9
10                95150    105430      0.10804
11
12               August              Gain (%)
13   Skiing       21270
14   Hunting      25900
15   Camping      11085
16   Apparel      23540
17   Other        23635
18
19              105430
20
21
 Ready
```

FIGURE 3-1. *The* ALSPORTS *worksheet with the August sales figures copied.*

You'll learn a quicker method of copying in a minute. First, though, we'll show you how to move data; that is, how to put the data in a different cell or range and delete it from its original location.

Moving Data

Like the copy operation, the move operation consists of two commands. You must use both the Cut and Paste commands from the Edit menu.

To learn how to move cell data from one part of a worksheet to another, start by entering the September sales figures. Enter *September* in cell E3, and then enter the following sales figures in the range E4:E8:

Cell	Value
E4	36560
E5	28710
E6	7250
E7	27800
E8	30840

Now suppose you decide to move the September data to the lower portion of the worksheet. Follow these steps:

1. Select the range E3:E8.

2. Choose the Cut command from the Edit menu, or hold down Shift and press Del (the keyboard shortcut for the Cut command). The marquee surrounds the selected range.

3. Select cell C12.

4. Press Enter to move the data to the range C12:C17. (Pressing Enter has the same effect as choosing Paste from the Edit menu.)

 Using the shortcut keys for copy and move operations saves you time. You should make a point of memorizing them right away. The Edit menu lends a hand by listing important keyboard shortcuts next to the associated command names as reminders.

Fast Copying

The Fill commands on the Edit menu let you quickly and easily copy data to an adjacent range of cells. For example, select the range B19:C19, and choose Fill Right from the Edit menu. Microsoft Excel copies the formula in cell B19 to cell C19. In this case, you copied only one cell to an adjacent cell, but you can imagine how handy this command would be for heavy-duty copying. For example, suppose you want to copy 20 rows of complex formulas into the 20 adjacent columns. You can select a 20-row-by-21-column range, with the formulas in the leftmost column, and then simply choose the Fill Right command. Excel copies all the formulas from the leftmost column, row-by-row, to the rest of the cells in the range.

The Fill Down command works in a similar way. Try using Fill Down to calculate the gain from August to September in the *ALSPORTS* worksheet:

1. Copy cell D4 to cell D13.

2. Select the range D13:D19.

3. Choose the Fill Down command from the Edit menu. Fill Down copies the formula to the entire selected range.

4. Cells B18 and C18 are empty, so cell D18 displays a #DIV/0! error value. To get rid of the value, delete the formula from this cell.

Your worksheet now looks like Figure 3-2.

	A	B	C	D	E	F	G	H	I
1	Alan's Sports								
2									
3	Dept.	July	August	Gain (%)					
4	Skiing	15600	21270	0.363462					
5	Hunting	27280	25900	-0.05059					
6	Camping	13750	11085	-0.19382					
7	Apparel	15920	23540	0.478643					
8	Other	22600	23635	0.045796					
9									
10		95150	105430	0.10804					
11									
12		August	Septembe	Gain (%)					
13	Skiing	21270	36560	0.718853					
14	Hunting	25900	28710	0.108494					
15	Camping	11085	7250	-0.34596					
16	Apparel	23540	27800	0.180969					
17	Other	23635	30840	0.304845					
18									
19		105430	131160	0.244048					
20									
21									

FIGURE 3-2. *The* ALSPORTS *worksheet with the August–September sales comparison.*

Like the Copy command, the Fill commands overwrite any existing data in the destination portion of the selected range.

INSERTING AND DELETING

Unlike paper worksheets, Microsoft Excel worksheets give you the ability to insert blank rows or columns to hold information that may have slipped your mind when you were creating the original worksheet layout.

Inserting Rows and Columns

Suppose you want to add a descriptive title to your worksheet, but you still want to retain the blank row above the sales data. To do so, you must insert a new row. To insert a new row above row 3 and add a title, follow these steps:

1. Select the entire row 3 by clicking its header.

2. Choose the Insert command from the Edit menu. The rows from 3 on move down, leaving a new, blank row 3. (If Excel displays a dialog box, you probably selected a cell or a range instead of the entire row. Press Esc, select row 3, and choose the Insert command again.)

3. In cell A2, enter *Month-to-Month Sales.*

Now suppose Alan's Sports has decided to break the Other category into two parts: Team Sports and Golf. To make this change, follow these steps:

1. Insert a new row above row 9.

2. Enter *Team Sports* in cell A9.

3. Enter *Golf* in cell A10.

4. Enter the following sales figures in columns B and C of rows 9 and 10 for the newly created departments. (The new Golf figures replace the old Other figures.)

Department	July sales	August sales
Team Sports	12500	13930
Golf	10100	9705

5. Copy cell D8 to cell D9 to compute the percentage gain for the Team Sports department.

Now you'll use a different method to add another new row immediately above row 19:

1. Select the entire row 9.

2. Choose Copy from the Edit menu.

3. Select cell A19.

4. Choose the Insert Paste command from the Edit menu.

Excel copies the data in row 9 to row 19, and in the process, moves everything below row 19 down a row to make room.

Now copy the August sales figures for the Team Sports and Golf departments from the upper portion of the worksheet to cells B19 and B20. In cells C19 and C20, enter *22570* and *8270* (the September sales figures for Team Sports and Golf). When you replace *Other* in cell A20 with *Golf*, your worksheet looks like Figure 3-3.

	A	B	C	D	E	F	G	H	I
1	Alan's Sports								
2	Month-to-Month Sales								
3									
4	Dept.	July	August	Gain (%)					
5	Skiing	15600	21270	0.363462					
6	Hunting	27280	25900	-0.05059					
7	Camping	13750	11085	-0.19382					
8	Apparel	15920	23540	0.478643					
9	Team Spc	12500	13930	0.1144					
10	Golf	10100	9705	-0.03911					
11									
12		95150	105430	0.10804					
13									
14		August	Septembe	Gain (%)					
15	Skiing	21270	36560	0.718853					
16	Hunting	25900	28710	0.108494					
17	Camping	11085	7250	-0.34596					
18	Apparel	23540	27800	0.180969					
19	Team Spc	13930	22570	0.620244					
20	Golf	9705	8270	-0.14786					

FIGURE 3-3. *The* ALSPORTS *worksheet with Other replaced by the Team Sports and Golf departments.*

Excel makes it easy to insert new columns in your worksheets. To insert a new column, simply select the entire column (by clicking its header) to the right of the location where you need the new column, and choose the Insert command from the Edit menu. Now practice by inserting a new column in front of the current column D.

Deleting Rows and Columns

Deleting rows and columns is as straightforward as inserting them. To delete the blank column you just inserted in the *ALSPORTS* worksheet, simply select column D, and choose the Delete command from the Edit menu.

 If you enter data in a remote area of the worksheet, you might forget it's there. It's a good policy always to scroll through the worksheet before deleting rows or columns, to ensure that important data is not inadvertently deleted.

Inserting Cells

You don't always have to insert entire rows or columns in a worksheet. When you want to insert only a few cells, simply select the same number of cells below or to the right of the location where you need the new cells, and choose the Insert command from the Edit menu. Microsoft Excel shifts other cells in the worksheet to make room for the new cells. You must choose between shifting the selected cells and all cells located to the right of them to the *right* and shifting the selected cells and all cells located below them *down*. To see how this works, follow these steps:

1. Select the range A4:A12.

2. Choose the Insert command from the Edit menu. The following dialog box appears:

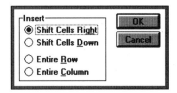

3. Confirm that Shift Cells Right is selected.

4. Click OK, or press Enter.

The labels in these cells move one column to the right.

Deleting Cells

The Delete command on the Edit menu works in much the same manner as the Insert command. To delete some cells, follow these steps:

1. Select the range A4:A12.

2. Choose the Delete command from the Edit menu.

3. Confirm that Shift Cells Left is selected.

4. Click OK, or press Enter.

The labels move left to column A, again without changing anything above or below the selection.

 Note that the Insert and Delete commands on the Edit menu work only with single, rectangular selections. You cannot select discontiguous ranges to insert or delete multiple rows or columns with one command.

USING RELATIVE AND FIXED CELL ADDRESSES

Revising worksheets can be fraught with danger unless you understand the difference between Microsoft Excel's two types of cell addresses: *relative* and *fixed*. (So far, we've used only relative cell addresses.) Relative addresses identify cells by their positions in relation to the active cell. Fixed cell addresses, on the other hand, refer to the fixed, or *absolute*, positions of the cells. The fixed addressing method uses dollar signs ($) to indicate the absolute portions of the cell address.

Look at the formula in cell D10 that we copied from cell D8, earlier in the chapter. Because we used the relative address (no dollar signs) in the function in cell D8, the function in cell D10 contains a different cell range, but one that occupies the same position *relative to cell D10* as the range in cell D8 occupies relative to cell D8.

To see the difference between using relative and fixed cell addresses, try copying a cell using a fixed address. First, save the *ALSPORTS* worksheet in case you make an error and want to get back to where you were. Then follow the steps on the next page.

1. Select cell B12.

2. Edit the formula to read as follows:

   `=SUM($B$5:$B$10)`

3. Copy the formula in cell B12 to cell C12.

Your worksheet now looks like Figure 3-4. Because the formula in cell B12 contains fixed cell references, the formula in cell C12 is exactly the same as the formula in cell B12. However, the formula now in cell C12 doesn't produce the result you want because it sums cells B5 through B10, rather than cells C5 through C10. Because the formula uses a fixed cell reference, copying it to other cells will yield unintended results.

To restore the original formula, choose the Undo Paste command from the Edit menu. Then press Esc to remove the marquee.

	Microsoft Excel - ALSPORTS.XLS								
File	**Edit**	**Formula**	**Format**	**Data**	**Options**	**Macro**	**Window**	**Help**	

Normal

C12   =SUM($B$5:$B$10)

	A	B	C	D	E	F	G	H	I
1	Alan's Sports								
2	Month-to-Month Sales								
3									
4	Dept.	July	August	Gain (%)					
5	Skiing	15600	21270	0.363462					
6	Hunting	27280	25900	-0.05059					
7	Camping	13750	11085	-0.19382					
8	Apparel	15920	23540	0.478643					
9	Team Spc	12500	13930	0.1144					
10	Golf	10100	9705	-0.03911					
11									
12		95150	95150	0					
13									
14		August	Septembe	Gain (%)					
15	Skiing	21270	36560	0.718853					
16	Hunting	25900	28710	0.108494					
17	Camping	11085	7250	-0.34596					
18	Apparel	23540	27800	0.180969					
19	Team Spc	13930	22570	0.620244					
20	Golf	9705	8270	-0.14786					
21									

Ready

FIGURE 3-4. *The* ALSPORTS *worksheet after a formula with fixed cell referencing is copied from cell B12 to cell C12.*

82

Be sure to press Esc and not Enter after you choose the Undo Paste command. Pressing Enter simply pastes the copied cell in place again.

You can mix the two cell-address modes by inserting a single dollar sign in front of either the column letter or the row number. The following example shows why you would want to do this. Follow these steps:

1. Select the range F1:F10.

2. Type *10*, hold down Ctrl, and press Enter.

3. Select the range G1:G10.

4. Type the formula

   ```
   =SUM(F$1:F1)
   ```

5. Hold down Ctrl, and press Enter.

Now look at the formulas in cells G2 through G10. The cell address to the left of the colon is F$1 in each formula; the cell address following the colon always reflects the active row. The result is a series of formulas in column G that return cumulative totals of the amounts in column F from row 1 through the current row. The dollar sign, in effect, ''anchors'' the row number of the first half of the range argument in place.

CLEARING DATA

The entries from the previous example are obviously not pertinent to the *ALSPORTS* worksheet, so this would be a good time to learn how to eliminate unwanted entries from your worksheets. You remove data with the Clear command on the Edit menu. Although you can choose Clear from the menu, the fastest way to clear cells is to simply press the Del key.

1. Select F1:G10, and press the Del key. This dialog box appears:

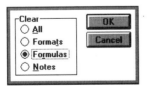

2. Click OK, or press Enter.

Excel erases the entries from the selected range.

The Clear dialog box lets you choose the kinds of data you want to delete. Usually, you will accept the default response (Formulas), which, as you've just seen, clears the contents of the selected cells. Any formatting you have applied to the contents remains, however, and any new entries you make in the cells will be displayed with that formatting. (We discuss formatting in detail in Chapter 4, "Enhancing Your Worksheets.") You can erase the formatting but not the contents by selecting the Formats option, and you can erase both the contents and the formatting by selecting the All option.

The Clear dialog box allows you to clear cell notes as well as formulas and formats. You'll learn more about cell notes later in this chapter.

> *The distinction between the Clear command and the Delete command is important. Clear erases data from a cell but leaves the cell in place; clearing data has no effect on surrounding cells. Delete removes the cell itself from the worksheet and moves adjacent cells up or to the left into the position formerly occupied by the deleted cell.*

UPDATING CELL REFERENCES

When data referenced by formulas in other cells is relocated in a worksheet, Microsoft Excel updates all the formulas that reference that data to reflect its new address. This is true whether the data was relocated by cutting and pasting or by the insertion or deletion of cells.

To see how cell-reference updating works, follow these steps:

1. Select the entire column C in the *ALSPORTS* worksheet.

2. Choose the Insert command from the Edit menu.

The August sales values now appear in column D, but notice that the values in the Gain (%) column didn't change. The gain formulas now refer to cells in column D instead of those in column C. Now choose the Undo command from the Edit menu to return the worksheet to its previous state.

Excel adjusts cell formulas whether the references to the relocated cells are relative, fixed, or mixed.

Updating SUM Functions

Sometimes, deleting a cell referenced by another cell produces a #REF! error value in the worksheet. However, when cells are inserted or deleted from a range referenced by a SUM function, Microsoft Excel adjusts the range argument to account for the revision.

To see how this works, select cell B22 of the *ALSPORTS* worksheet. The formula currently reads

```
=SUM(B15:B20)
```

Now select the entire row 17, and choose the Insert command from the Edit menu. Look again at the SUM formula (now located in cell B23). It now reads

```
=SUM(B15:B21)
```

Microsoft Excel has stretched the range argument to include the newly inserted row. (Choose the Undo command again to undo the row insertion.)

 Of course, if you delete the entire range referenced by a SUM function—rows 15 through 20, for example—you will get a #REF! error.

CONTROLLING WORKSHEET CALCULATION

By default, Microsoft Excel recalculates worksheets whenever you make any kind of change. It does not, however, automatically recalculate every cell in the worksheet. To save time, Excel determines which cells are affected by your change and recalculates only those cells. Even so, automatic recalculation can slow you down when you're working with large documents. Luckily, Excel provides a way to turn off recalculation.

Choose the Calculation command from the Options menu to display the dialog box shown in Figure 3-5 on the next page. The Calculation option group offers you three selections: Automatic, Automatic Except Tables, and Manual. The Automatic option turns automatic recalculation back on after you have turned it off. The Automatic Except Tables option turns automatic recalculation on except for cells in data tables. (The subject of data tables is beyond the scope of this book. For more information on this topic, see the Microsoft Excel documentation.) The Manual option postpones recalculation until you specifically ask Microsoft Excel to recalculate the worksheet.

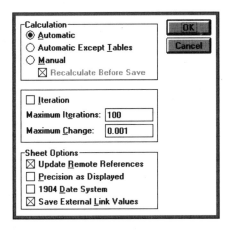

FIGURE 3-5. *The Calculation dialog box.*

To see how manual recalculation works, follow these steps:

1. Select the Manual option in the Calculation dialog box.

2. Click OK, or press Enter.

3. Select cell B9, and change the value in the cell to *10000*. Before you press Enter, look at cell B12.

4. Press Enter. Notice that the total value in cell B12 doesn't change to reflect the lower amount you entered in cell B9.

5. Keeping your eye on cell B12, press F9. The value of cell B12 decreases from $95,150 to $92,650.

The F9 key is the keyboard shortcut for the Calculate Now command, which recalculates values in a worksheet that is set to Manual recalculation.

Before you continue, re-enter *12500* in cell B9. Then choose the Calculation command from the Options menu again, select the Automatic option, and click OK or press Enter.

PROTECTING DATA FROM CHANGE

You may eventually create worksheets to be used primarily by people who are less familiar with Microsoft Excel than you are. Or you may want to hide certain private areas of your worksheet. In such cases, you may want to prevent other users from changing or viewing certain vital parts of the worksheet. (You may not mind a little editing of the department names or column headings in the *ALSPORTS* worksheet, but you don't want anyone to change the monthly figures or other formulas.) Microsoft Excel lets you protect such important data. Let's look at the protection process in detail.

If you are working on a network, consult the Microsoft Excel documentation or your network system manager for document-protection procedures.

Locking and Unlocking Cells

By default, the status of all cells in a worksheet is locked, but because you haven't activated Microsoft Excel's cell-protection system, this status hasn't affected your work so far. If you intend never to activate cell-protection, you can leave the status of all cells locked. You can also leave it locked if you want to protect every cell in the worksheet. If, however, you want to protect some cells but not others, you must first unlock the entire worksheet. To unlock the *ALSPORTS* worksheet, follow these steps:

1. Select the entire worksheet by clicking the small, empty square at the left of column header A and above row header 1 (the circled area shown here):

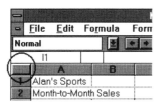

2. Choose the Cell Protection command from the Format menu. The following dialog box appears:

3. Turn off the Locked option.

4. Click OK, or press Enter.

The second step in protecting specific cells is to change the appropriate cells back to locked status. To lock certain cells, follow these steps:

1. Select the portions of the worksheet you want to protect. (Use the ranges B5:D12 and B15:D22 in this example. To select the second range, hold down the Ctrl key, and drag from cell B15 through cell D22.)

2. Choose Cell Protection from the Format menu again. This time, the Locked option in the dialog box is turned off.

3. Turn on the Locked option.

4. Click OK, or press Enter.

Turning on Cell Protection

Now only the cells you want to protect are locked. However, the cell contents can still be changed, because you haven't yet activated the Microsoft Excel cell-protection system—the final step in protecting your worksheet's cells. To turn on the cell-protection system, follow these steps:

1. Choose the Protect Document command from the Options menu. The following dialog box appears:

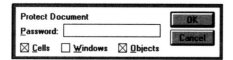

2. Type a password in the text box (for this example, type your initials). Notice that asterisks appear instead of the characters you type so that no one can read your password as you type it.

3. Click OK, or press Enter.

4. Re-enter the password in response to the prompt.

5. Click OK, or press Enter.

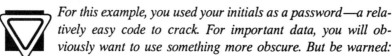 *For this example, you used your initials as a password—a relatively easy code to crack. For important data, you will obviously want to use something more obscure. But be warned: After you protect cells with a password, you cannot change the data without unprotecting the cells, and you cannot unprotect the cells without supplying the password. Always record passwords, and store the record in a secure place.*

Now try to enter data in one of the protected cells. You won't be able to do so; instead, you'll see the message shown in Figure 3-6. Click OK, or press Enter, to remove the error message.

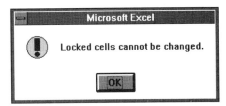

FIGURE 3-6. *This message appears when you try to enter data in a protected cell.*

To remove protection, you simply choose the Unprotect Document command from the Options menu. To practice, follow these steps:

1. Choose Unprotect Document from the Options menu.

2. Deliberately enter the wrong password. Microsoft Excel displays an error message.

3. Click OK, or press Enter, to remove this message.

4. Choose the Unprotect Document command again.

5. Type the correct password in the Password text box.

6. Click OK, or press Enter.

Now you can make changes to any cell in the worksheet.

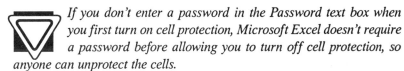

If you don't enter a password in the Password text box when you first turn on cell protection, Microsoft Excel doesn't require a password before allowing you to turn off cell protection, so anyone can unprotect the cells.

If you forget your password and you haven't heeded our earlier warning to write the password down, all is not lost. You can select the entire worksheet and copy it to a blank worksheet. Because protection status is not copied, you will be able to select cells and change their data.

Using Various Types of Protection

Unless you specify otherwise, Microsoft Excel protects both cell contents and screen objects (such as charts and text boxes). By choosing the Windows option from the Protect Document dialog box, you can prevent windows from being moved or resized.

You can also prevent users who don't have the password from opening a document in the first place. To see how this works, follow these steps:

1. Choose the Save As command from the File menu.

2. Click the Options button. The following dialog box appears:

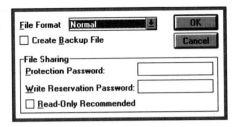

3. Select the Protection Password text box, type your initials, and then press Enter.

4. Re-enter the password as requested, and then press Enter.

5. Click OK, or press Enter, in the Save Worksheet As dialog box.

6. When Microsoft Excel displays a message asking you to confirm that you want the revised file to replace the current one on disk, press Enter.

7. Close the *ALSPORTS* worksheet, and then reopen it. The following dialog box appears:

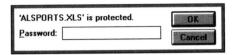

8. Type the password.

Microsoft Excel opens the file.

To remove the password protection, follow these steps:

1. With the file open, choose the Save As command from the File menu.

2. Click the Options button.

3. Delete the password from the Protection Password text box, and then click OK or press Enter.

4. In the Save Worksheet As dialog box, click OK, or press Enter.

5. When Microsoft Excel displays a message asking you to confirm that you want to replace the old version of the file with the new (un-protected) version, click OK, or press Enter.

Suppose you have a file that you'd like to protect but that others must have access to. In that case, you would enter the password in the Write Reservation Password box instead of in the Protection Password box. Excel will not require that a password be entered to open the file, but will require that a password be entered to save changes to the file.

OUTLINING YOUR WORKSHEETS

Microsoft Excel allows you to arrange the rows and columns of your worksheet in outline form. Outlining is useful when you want to organize the data in your worksheet and present it in the best possible way. Outlining is a familiar pro-cedure to people who use high-powered word-processing programs, but it can be confusing to spreadsheet users. To help you see how outlining can make reviewing and revising your worksheets easier, let's take a look at an example.

Entering the Data

Suppose you work in the marketing department of a company called Junk Food Distributors. Your company has four sales regions, and it's your responsibility to summarize monthly sales data by sales office (region).

Open a new worksheet, and enter in the cells designated in the first column of the following table the descriptions for the various Junk Food Distributors product lines listed in the second column:

Cell	Entry
A2	Salted snacks
A3	Candy
A4	Beverages
A5	Cakes & pies
A6	Ice cream

Then add the following data:

1. Enter *100*—the number of units sold—in each of the cells in the range B2:B6.

2. Using the Autosum button on the tool bar, enter the formula

   ```
   =SUM(B1:B6)
   ```

   in cell B8.

3. Now copy the range A2:B8 to the ranges A10:B16, A18:B24, and A26:B32. (Remember, you can do this quickly by selecting cells A10, A18, and A26 before pressing Enter to carry out the Paste command.)

Next type the names of the regional offices in the cells indicated in the following table:

Cell	Entry
A8	New York
A16	Chicago
A24	Detroit
A32	Atlanta

You may want to increase the width of column A so that you can see the labels in their entirety.

To show the grand sales total, select cell B34, and enter the formula

```
=SUM(B8,B16,B24,B32)
```

Creating the Outline

Now that you've entered the basic sales data in your worksheet, you're ready to create the outline. Follow these steps:

1. Select the range A1:B32 by dragging from cell B32 through cell A1.

2. Choose the Outline command from the Formula menu. The following dialog box appears:

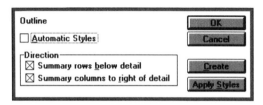

3. Select Create to accept the defaults in the dialog box.

Your worksheet now looks like Figure 3-7. Notice the outline symbols displayed at the left of the screen.

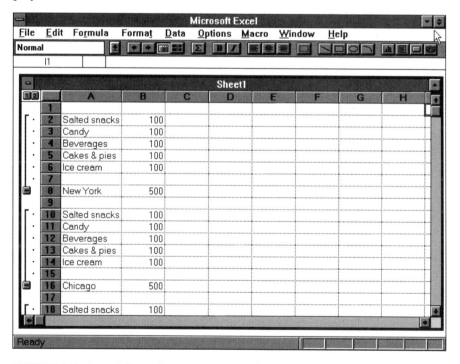

FIGURE 3-7. *A worksheet after creating an outline.*

Microsoft Excel has assigned each row to either level 1 or level 2 in the outline, based on the cell references. Excel assumes that rows containing references to other cells (that is, rows containing SUM functions) are level 1, and that "supporting" rows (that is, rows containing the cells referenced by those SUM functions) are level 2. The small boxes containing minus signs to the left of the worksheet indicate the level 1 rows, which contain totals. The lines connected to these boxes indicate the level 2 rows, which contain cells that are referenced by the formulas in level 1.

Working with Outlines

What you've done so far is really setup work. Now it's time to demonstrate how Excel's outlining feature can help you reorganize and summarize data.

Collapsing outline levels

Suppose your manager wants to see a summary sales report by region, without the product-line detail. You can provide such a report very quickly by collapsing the outline to level 1. Click the square with the number 1 in the top-left corner of the document window. (These squares are called *row-level buttons*. Excel displays a button for every level in the worksheet. Only buttons for levels 1 and 2 are currently displayed, but you can have seven levels, each represented by a button with the corresponding number.) Your worksheet now looks like Figure 3-8. (So that you can see the results clearly in the figure, we have deselected the range. For clarity, we will deselect ranges in figures throughout the rest of the book.)

To expand the outline back to two levels, simply click the level 2 button in the top-left corner of the document window.

 You can collapse part of this outline by clicking the minus button to the left of one of the level 1 rows. All the level 2 rows bracketed by the line connected to that particular minus button collapse, and the minus button changes to a plus button. Clicking the plus button expands the outline to once again display the level 2 rows.

Promoting and demoting items in the outline

As you organize your worksheet, you may need to change the level of some rows. You do this with the Promote and Demote buttons, located near the left end of the tool bar. The Promote button is designated by the left-pointing arrow, and the Demote button is designated by the right-pointing arrow.

A screenshot of a Microsoft Excel window.

Window title bar: **Microsoft Excel**

Menu bar: **File Edit Formula Format Data Options Macro Window Help**

Toolbar row showing: **Normal** and various buttons. Cell reference box: **I1**

Sheet window title: **Sheet1**

Columns: A, B, C, D, E, F, G, H

Row	A	B
1		
8	New York	500
9		
16	Chicago	500
17		
24	Detroit	500
25		
32	Atlanta	500
33		
34		2000
35		
36		
37		
38		
39		
40		
41		
42		

Status bar: **Ready**

FIGURE 3-8. *The worksheet after collapsing its outline to level 1.*

To see how to promote and demote items, select cell A4, click the Promote button, and press Enter to accept the default response in the dialog box that appears. Your worksheet now looks like Figure 3-9 on the next page. Notice the outline symbols to the left of the worksheet, which indicate that row 4 has been promoted to level 1.

To return the New York beverage sales row to level 2, click the Demote button, and press Enter when the dialog box appears.

 If this worksheet had more than two levels, you could advance a row from the lowest to the highest level by repeatedly clicking the Promote button. Similarly, you could demote a row by clicking Demote the appropriate number of times.

Using outlining to build large worksheets

Outlining can come in handy when you need to copy ranges that are so large that they extend past the limits of the screen. By creating an outline and collapsing the rows, you can easily copy and move large areas.

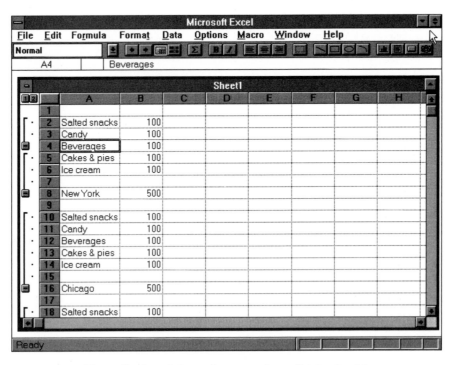

FIGURE 3-9. *The outlined worksheet after promoting cell A4 to level 1.*

To see how copying in outline mode works with your sales figures, follow these steps:

1. Collapse the outline to level 1 so that only the city names show.

2. Select the range A1:B33.

3. Copy the selected range to cell D1.

4. Expand the outline to show two levels.

Your worksheet now looks like Figure 3-10. (We have increased the width of column D.)

Collapsing an outline, as you can see, is a handy way of compressing a large range into a relatively small area on the screen.

 If you want to get out of Outline mode, simply select all the cells containing entries, and then click the level 1 button to promote all rows to level 1.

	A	B	C	D	E	F	G	H
1								
2	Salted snacks	100		Salted snacks	100			
3	Candy	100		Candy	100			
4	Beverages	100		Beverages	100			
5	Cakes & pies	100		Cakes & pies	100			
6	Ice cream	100		Ice cream	100			
7								
8	New York	500		New York	500			
9								
10	Salted snacks	100		Salted snacks	100			
11	Candy	100		Candy	100			
12	Beverages	100		Beverages	100			
13	Cakes & pies	100		Cakes & pies	100			
14	Ice cream	100		Ice cream	100			
15								
16	Chicago	500		Chicago	500			
17								
18	Salted snacks	100		Salted snacks	100			

FIGURE 3-10. *The results of a copy-and-paste operation performed while the copy range was collapsed to level 1 in the outline.*

Selecting visible cells

When we copied the collapsed outline in the previous example, we copied all the data, both visible and invisible. Sometimes you may want to copy only summary figures, such as totals, to another range or another worksheet. You can easily copy selected parts of the worksheet by hiding the cells you don't want to copy and then selecting only the visible cells. Before we see how to selectively copy, tidy up the worksheet by deleting columns D and E. Then follow these steps:

1. Collapse the outline to level 1 again.

2. Select the range A1:B33.

3. Click the Select Visible Cells button (shown below) on the tool bar.

4. Copy the selected range to cell D1.

5. Expand the outline to show two levels.

Your worksheet now looks like Figure 3-11. Notice that because you clicked the Select Visible Cells button before copying the data, Excel copied only the visible cells. You cannot expand the data in column D to display level 2, because there is no level 2 data in column D.

The concept of outlining is presented here in order to familiarize you with a useful worksheet organization tool. However, putting it into practice in your day-to-day work can be a real challenge. If you need more information about outlining, see the Microsoft Excel documentation.

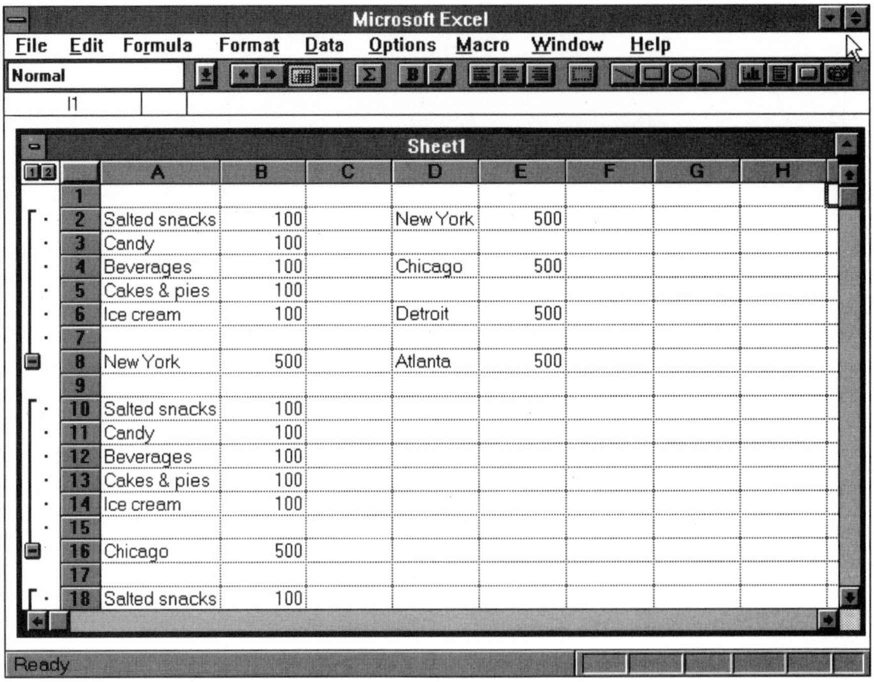

FIGURE 3-11. *The results of clicking the Select Visible Cells button before copying data in an outlined worksheet.*

CONCLUSION

In this chapter, you've learned the basics of revising, protecting, and outlining worksheets. Next we'll cover worksheet formatting techniques.

Chapter 4

Enhancing Your Worksheets

So far, we've covered the basics of entering, calculating, and revising data in your worksheets. In this chapter, we look at ways to format the data to make it easier to interpret or to give it more impact. First, we cover ways to change the width of columns, format numeric data, and align the data within cells. Then we discuss how to change the appearance of both numbers and text. Finally, we look at ways you can add design elements, such as borders and colors, to guide a reader's eye to specific parts of a worksheet.

CHANGING COLUMN WIDTH

When you create a worksheet, all cells have the same width, and all text and numbers appear in the same format. By formatting cells, you can display information in your worksheets in more comprehensible, easy-to-read formats. First, open the *ALSPORTS* worksheet. Notice that all the entries are displayed in a simple, unembellished way known as the General format. Now you're ready to change this format to accommodate more information and to clarify the information the worksheet contains.

Some cell entries are too long to fit into the Microsoft Excel standard columns, which hold eight numeric characters in the default 10-point Helvetica font. Sometimes an entry with the General format may fit in the cell, but the same entry may become too long to fit in the cell when you apply a different format. Entries that are too long appear truncated, or partially hidden, but the entire entry is still stored in the column.

You have already seen an example of long text in the *ALSPORTS* worksheet, shown in Figure 4-1. In Chapter 3, "Revising and Reviewing Worksheets,"

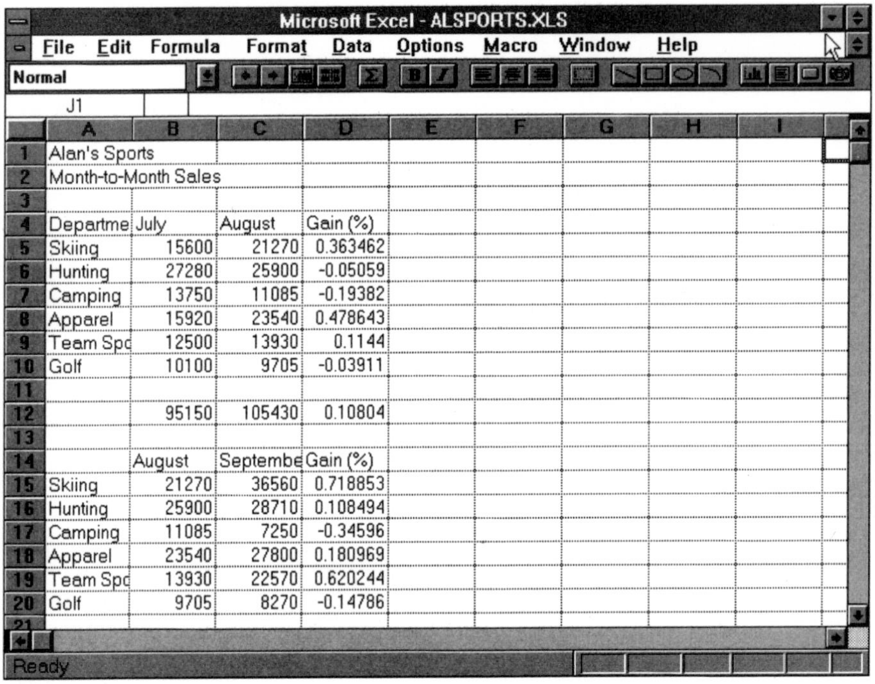

	A	B	C	D
1	Alan's Sports			
2	Month-to-Month Sales			
3				
4	Departme	July	August	Gain (%)
5	Skiing	15600	21270	0.363462
6	Hunting	27280	25900	-0.05059
7	Camping	13750	11085	-0.19382
8	Apparel	15920	23540	0.478643
9	Team Spc	12500	13930	0.1144
10	Golf	10100	9705	-0.03911
11				
12		95150	105430	0.10804
13				
14		August	Septembe	Gain (%)
15	Skiing	21270	36560	0.718853
16	Hunting	25900	28710	0.108494
17	Camping	11085	7250	-0.34596
18	Apparel	23540	27800	0.180969
19	Team Spc	13930	22570	0.620244
20	Golf	9705	8270	-0.14786

FIGURE 4-1. *The truncated text entries in cells A4, A9, A19, and C14 are too long to be fully displayed.*

you replaced the *Other* department with the *Team Sports* and *Golf* departments. The *Team Sports* label is too long to fit in column A of the worksheet, and because the adjacent cell in column B contains an entry, Excel has truncated the *Team Sports* label. Similarly, the word *September* is too long to fit in cell C14. To see how Excel truncates a label, replace the entry in cell A4 of the *ALSPORTS* worksheet (*Dept.*) with the longer word *Department*. If cells B4, B9, B19, and D14 were blank, *Department, Team Sports*, and *September* would overlap into them, just as the company name (*Alan's Sports*) in cell A1 overlaps into cell B1.

Adjusting Columns with the Mouse

When an entry is too long to be fully displayed, you can remedy the situation by widening the column. To widen column A, follow these steps:

1. Point to the right edge of the column A header. Notice that when the pointer is over the vertical line, called a *border*, between the column A and column B headers, it changes into the shape shown here:

2. To widen the column, drag the border to the right. As you move the pointer, a shaded vertical line moves with it. The shaded line shows where the new column border will appear if you release the mouse button at that moment.

3. When the column is wide enough to accommodate the words *Department* and *Team Sports*, release the mouse button. Column A expands to the position of the shaded vertical line.

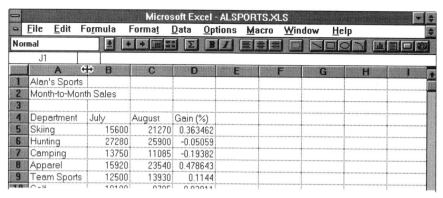

If the column is still not wide enough to display the long labels, drag the border to the right again. If the column is now too wide, simply drag the border back to the left.

Using the Column Width Command

Another method of changing the width of columns is to use the Column Width command on the Format menu. Follow these steps:

1. Select any cell in column C.

2. Choose the Column Width command from the Format menu. The following dialog box appears:

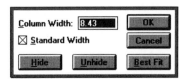

3. Type the new column-width value (the number of characters) in the Column Width text box.

4. Press Enter.

The character unit Excel uses is that of a fixed-width numeric character. Because text characters can vary in width, you will probably have to use trial and error to get the width you want.

To reset a column to the standard width (8.43 numeric characters), follow these steps:

1. Select any cell in the column you want to reset.

2. Choose Column Width from the Format menu.

3. Click the Standard Width check box.

4. Click OK, or press Enter, to carry out the command.

The Effect of Column Width on Numeric Entries

Microsoft Excel treats a long numeric entry differently from a text entry. Instead of truncating the entry, Excel changes the entry's format so that the number can fit within the current cell width.

To see this change, select any standard-width cell in the worksheet and enter a ten-digit number. In a standard-width cell with the General format, Excel displays the number in exponential form. For example, if you enter the number 7777777777, Excel displays the value 7.78E+09.

Now reduce the width of the column containing the ten-digit number to about half the standard width. Simply drag the column's right border to the left. Because there's no longer sufficient room to display the number even in exponential format, Excel fills the cell with pound signs (#) to indicate that the cell contains an entry that cannot be displayed. (You might recall seeing these pound signs earlier when you worked with date and time values in Chapter 2, "Using Formulas and Functions.")

Finally, drag the right column border to the right until the column is wide enough to display the entire number.

Changing the Width of Several Columns

With Microsoft Excel, you can change the width of several columns at a time. For example, select columns B through F, and drag the right border of any selected column to widen that column. When you release the mouse button, Excel widens all five columns.

You can also widen multiple columns by selecting them, choosing the Column Width command from the Format menu, and then entering a new width in the Column Width text box and pressing Enter.

Now before continuing, delete the ten-digit numeric entry, and restore any columns you have widened, except columns A and C, to standard width.

CHANGING ROW HEIGHT

Because you inserted rows into the *ALSPORTS* worksheet in Chapter 3, "Revising and Reviewing Worksheets," the data in the worksheet no longer fits on one screen. If you want to see all the data at once, you can squeeze more rows onto the screen by reducing the height of blank rows.

Adjusting Rows with the Mouse

To reduce the row height in your *ALSPORTS* worksheet, follow these steps:

1. Click the row 3 header, and then hold down the Ctrl key while clicking the row 11 and row 21 headers.

2. Point to the row 3 header's bottom border. The pointer changes to the following shape:

3. Drag the border up until the row height is about one-third the height of the other rows.

4. Release the mouse button to complete the operation.

All three selected rows are now about one-third normal height. Your worksheet now looks like Figure 4-2.

	A	B	C	D	E	F	G	H	I
1	Alan's Sports								
2	Month-to-Month Sales								
4	Department	July	August	Gain (%)					
5	Skiing	15600	21270	0.363462					
6	Hunting	27280	25900	-0.05059					
7	Camping	13750	11085	-0.19382					
8	Apparel	15920	23540	0.478643					
9	Team Sports	12500	13930	0.1144					
10	Golf	10100	9705	-0.03911					
12		95150	105430	0.10804					
13									
14		August	September	Gain (%)					
15	Skiing	21270	36560	0.718853					
16	Hunting	25900	28710	0.108494					
17	Camping	11085	7250	-0.34596					
18	Apparel	23540	27800	0.180969					
19	Team Sports	13930	22570	0.620244					
20	Golf	9705	8270	-0.14786					
22		105430	131160	0.244048					
23									

Microsoft Excel - ALSPORTS.XLS
File Edit Formula Format Data Options Macro Window Help
Normal
I1
Ready

FIGURE 4-2. *The* ALSPORTS *worksheet with the height of rows 3, 11, and 21 reduced and the height of row 1 increased.*

Using the Row Height Command

Here's an alternative method of changing the height of rows:

1. Click the row 1 header to select the entire row, and choose the Row Height command from the Format menu. This dialog box appears:

2. Type *24* in the Row Height box, and press Enter.

Before continuing, return row 1 to its original height by selecting it, choosing the Row Height command, clicking the Standard Height box, and then clicking OK.

HIDING CELLS

On occasion, you may want to hide some of the data in a worksheet. Perhaps you simply want to reduce clutter. Or you might want to protect certain parts of your worksheet from being changed.

To practice hiding cells, follow these steps:

1. Select any cell in row 2.

2. Choose the Row Height command from the Format menu. The Row Height dialog box (shown earlier) appears.

3. Click the Hide button.

4. Click OK, or press Enter, to hide row 2.

While row 2 is still selected, unhiding the row is a simple matter of choosing the Row Height command and clicking the Unhide button. If you have moved the selection to another part of the worksheet, you can select a hidden cell by following these steps:

1. Choose the Goto command from the Formula menu, type *A2* (or any other cell reference in row 2), and click OK or press Enter.

2. Having selected row 2, choose Row Height from the Format menu.

3. Click the Unhide button.

4. Click OK, or press Enter.

You can hide and unhide columns in a similar way, using the Hide and Unhide buttons in the Column Width dialog box.

You can drag through the headers on either side of a hidden column or row to select a block of rows. The hidden row will be among those selected. For example, if row 2 is hidden, you can drag through the headers for rows 1 and 3 to select rows 1, 2, and 3. You can then choose the Row Height command from the Format menu and click the Unhide button to display row 2.

USING NUMBER FORMATS

As you use Microsoft Excel in your day-to-day work, you'll discover that for the sake of clarity you need to display numeric values in a number of different ways. As we mentioned earlier, Excel lets you adjust the way numbers are displayed.

Excel's General number format (the default) does not automatically insert special characters, such as dollar signs, embedded commas, and percent signs. As a result, the numbers in the Alan's Sports sales analysis worksheet are not immediately identifiable as dollar amounts and percentages. A few simple improvements—dollar signs, commas between the thousands and hundreds digits, percent signs after values in the percentage column, and parentheses around negative numbers—would make a big difference. Excel offers numerous built-in formats that make it easy for you to add these special characters. We'll look at some typical built-in formats, and then we'll show you how to design custom formats.

Using the Built-in Number Formats

As with most Microsoft Excel procedures, you first select the cells you want to format. To format the sales figures in the *ALSPORTS* worksheet, follow these steps:

1. Select the range B5:C22.

2. Choose the Number command from the Format menu. The Number dialog box appears, listing the available formats as combinations of symbols. (We'll talk more about these symbols in a minute.).

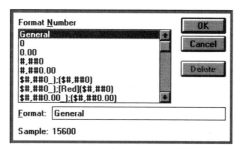

3. To display commas, dollar signs, and parentheses with your data, select the $#,##0_);($#,##0) format.

4. Click OK, or press Enter.

Your worksheet now looks like Figure 4-3.

Microsoft Excel - ALSPORTS.XLS								
File **Edit** **Formula** **Format** **Data** **Options** **Macro** **Window** **Help**								

Normal

I1

	A	B	C	D	E	F	G	H	I
1	Alan's Sports								
2	Month-to-Month Sales								
4	Department	July	August	Gain (%)					
5	Skiing	$15,600	$21,270	0.363462					
6	Hunting	$27,280	$25,900	-0.05059					
7	Camping	$13,750	$11,085	-0.19382					
8	Apparel	$15,920	$23,540	0.478643					
9	Team Sports	$12,500	$13,930	0.1144					
10	Golf	$10,100	$9,705	-0.03911					
12		$95,150	$105,430	0.10804					
13									
14		August	September	Gain (%)					
15	Skiing	$21,270	$36,560	0.718853					
16	Hunting	$25,900	$28,710	0.108494					
17	Camping	$11,085	$7,250	-0.34596					
18	Apparel	$23,540	$27,800	0.180969					
19	Team Sports	$13,930	$22,570	0.620244					
20	Golf	$9,705	$8,270	-0.14786					
22		$105,430	$131,160	0.244048					
23									

Ready

FIGURE 4-3. *The* ALSPORTS *worksheet with the sales figures formatted.*

Notice that some of the formats you see in the Format Number dialog box use zero (0) as a placeholder and others use the pound sign (#). Here's the difference: Choosing a format with 0 in any digit position causes Microsoft Excel to display that digit even if it is a zero. Choosing a format with # causes Excel to suppress the display of nonsignificant zeros. For example, when you display dollar-and-cents amounts, you will generally prefer a format like $#,##0.00, which suppresses all but one leading zero to the left of the decimal point but always displays the two digits to the right of the decimal point.

Table 4-1 illustrates the effects of the Microsoft Excel built-in formats on cell entries of various types.

Format	Entry	Display
General	1648.2357	1648.2357
0	1648.2357	1648
0.00	1648.2357	1648.24
#,##0	1648.2357	1,648
#,##0.00	2374.1	2,374.10
$#,##0_);($#,##0)	2374.1	$2,374
$#,##0_);[Red]($#,##0)	–2374.1	($2,374)
$#,##0.00_);($#,##0.00)	–2374.1	($2,374.10)
$#,##0.00_);[Red]($#,##0.00)	2374.1	$2,374.10
0%	1.179	118%
0.00%	1.179	117.90%
0.00E+00	34586792.51	3.46E+07
# ?/?	3.9375	4
# ??/??	3.9375	3 15/16

TABLE 4-1. *Excel's built-in number formats and their effects.*

Notice that several of the formats in Table 4-1 actually contain two formats separated by a semicolon (;). In these cases, Excel applies the format on the left of the semicolon to positive values and the format on the right to negative

108

values. The formats that include the word *Red* in brackets display negative numbers in red on a color monitor. (You can also apply formats to zero values only and to text entries only, but this Excel feature is beyond the scope of this book. For more information, see the Microsoft Excel documentation.)

Some of the formats include an underscore (_) followed by a right parenthesis. The underscore tells Excel to skip the width of the character that follows it, so the effect of _) is to make positive numbers line up with negative numbers that are enclosed in parentheses.

 You can apply certain number formats as you enter data. Typing a dollar sign ($) at the beginning of a numeric entry turns on the $#,##0_);($#,##0) or $#,##0.00_);($#,##0.00) format, depending on whether the entry contains a decimal point. Typing a trailing percent sign (%) selects the 0% or 0.00% format. Typing embedded commas, however, has no effect.

Using the Built-in Date Formats

To help you format dates, Microsoft Excel also offers a wide variety of date formats. Table 4-2 illustrates how various built-in date formats affect the appearance of the date July 4, 1991, in a worksheet.

Format	Display
m/d/yy	7/4/91
d-mmm-yy	4-Jul-91
d-mmm	4-Jul
mmm-yy	Jul-91

TABLE 4-2. *Excel's built-in date formats and their effects.*

To see how date formats work, enter *7/31/91* in cell B4 and *8/31/91* in cell C4 of the *ALSPORTS* worksheet. Although it may appear that Excel treats your entries as text, the program actually recognizes them as dates.

Suppose you don't like the date format used in the worksheet. You'd rather show the month's three-letter abbreviation and the year. To apply the new format (mmm-yy), follow the steps on the next page.

1. Select cells B4 and C4.

2. Choose the Number command from the Format menu.

3. Scroll through the list box, and select the mmm-yy format.

4. Click OK, or press Enter, to apply the format.

The month names now read *Jul-91* and *Aug-91*, respectively. You'll learn more about date formats in a minute, when we look at custom formats.

Creating Custom Formats

You're not limited to the built-in formats Microsoft Excel provides. You can create your own formats by customizing one of the built-in formats.

Let's build a custom format for the percentage gains and losses shown in column D of the *ALSPORTS* worksheet. Simply follow these steps:

1. Select the range *D5:D22*.

2. Choose the Number command from the Format menu.

3. Scroll through the list box and select the 0.00% format, but don't press Enter yet. The format now appears in the Format text box, and you can edit it there.

4. To display the figures in column D in percentage format rounded off to one decimal place and with parentheses to indicate negative values, select the Format text box, and then delete one of the two zeros to the right of the decimal point. At the end of the entry, add an underscore, a right parenthesis, and a semicolon followed by (0.0%). (The underscore and parenthesis are necessary to make positive numbers line up properly with the negative numbers.) The dialog box now looks like this:

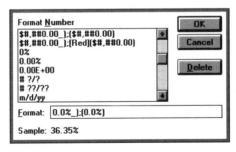

5. Click OK, or press Enter.

Your worksheet now looks like Figure 4-4.

	A	B	C	D	E	F	G	H	I
1	Alan's Sports								
2	Month-to-Month Sales								
4	Department	Jul-91	Aug-91	Gain (%)					
5	Skiing	$15,600	$21,270	36.3%					
6	Hunting	$27,280	$25,900	(5.1%)					
7	Camping	$13,750	$11,085	(19.4%)					
8	Apparel	$15,920	$23,540	47.9%					
9	Team Sports	$12,500	$13,930	11.4%					
10	Golf	$10,100	$9,705	(3.9%)					
12		$95,150	$105,430	10.8%					
13									
14		August	September	Gain (%)					
15	Skiing	$21,270	$36,560	71.9%					
16	Hunting	$25,900	$28,710	10.8%					
17	Camping	$11,085	$7,250	(34.6%)					
18	Apparel	$23,540	$27,800	18.1%					
19	Team Sports	$13,930	$22,570	62.0%					
20	Golf	$9,705	$8,270	(14.8%)					
22		$105,430	$131,160	24.4%					

FIGURE 4-4. *The* ALSPORTS *worksheet with the percentages formatted.*

Now choose the Number command again, and scroll to the bottom of the list box. You'll see your custom format there. Excel adds it to the format list so that you can use it again later.

Table 4-3, on the next page, lists a series of custom formats and the resulting worksheet displays. These formats may give you some ideas for putting Excel to work in your own worksheets.

The 00000-0000 and (000) 000-0000 formats can be particularly useful in entering nine-digit ZIP codes and ten-digit telephone numbers, respectively. They streamline data entry by inserting the non-numeric characters for you.

Let's look more closely at the date-format symbols. Table 4-4, on the next page, shows the format symbols for each of the elements of a date (month, day, and year) and their effects on the date July 4, 1991. You can use any of these symbols in your custom date formats.

Format	Entry	Display
$#,###.00_C_R;$#,###.00CR	−437.59	$437.59CR
#,###_);(#,###)	−437.59	(438)
0.####%	0.918	91.8%
0.##%	0.918369	91.84%
00000-0000	487063034	48706-3034
(000) 000-0000	2137645555	(213) 764-5555
d mmmm yyyy	11/8/90	8 November 1990
mm-dd-yy	11/8/90	11-08-90

TABLE 4-3. *Custom number formats and their effects.*

Format	Display	Format	Display
m	7	dd	04
mm	07	ddd	Thu
mmm	Jul	dddd	Thursday
mmmm	July	yy	91
d	4	yyyy	1991

TABLE 4-4. *Excel's date-format symbols and their effects.*

Now try another custom-format example. Suppose you've decided to display the full month name without the year in the *ALSPORTS* worksheet. To assign this format, follow these steps:

1. Select cells B4 and C4.

2. Choose the Number command from the Format menu.

3. Select the default entry in the Format text box.

4. Type *mmmm.*

5. Click OK, or press Enter.

The *ALSPORTS* worksheet now displays *July* in cell B4 and *August* in cell C4. Although these entries appear to be text rather than numbers, they remain numeric values to Excel.

For some of the later examples in this chapter to work properly, you must restore the original text entries in cells B4 and C4, so before you continue, select each cell, type the appropriate month name, and press Enter.

POSITIONING DATA WITHIN CELLS

Unless you specify otherwise, Microsoft Excel left-aligns text and right-aligns numbers; that is, text fills cell space from left to right, and numbers fill cell space from right to left. You can change this placement by using the Alignment command on the Format menu. The Alignment command displays the dialog box shown in Figure 4-5.

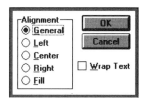

FIGURE 4-5. *The Alignment dialog box.*

Aligning and Centering Entries

The first option in the Alignment dialog box, General, is the default alignment we just described. Right, Left, and Center are self-explanatory. You can use any of these alignment settings with either numeric or text entries. Figure 4-6 shows how these alignments (column A) affect text entries (column B) and numeric entries (column C).

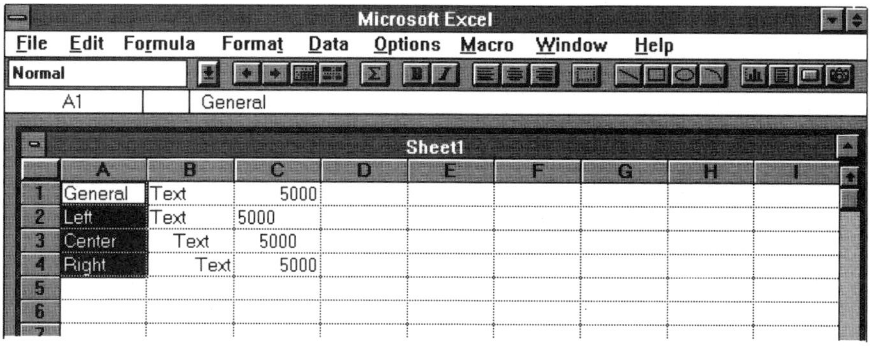

FIGURE 4-6. *The four data alignments available for Excel worksheets.*

113

To see the effects of these alignment settings in the *ALSPORTS* worksheet, follow these steps:

1. Select cell A5.

2. Choose the Alignment command from the Format menu.

3. Select the Right option.

4. Click OK, or press Enter.

Alternatively, you can use the Alignment buttons on the tool bar to align data in cells:

Clicking the left Alignment button left-aligns the selection, clicking the center Alignment button centers the selection, and clicking the right Alignment button right-aligns the selection. Follow these steps to use the Alignment buttons:

1. Select cell A6.

2. Click the Center Alignment button on the tool bar.

3. Select cell A7

4. Click the Left Alignment button.

Notice that the formatting change does not affect the appearance of cell A7, because that cell was already set to the default General alignment, which left-aligns text.

If a left-aligned cell entry is too long and the adjacent cell to the right is empty, the excess spills over to the right. If a right-aligned cell entry is too long and the adjacent cell to the left is empty, the excess spills over to the left. If a centered entry is too long and both adjacent cells are empty, the overflow is evenly divided between the right and left edges of the cell, as shown in Figure 4-7.

You can restore the alignment of cells to General alignment by choosing the Alignment command from the Format menu, selecting the General option, and then clicking OK. Do that now to restore cells A5:A7 to General alignment. Then we'll cover the other options in the Alignment dialog box.

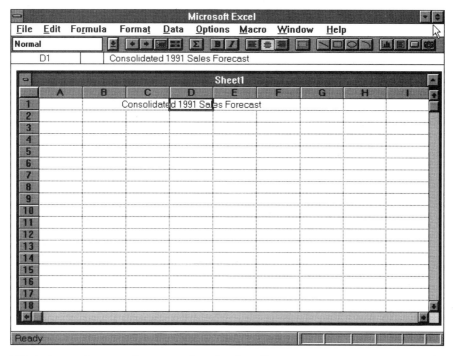

FIGURE 4-7. *A centered entry too long for the cell containing it.*

Filling a Range

You can also use the Alignment command to fill a range of cells with a single character or a repeating series of characters. Any characters you enter are repeated to fill the entire range. Filling ranges with such characters as hyphens (-) or equal signs (=) can be useful for creating dividing lines and borders around areas of a worksheet.

To create a dividing line between the two sections of the *ALSPORTS* worksheet:

1. Enter an asterisk (*) in cell A13.

2. Select the range A13:D13.

3. Choose the Alignment command from the Format menu.

4. Select the Fill option.

5. Click OK, or press Enter.

Your worksheet now looks like Figure 4-8. Because you applied the Fill format to the range A13:D13, and you entered no data in cells B13 through D13, Excel filled the entire range A13:D13 with the character you entered in cell A13.

Although the asterisks appear in cells A13:D13, the actual entry is contained only in cell A13. To see this for yourself, select cell A13, and press the Del key. In the dialog box that appears, select the All option, and click OK. The line of asterisks disappears.

	A	B	C	D	E	F	G	H	I
1	Alan's Sports								
2	Month-to-Month Sales								
4	Department	July	August	Gain (%)					
5	Skiing	$15,600	$21,270	36.3%					
6	Hunting	$27,280	$25,900	(5.1%)					
7	Camping	$13,750	$11,085	(19.4%)					
8	Apparel	$15,920	$23,540	47.9%					
9	Team Sports	$12,500	$13,930	11.4%					
10	Golf	$10,100	$9,705	(3.9%)					
12		$95,150	$105,430	10.8%					
13	**								
14		August	September	Gain (%)					
15	Skiing	$21,270	$36,560	71.9%					
16	Hunting	$25,900	$28,710	10.8%					
17	Camping	$11,085	$7,250	(34.6%)					
18	Apparel	$23,540	$27,800	18.1%					
19	Team Sports	$13,930	$22,570	62.0%					
20	Golf	$9,705	$8,270	(14.8%)					
22		$105,430	$131,160	24.4%					

FIGURE 4-8. *The* ALSPORTS *worksheet after the Alignment command creates a line of asterisks.*

Wrapping Text

Sometimes you may want to keep a long text entry within a single cell. In such cases, you can choose the Wrap Text option in the Alignment dialog box. To see how this works, open a blank worksheet, and do the following:

1. In cell A1, type the following:

```
These figures have not been audited. Please do not release
this information outside the company.
```

Notice that the formula bar expands to display the entire entry.

2. Press Enter. If this entry were any longer, it would run off the edge of the screen:

3. Widen column A so that it occupies about half the width of the screen.

4. Choose the Alignment command from the Format menu.

5. Click the Wrap Text option, and press Enter.

Your worksheet now looks like Figure 4-9.

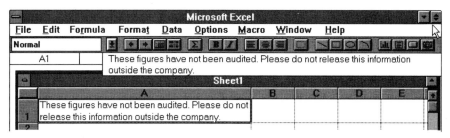

FIGURE 4-9. *A wrapped text entry.*

Justifying Text

Sometimes you may need to fit some lengthy text into a specific range of cells in a worksheet by breaking the text into several lines. You do this by using the Justify command on the Format menu. To practice, use the Clear command to erase only the formatting from cell A1, and then follow these steps:

1. Select the range A1:E2.

2. Choose the Justify command from the Format menu.

The text is now split between cells A1 and A2.

When you want your text to fit within a single cell, use the Wrap Text option of the Alignment command. If it's necessary for your text to occupy more than one column or more than one row, use the Justify command.

CHANGING THE APPEARANCE OF CHARACTERS

The word *font* is commonly used in two ways. Sometimes it refers to a specific typeface, such as Helvetica, Script, or Roman. More commonly, the word *font* refers to the aggregate of all the attributes—size, style (such as bold or italic), typeface, and color—that determine how a character looks on the Microsoft Excel screen and when printed.

The default Excel font is 10-point, plain Helvetica. By using the Font command on the Format menu, you can control the appearance of onscreen and printed characters. Altering the typeface, the size, or the style is the easiest way to spruce up your worksheet. To experiment with this type of formatting, activate the *ALSPORTS* worksheet now, and practice changing its appearance.

Selecting Styles

We'll start by changing the appearance of the worksheet title. First, select the range A1:A2 in the *ALSPORTS* worksheet, and choose Insert from the Edit menu to move the title and subtitle of the worksheet one column to the right. Then select the range B1:B2, and choose the Font command from the Format menu. The dialog box shown in Figure 4-10 appears.

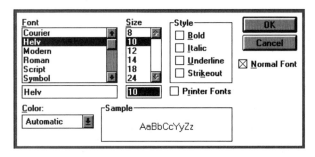

FIGURE 4-10. *The Font dialog box.*

118

The Font dialog box lists all of Microsoft Excel's font-formatting options. You can choose different fonts from the Font list box, change the size of the font by selecting a new size from the Size list box, and alter the font style by turning on and off options in the Style section. The Sample box shows some sample text formatted with the options you have selected.

Suppose you decide to add emphasis and polish to the worksheet by changing the title and subtitle to bold and italic. Be sure the range B1:B2 is selected, and then follow these steps:

1. Click the Bold check box to turn on the bold style.

2. Click OK, or press Enter.

The titles *Alan's Sports* and *Month-to-Month Sales* are now bold.

As you know, the tool bar provides formatting shortcuts. Let's use the Italic button on the tool bar to italicize the titles. With the range B1:B2 selected, click the Italic button shown below.

That's all you need to do to italicize a range of cells. You can also use the tool bar to add bold formatting. Simply click the Bold button shown below.

Like the check boxes in the Font dialog box, the Bold and Italic buttons can be used as *toggle switches*, meaning that you click them once to turn on their attributes and click them again to turn off their attributes. For example, if the current selection is bold, clicking the Bold button removes the bold formatting. Click the Bold or Italic buttons now to see how this works.

Formatting More Than One Range at a Time

Suppose you want to make certain headings in your worksheet bold. Rather than select each heading and then make it bold, a faster way is to select all the headings you want to change and format them all at once. To select multiple ranges, hold down Ctrl while you click the cells you want to format.

For example, to select the entries in rows 4 and 14 of the *ALSPORTS* worksheet and make them bold, follow these steps:

1. Select the range A4:D4.

2. Hold down Ctrl, and select the range B14:D14. Your worksheet should look like this:

	A	B	C	D	E	F	G	H	I
		Alan's Sports							
1		**Alan's Sports**							
2		**Month-to-Month Sales**							
4	Department	July	August	Gain (%)					
5	Skiing	$15,600	$21,270	36.3%					
6	Hunting	$27,280	$25,900	(5.1%)					
7	Camping	$13,750	$11,085	(19.4%)					
8	Apparel	$15,920	$23,540	47.9%					
9	Team Sports	$12,500	$13,930	11.4%					
10	Golf	$10,100	$9,705	(3.9%)					
12		$95,150	$105,430	10.8%					
13									
14		August	September	Gain (%)					
15	Skiing	$21,270	$36,560	71.9%					
16	Hunting	$25,900	$28,710	10.8%					
17	Camping	$11,085	$7,250	(34.6%)					
18	Apparel	$23,540	$27,800	18.1%					
19	Team Sports	$13,930	$22,570	62.0%					
20	Golf	$9,705	$8,270	(14.8%)					
22		$105,430	$131,160	24.4%					

3. Click the Bold button in the tool bar.

Selecting Fonts

In addition to adding bold or italic formatting, you can also change the font used in your worksheet. You might want to use a different font for titles to make them distinct from numeric values. Or you might want to use different fonts for totals to make summary information stand out.

To add a more distinctive font to your worksheet title, follow these steps:

1. Select cell B1.

2. Choose the Font command from the Format menu.

3. Scroll to the end of the Font list box, and select Tms Rmn. Notice that the letters displayed in the Sample box change to reflect the selected font.

4. In the Size list box, select 18, and then click the Italic check box to turn off the italic attribute.

5. Click OK, or press Enter.

Your worksheet now looks like Figure 4-11. Notice that Excel automatically increased the row height to make room for the larger characters. However, if you've previously changed the row height, Excel does not adjust the height.

 Bold fonts sometimes make entries too wide to display in their entirety. If this happens, increase the width of the affected columns by dragging the column-header border or by choosing the Column Width command from the Format menu.

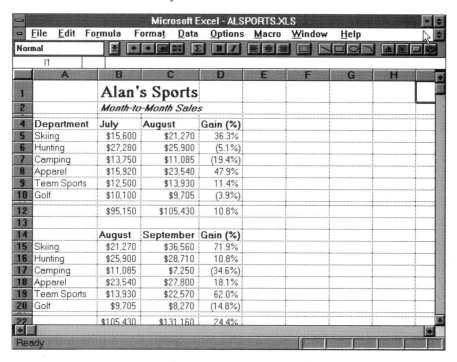

FIGURE 4-11. *The* ALSPORTS *worksheet with a new font for the title.*

Repeating Font Commands

With Microsoft Excel, you can repeat certain commands without having to set up the entire command again. After you carry out a repeatable command, such as Font, Insert, or Paste, the command name is preceded by the word *Repeat* on the Edit menu. By choosing the Repeat command, you can repeat your last action, even if you have selected another cell or range of cells.

Try this for yourself. To use the font you just applied to cell B1, select cell B2, and then choose the Repeat Font command. Excel applies the 18-point Tms Rmn font to the title in cell B2.

Before you continue, change the font in cells B1 and B2 again, this time to 10-point Helvetica. You can then see all the data in the *ALSPORTS* worksheet without scrolling.

Limiting Fonts to Those You Can Print

Most printers don't support the full range of Microsoft Excel screen fonts, so Excel provides a special roster of the fonts that your printer does support. To limit the Font list box display to the fonts you can print, choose the Font command from the Format menu, and click the Printer Fonts check box.

HIGHLIGHTING DATA WITH LINES, BOXES, AND SHADING

Lines, boxes, and shading can emphasize important information in a worksheet. For example, if totals are important, you can frame them with a box. Or if negative numbers are important, you can shade them so that they can be seen at a glance.

In a moment, we'll use lines, boxes, and shading to dress up the Alan's Sports sales analysis. First, though, save the *ALSPORTS* worksheet so that you can return to it in its present state after you've finished experimenting.

Underlining Cells

Underlining can be useful for formatting certain kinds of reports. To add underlining to the *ALSPORTS* worksheet, follow these steps:

1. Select the ranges B10:D10 and B20:D20.

2. Choose the Border command from the Format menu. The following dialog box appears.

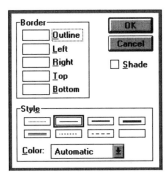

3. To underline the selected cells, turn on the Bottom option.

4. Click OK, or press Enter.

The selected cells now have a single underline. This underline doesn't show up well on the screen because of the gridlines. To make the underline more visible, you can select a thicker line or, when printing the worksheet, you can turn off the gridlines, as explained in Chapter 6, "Printing Microsoft Excel Documents."

Now suppose you want to double-underline the totals. Follow these steps:

1. Select the ranges B12:D12 and B22:D22.

2. Choose the Border command from the Format menu to redisplay the Border dialog box. This time, select the double-underline style in the Style box, as shown here:

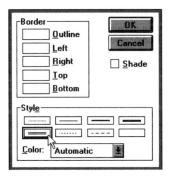

3. Select the Bottom option, and click OK or press Enter.

Enclosing Cells in Boxes

Suppose you want to draw attention to the percentage differences shown in column D, including the total percentage gain for all departments. To emphasize the percentage differences, follow these steps:

1. Select the ranges D4:D12 and D14:D22.

2. Choose the Border command from the Format menu.

3. Click the Outline option.

4. Click OK, or press Enter.

Your worksheet now looks like Figure 4-12.

Do you notice anything wrong with the worksheet? When you applied the Outline format, you lost the double-underline format in column D. To reinstate this format, use the Border command to add double-underlining to cells D12 and D22.

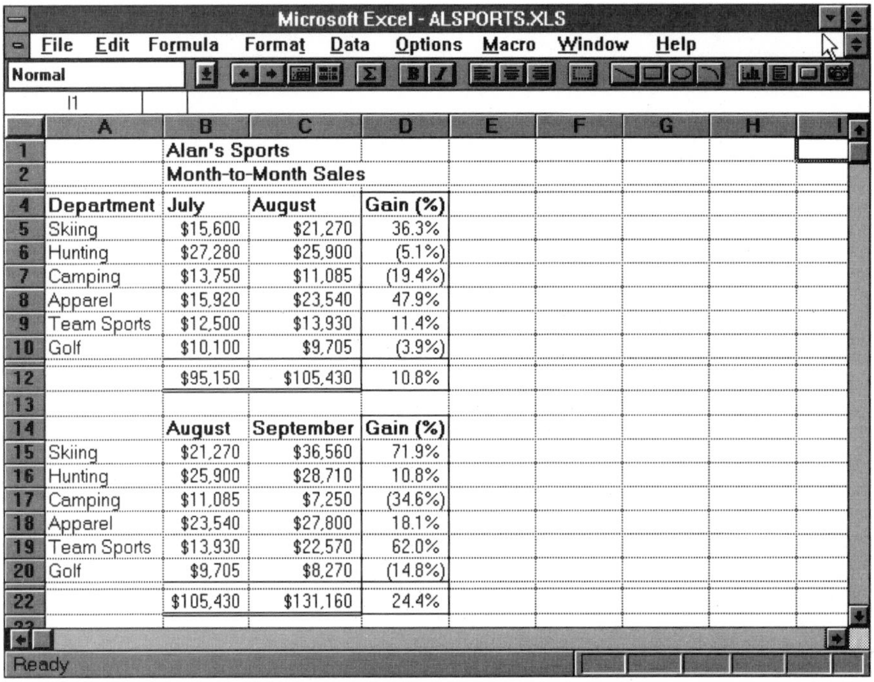

	A	B	C	D	E	F	G	H	I
1		Alan's Sports							
2		Month-to-Month Sales							
4	Department	July	August	Gain (%)					
5	Skiing	$15,600	$21,270	36.3%					
6	Hunting	$27,280	$25,900	(5.1%)					
7	Camping	$13,750	$11,085	(19.4%)					
8	Apparel	$15,920	$23,540	47.9%					
9	Team Sports	$12,500	$13,930	11.4%					
10	Golf	$10,100	$9,705	(3.9%)					
12		$95,150	$105,430	10.8%					
13									
14		August	September	Gain (%)					
15	Skiing	$21,270	$36,560	71.9%					
16	Hunting	$25,900	$28,710	10.8%					
17	Camping	$11,085	$7,250	(34.6%)					
18	Apparel	$23,540	$27,800	18.1%					
19	Team Sports	$13,930	$22,570	62.0%					
20	Golf	$9,705	$8,270	(14.8%)					
22		$105,430	$131,160	24.4%					

FIGURE 4-12. *The* ALSPORTS *worksheet with underlining and boxes.*

Shading Cells

You have many choices when it comes to presenting the information in your worksheets. For example, you can use shading for emphasis; or you can use underlining, double-underlining, and boxes to emphasize some cells and shading to de-emphasize others.

To add shading to the *ALSPORTS* worksheet, follow these steps:

1. Select the range A1:E23.

2. Choose the Border command from the Format menu. In the Border dialog box, notice that the Left, Right, Top, and Bottom check boxes are gray. Gray boxes indicate that some of the selected cells have the corresponding attributes turned on but some don't. Clicking any of these gray boxes turns on the attribute for the entire selection. Clicking the box a second time turns off the attribute for the entire selection. Clicking it a third time turns the box gray again, indicating no change.

3. Click the Shade check box.

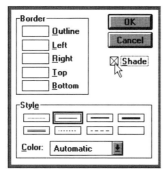

4. Click OK, or press Enter, to apply shading to the range A1:E23.

5. Select the ranges B1:D2 and A4:D22.

6. Choose the Border command again.

7. Click the Shade option to turn it off.

8. Click OK, or press Enter.

Your worksheet now looks like Figure 4-13 on the next page.

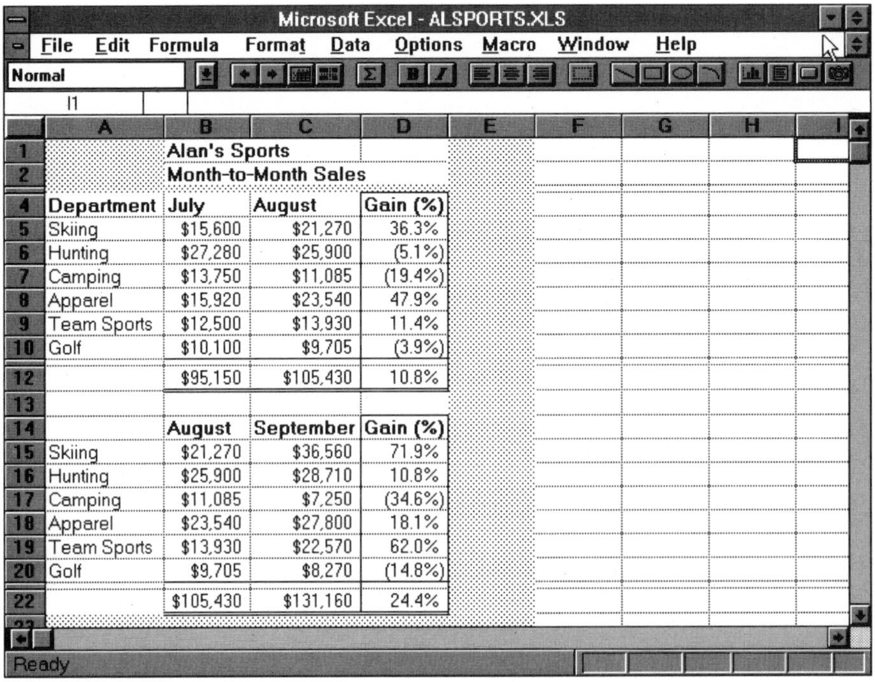

	A	B	C	D
1		Alan's Sports		
2		Month-to-Month Sales		
4	Department	July	August	Gain (%)
5	Skiing	$15,600	$21,270	36.3%
6	Hunting	$27,280	$25,900	(5.1%)
7	Camping	$13,750	$11,085	(19.4%)
8	Apparel	$15,920	$23,540	47.9%
9	Team Sports	$12,500	$13,930	11.4%
10	Golf	$10,100	$9,705	(3.9%)
12		$95,150	$105,430	10.8%
13				
14		August	September	Gain (%)
15	Skiing	$21,270	$36,560	71.9%
16	Hunting	$25,900	$28,710	10.8%
17	Camping	$11,085	$7,250	(34.6%)
18	Apparel	$23,540	$27,800	18.1%
19	Team Sports	$13,930	$22,570	62.0%
20	Golf	$9,705	$8,270	(14.8%)
22		$105,430	$131,160	24.4%

FIGURE 4-13. *The* ALSPORTS *worksheet with shading added.*

If you like the results, save the document under a new name. If you don't like the results, go ahead and experiment some more.

USING COLORS AND PATTERNS

Suppose you are creating a worksheet for a special report or slide presentation that will use color. To heighten the impact of your presentation, you can use colors and patterns in your worksheet. (Even if you have a monochrome monitor, you can apply colors that will appear when the worksheet is opened on a computer with a color monitor.)

To assign a new pattern to the title and subtitle of the *ALSPORTS* worksheet, follow these steps:

1. Select the range B1:D2.

2. Choose the Patterns command from the Format menu. The following dialog box appears.

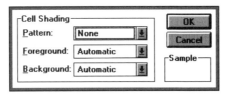

3. Click the arrow button at the right of the Pattern list box. The following list box appears:

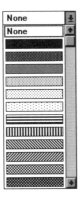

4. Select a pattern that appeals to you. (For the example worksheet, we used the third pattern from the top.)

5. Select foreground and background colors from their respective list boxes, and press Enter.

Your worksheet now looks like Figure 4-14 on the next page.

The concept of foreground and background colors can be confusing. The terms foreground *and* background *apply to the areas that make up a pattern. For example, if you have an even gray pattern (50 percent black and 50 percent white) and you change the foreground color from black to red and the background color from white to blue, you get an even purple pattern. The color of characters that appears against the pattern is controlled by the Color options in the dialog box that appears when you choose Font from the Format menu. To ensure that the characters stand out, you might want to change the color of characters after you have changed the color of the pattern. For example, if you select a dark pattern, you might want to change the color of characters to white to maintain contrast.*

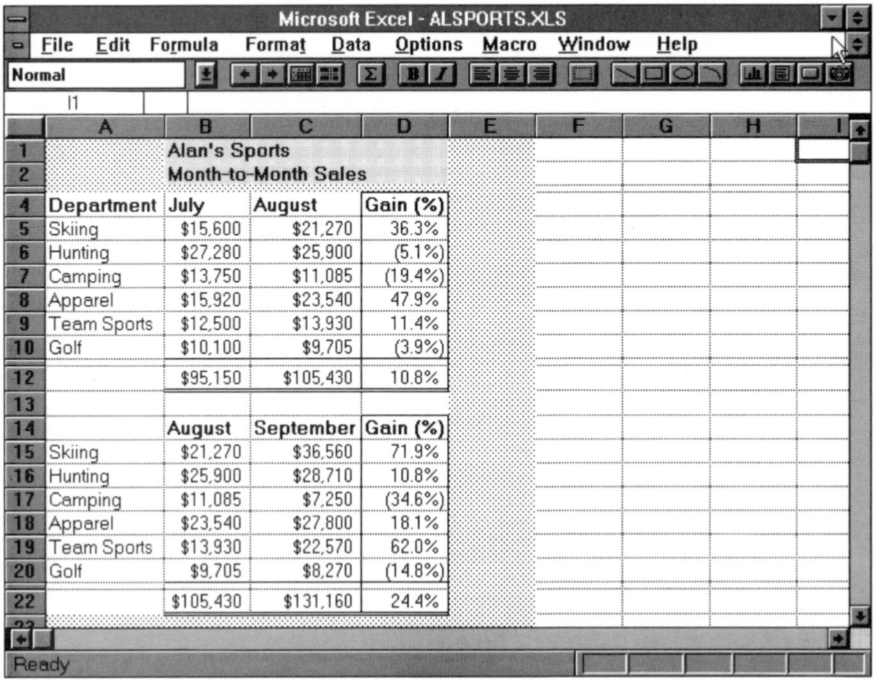

FIGURE 4-14. *The* ALSPORTS *worksheet with patterns applied to cells in the first two rows.*

ATTACHING NOTES TO CELLS

Sometimes, you might need to submit a preliminary report before you have collected all the information you need. At other times, you might want to record important assumptions or document your work. With Microsoft Excel, you can easily attach notes to cells without having to clutter up the worksheet itself. The notes are hidden unless you specifically choose to display them, and they can be printed on a separate page as a handy way of annotating printed worksheets. (You'll learn how to print notes in Chapter 6, "Printing Microsoft Excel Documents.")

To attach a note to a cell, follow these steps:

1. Select the cell to which you want to attach the note. (Select cell C9 in the *ALSPORTS* worksheet.)

2. Choose the Note command from the Formula menu. The following dialog box appears.

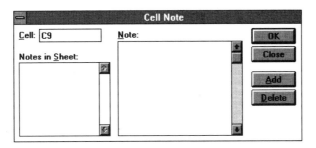

3. Type the following note in the Note box:

```
We usually get a big increase in August.
Ask Bob what happened last month.
```

Notice that you don't need to press Enter to start a new line when your text reaches the right edge of the Note box. Excel automatically moves the text to the next line. (If you want to start a new paragraph, hold down Shift, and press Enter.)

4. Click OK, or press Enter, to attach the note to the cell.

When you return to the worksheet, notice the small square in the top-right corner of cell C9, indicating that this cell has a note attached to it.

Now choose the Note command again, or double-click cell C9 to display the Note dialog box. Excel displays C9 (the cell reference of the note you added) in the Notes In Sheet list box and the note you typed for that cell in the Note box.

If you have more than one note in a worksheet, the Notes In Sheet box lists all their references, and the Note box displays the text of the note whose cell reference you select.

To delete a note, simply select its cell reference in the list box, click the Delete button, and press Enter to confirm the deletion. (An easier way to delete a note directly from the worksheet is to select the cell to which the note is attached, press Del, and then select Notes from the dialog box that appears.)

ADDING TEXT BOXES

If you want to make your notes and comments immediately noticeable to those who look at your worksheet, you can put your comments in text boxes that appear on the worksheet itself, instead of attaching them to cells as notes.

The text-box tool, shown here, allows you to create a box on the worksheet. This tool is found toward the right end of the tool bar.

To practice creating text boxes, suppose you want to add a few words of congratulations on the *ALSPORTS* worksheet to Harvey Johnson, the manager of the Team Sports department. Follow these steps:

1. Click the text-box tool. The mouse pointer changes to a cross.

2. Point to the top-left corner of cell F18.

3. Drag the pointer to about the middle of cell H20. A dotted box follows the pointer. When you release the mouse button, a text box appears on the worksheet.

4. Type

   ```
   Good job, Harvey. Go Team Sports!
   ```

Your screen now looks like Figure 4-15.

	A	B	C	D	E	F	G	H	I
1		Alan's Sports							
2		Month-to-Month Sales							
4	Department	July	August	Gain (%)					
5	Skiing	$15,600	$21,270	36.3%					
6	Hunting	$27,280	$25,900	(5.1%)					
7	Camping	$13,750	$11,085	(19.4%)					
8	Apparel	$15,920	$23,540	47.9%					
9	Team Sports	$12,500	$13,930	11.4%					
10	Golf	$10,100	$9,705	(3.9%)					
12		$95,150	$105,430	10.8%					
13									
14		August	September	Gain (%)					
15	Skiing	$21,270	$36,560	71.9%					
16	Hunting	$25,900	$28,710	10.8%					
17	Camping	$11,085	$7,250	(34.6%)					
18	Apparel	$23,540	$27,800	18.1%		Good job, Harvey. Go			
19	Team Sports	$13,930	$22,570	62.0%		Team Sports!			
20	Golf	$9,705	$8,270	(14.8%)					
22		$105,430	$131,160	24.4%					

Microsoft Excel - ALSPORTS.XLS — File Edit Formula Format Data Options Macro Window Help — Normal — Ready

FIGURE 4-15. *The worksheet with a text box.*

As with all tool-bar buttons, you can use the text-box tool only if you have a mouse; you cannot create text boxes with the keyboard.

You can apply the full range of Microsoft Excel formatting options to text boxes. Experiment on your own with fonts, patterns, and colors. To select the box, simply click it. If you want to adjust its size, drag one of the handles that appear when the box is selected. To delete the box, press the Del key while the box is selected.

ADDING GRAPHICS

Near the right end of the tool bar is a group of four buttons labeled with geometric lines and shapes. These buttons are called the *drawing tools*. With these tools, you can draw lines, curves, boxes, and circles on your worksheets. We won't go into detail about how to use these tools in this book. For more information, consult the Microsoft Excel documentation.

FAST FORMATTING TECHNIQUES

You now have a good command of Microsoft Excel's worksheet formatting options. In the remainder of this chapter, we'll show you a few useful labor-saving techniques.

Copying Cell Formats

When you copy cell contents, Microsoft Excel also copies cell formats. Copying cell formats along with contents can be very useful if you plan carefully. For example, if you build a worksheet in sections (as we did with the Alan's Sports example), you can save time by formatting the first section before copying it to create the next section.

Excel also lets you specify what information you want to copy. To see how, follow these steps:

1. Select cell B1 in the *ALSPORTS* worksheet.

2. Hold down Ctrl, and press Ins. The marquee appears.

3. Select the range B4:D4. Instead of pressing Enter, choose the Paste Special command from the Edit menu. The following dialog box appears, allowing you to specify which elements of cell B1 to copy.

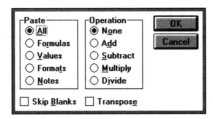

4. Select the Formats option.

5. Click OK, or press Enter.

Microsoft Excel copies the pattern you applied to cell B1 to the range B4:D4 without changing the data in the paste range. Notice that the marquee remains active, allowing you to paste to another range in the worksheet. To turn off the marquee, simply press Esc.

Using Worksheet Format Templates

If you repeatedly create worksheets with specific formatting, you might want to save one of these worksheets as a *template*. Follow these steps to create a template from the *ALSPORTS* worksheet:

1. With the *ALSPORTS* worksheet active, choose the Save As command from the File menu.

2. Click the Options button.

3. Click the right end of the File Format drop-down list box to open it, and select the Template option.

4. Press Enter. The File Save As dialog box reappears.

5. Notice that Microsoft Excel has attached the extension XLT to the ALSPORTS filename. Now double-click [xlstart] in the Directories list box to change the current directory to XLSTART.

6. You can now edit the filename, or press Enter to accept the name ALSPORTS.XLT.

Because you saved the file as a template, the next time you choose New from the File menu (after having exited and restarted Excel), the file appears as an option in the New dialog box, as shown in Figure 4-16. (If the template is not listed in the New dialog box when you restart Excel, check whether you saved the file in the XLSTART directory. It must be in this directory to appear in the New dialog box.)

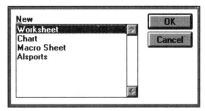

FIGURE 4-16. *The New dialog box with the template option.*

 Instead of creating a template, you can open an existing worksheet that has the format you want and enter new data. However, by using a template you avoid having to search through your directories for the right worksheet, and you don't have to worry about accidentally overwriting the existing worksheet with the new one.

Saving Time with Cell Styles

With Microsoft Excel, you can define a collection of cell formats as a *style.* Then using the Style command from the Format menu, you can give the style a name so that you can later select the style from the Style list box at the left end of the tool bar.

By default, this drop-down box lists a few common styles that Excel has defined for you. Experiment by selecting various cells in the *ALSPORTS* worksheet and applying styles from the list box to see how you can change the look of entries in one operation.

Defining custom cell styles is beyond the scope of this book. If Excel's predefined styles don't meet your needs, see the Microsoft Excel documentation for more information.

CONCLUSION

This chapter has covered basic formatting techniques for dressing up your data. You should now be able to produce worksheets that not only perform useful calculations, but also present their information in ways that are easy to read and easy to understand. In the next chapter, we discuss working with more than one worksheet at a time. We also show you how to link worksheets so that you can enter information in one worksheet and then use it in several worksheets.

Chapter 5

Working with Multiple Worksheets

As you've already seen, you can open several Microsoft Excel worksheets at one time—each worksheet in a separate window. With Excel, you can link one worksheet to another so that one worksheet can feed the results of its computations into another worksheet. In this chapter, we show you how to use linking to enhance efficiency, and then we briefly look at methods of transferring information to and from documents created with other programs. Finally, we discuss two other Excel features, workgroups and workspaces, that make working with multiple worksheets easier.

MOVING DATA BETWEEN WORKSHEETS

Before you can link worksheets, you need to know how to copy data from one worksheet to another. Copying data saves time when you need to create worksheets that are similar in structure to a worksheet you created earlier; it also reduces the chance of error.

To experiment with copying data, open a blank worksheet, and enter the sales data for the Balloon City Co., as shown in Figure 5-1. (We added bold formatting to the worksheet title and subtitle.)

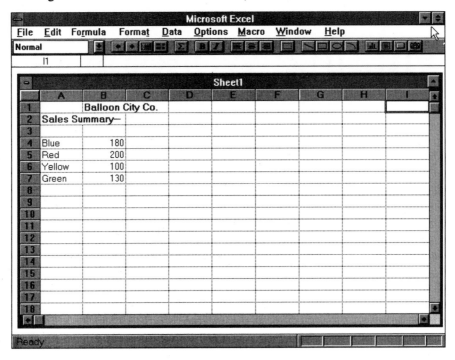

FIGURE 5-1. *The Balloon City Co. data.*

Save the worksheet with the name *BALLOONS*. To copy the Balloon City Co. data from the first worksheet, follow these steps:

1. Open a new worksheet. It will have the name *Sheet2* in its title bar.

2. Pull down the Window menu, which looks like the following.

The open worksheets are listed at the bottom of the menu.

3. Choose BALLOONS.XLS from the bottom of the menu. This work-sheet's window becomes the active window.

4. Select the range A1:B7, and then choose Copy from the Edit menu.

5. Choose the *Sheet2* window from the Window menu.

6. Select cell A1, and choose Paste from the Edit menu.

As you can see, copying data from one worksheet to another is very straight-forward.

In this instance, we used the Window menu to move from one worksheet to another. Often, simply clicking any part of a win-dow that displays the worksheet to which you want to move is quicker than using the Window menu.

LINKING WORKSHEETS

In a minute, you'll copy the worksheet again, thereby creating three work-sheets that summarize sales for the three Balloon City Co. regions: North, Central, and South. From these three *supporting worksheets* you'll create a fourth worksheet, called a *dependent worksheet*, that is linked to the other three in such a way that it can consolidate regional sales into total company sales. The links allow Microsoft Excel to update the information in the dependent worksheet if the information in any of the supporting worksheets changes. After you've created the four worksheets, we'll show you some important labor-saving techniques for editing groups of linked worksheets. First, though, let's answer a very important question.

Why Use Linked Worksheets?

Using linked worksheets can make your work simpler, faster, and more accurate. Here are some of the benefits of using linked worksheets:

- Easier summarizing of data. When you need to summarize information from several locations or departments, maintaining the consolidated totals in a separate worksheet can be helpful.

- Easier reporting. Generating a variety of reports from one large worksheet can be cumbersome and error-prone. By breaking the large worksheet into sections and maintaining each section as a separate worksheet, you can keep the reports accessible. When you want a particular report, simply print the appropriate worksheet.

- Less clutter on the screen. Instead of scrolling through a massive worksheet looking for the information you need, you can view only the data that interests you by opening the worksheet in which that data is stored.

- Conservation of memory. You do not have to open the supporting worksheets to work with the dependent worksheet. Breaking up a large worksheet into small worksheets allows you to work easily with the information when you might otherwise encounter memory limitations.

Summarizing Data from Multiple Worksheets

Now we'll explore the concept of linked worksheets by working through an example. Before you continue, follow these steps:

1. Save the *BALLOONS* worksheet with the name *NORTH*.

2. Save the *Sheet2* worksheet, which contains identical data, with the name *SOUTH*.

3. Open two new worksheets.

4. Copy the range A1:B7 from the *NORTH* worksheet to the two new worksheets.

5. Save one new worksheet with the name *CENTRAL* and the other with the name *TOTALS*.

You now have four worksheets, three with regional sales data and one that will contain total sales for the company.

 We used this exercise to demonstrate copying between worksheets, but there's an even quicker way to create dependent worksheets. You can use the Save As command on the File menu three times to save one worksheet with three different names. Then you can open the newly created worksheets by double-clicking their names at the bottom of the Window menu.

Arranging windows on the screen

The four open worksheets are somewhat awkward to work with as they appear on the screen right now. Fortunately, there's a simple way to overcome this problem. Choose the Arrange All command from the Window menu. Your screen now looks something like the one shown in Figure 5-2. (Your worksheets may appear in a different order, depending on the order in which you created them.)

```
┌─────────────────────── Microsoft Excel ──────────────────────┐
│ File  Edit  Formula  Format  Data  Options  Macro  Window  Help │
│ Normal                                                          │
│           E1                                                    │
│  ┌─── CENTRAL.XLS ───┐        ┌─── NORTH.XLS ───┐              │
│  │    A    B    C  D │        │   A    B    C  D │              │
│  │ 1    Balloon City Co.│     │ 1   Balloon City Co.│           │
│  │ 2 Sales Summary─  │        │ 2 Sales Summary─  │            │
│  │ 3                 │        │ 3                 │            │
│  │ 4 Blue    180     │        │ 4 Blue    180     │            │
│  │ 5 Red     200     │        │ 5 Red     200     │            │
│  │ 6 Yellow  100     │        │ 6 Yellow  100     │            │
│  │ 7 Green   130     │        │ 7 Green   130     │            │
│  │ 8                 │        │ 8                 │            │
│  │ 9                 │        │ 9                 │            │
│  ┌─── TOTALS.XLS ───┐         ┌─── SOUTH.XLS ───┐              │
│  │    A    B    C  D │        │   A    B    C  D │              │
│  │ 1    Balloon City Co.│     │ 1   Balloon City Co.│           │
│  │ 2 Sales Summary─  │        │ 2 Sales Summary─  │            │
│  │ 3                 │        │ 3                 │            │
│  │ 4 Blue    180     │        │ 4 Blue    180     │            │
│  │ 5 Red     200     │        │ 5 Red     200     │            │
│  │ 6 Yellow  100     │        │ 6 Yellow  100     │            │
│  │ 7 Green   130     │        │ 7 Green   130     │            │
│  │ 8                 │        │ 8                 │            │
│  │                   │        │ 9                 │            │
│ Ready                                                           │
└─────────────────────────────────────────────────────────────┘
```

FIGURE 5-2. *The Balloon City Co. worksheets after you choose the Arrange All command.*

Creating linking formulas

Now that you have created the necessary worksheets, you can summarize the regional sales information in the *TOTALS* worksheet. You summarize the data by creating a *linking formula*. Follow these steps:

1. Select cell B4 in the *TOTALS* worksheet, and type *=*.

2. Select cell B4 in the *NORTH* worksheet, and type *+*.

3. Select cell B4 in the *SOUTH* worksheet, and type *+*.

4. Select cell B4 in the *CENTRAL* worksheet, and press Enter.

Your worksheet now looks like Figure 5-3. Notice the linking formula in the formula bar.

The linking formula contains *external cell references* that link the *TOTALS* worksheet (the dependent worksheet) to the three supporting worksheets. An external cell reference consists of two components: the name of the supporting worksheet followed by an exclamation point (!) and a reference to a cell or range within that worksheet.

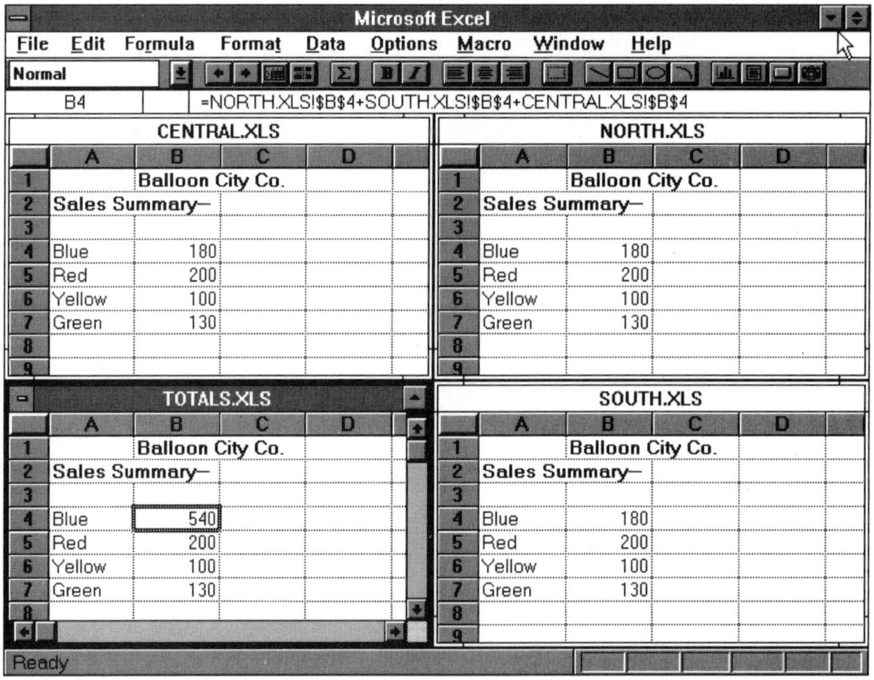

FIGURE 5-3. *The* TOTALS *worksheet with a linking formula in the formula bar.*

You could have entered this formula by typing it in the formula bar, but when the supporting worksheet is open, it's usually easier to simply click the cell that you want to reference. When you create an external cell reference by clicking a cell in a supporting worksheet, Microsoft Excel uses the cell's fixed address in the formula. (Recall from Chapter 3, ''Revising and Reviewing Worksheets,'' that a fixed address always refers to a specific cell, whereas a relative address refers to a cell that is a certain number of columns and rows from the cell containing the reference.) If you anticipate copying a formula containing an external cell reference to other parts of your worksheet, fixed addresses might yield inaccurate results. To avoid problems, follow these steps:

1. Be sure that cell B4 in the *TOTALS* worksheet is selected.

2. Choose the Replace command from the Formula menu.

3. Type *$* in the Find What text box, and click the Replace button.

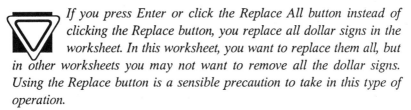

If you press Enter or click the Replace All button instead of clicking the Replace button, you replace all dollar signs in the worksheet. In this worksheet, you want to replace them all, but in other worksheets you may not want to remove all the dollar signs. Using the Replace button is a sensible precaution to take in this type of operation.

The Replace command on the Formula menu works just like the replace features of most word-processing programs. In this case, we substituted ''nothing'' for the dollar signs in the formula, which removed the dollar signs and transformed the fixed cell addresses into relative addresses.

Now, to display the company sales totals for all regions in the *TOTALS* worksheet, choose the Fill Down command from the Edit menu to copy the formula in B4 to the range B5:B7.

Updating the Dependent Worksheet

When you open a worksheet containing one or more linking formulas, Microsoft Excel checks to see if the supporting worksheets are open. If they are open, Excel simply updates the dependent worksheet with the current values from the supporting worksheets. If they are not open, Excel displays the message shown in Figure 5-4. To tell Excel to read all supporting worksheets and supply the current values for all external cell references, click Yes, or press Enter. To retain the values the cells had when you last saved the dependent worksheet, click No.

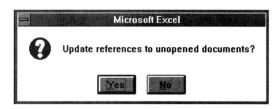

FIGURE 5-4. *The message displayed when a dependent worksheet's supporting worksheets are not open.*

At this point, the Balloon City Co. worksheets are not complete. First, to properly identify the regions, you must revise the text entries in cell A2 of each worksheet. Add the text in the second column of the following table at the end of the existing entries in the worksheet indicated in the first column:

Worksheet	Text to add to cell A2
TOTALS	Company Totals
NORTH	North Region
SOUTH	South Region
CENTRAL	Central Region

You need to make a number of other changes to these worksheets, but because these changes are identical for each of the four worksheets, we'll save those changes for the discussion of workgroups, later in this chapter.

Saving Linked Worksheets

You save linked worksheets the same way you save any other file, by choosing Save or Save As from the File menu. However, you should make a point of saving the supporting worksheets before saving the dependent worksheet. Here's why: If you save a supporting worksheet under a new name while the dependent worksheet is open, Microsoft Excel updates the name of the supporting worksheet in the external cell reference in the linking formulas. If you save and close the dependent worksheet and then save a supporting worksheet under a new name, Excel cannot update the external cell reference. The next time you open the dependent worksheet, Excel won't be able to update the information from the new supporting worksheet.

Save the supporting worksheets (*NORTH*, *SOUTH*, and *CENTRAL*) now, and then save the *TOTALS* dependent worksheet.

 It is best to save linked worksheets in the same directory. If you save linked worksheets in different directories, you must use the Save As command on the File menu to save all supporting worksheets. This ensures that the external references in the dependent worksheet are saved correctly. See the Microsoft Excel documentation for more information.

Opening Linked Worksheets

In a moment, we'll show you a technique for opening a group of linked worksheets with one command. For now, suppose you have opened only the dependent worksheet and then find that you need to revise one or more of the supporting worksheets. Instead of opening the supporting worksheet with the Open command, you can use the Links command on the File menu.

To see how the Links command works, close all the open worksheets. Then follow these steps:

1. Open the TOTALS.XLS worksheet. Press Enter in response to the dialog box that appears.

2. Choose the Links command from the File menu. The following dialog box appears:

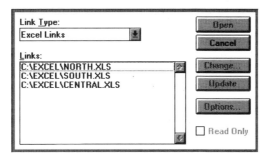

3. Be sure Excel Links is shown as the selected option in the Link Type drop-down list box.

4. Select NORTH.XLS, SOUTH.XLS, and CENTRAL.XLS by holding down the Shift key and clicking their filenames.

5. Click the Open button. Your screen now looks like this:

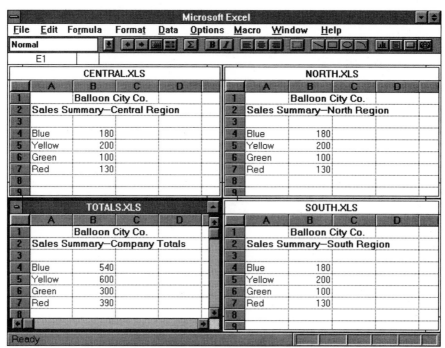

MOVING DATA BETWEEN EXCEL AND OTHER PROGRAMS

As you become more proficient with Microsoft Excel, you'll probably start to see ways that you could use the information in your Excel files in documents you create with other programs. Or you might want to import information into Excel from documents created with other programs. You might, for example, want to transfer a table of Excel data into a report you are writing with your word processor, or you might want to include in an Excel worksheet data obtained from a colleague who uses a different spreadsheet program.

Microsoft Excel provides three methods of sharing your information with other programs:

- You can save Excel files in formats that can be directly imported into other programs, by using the Save As command on the File menu and selecting a format from the File Format drop-down list box. (We discussed these formats briefly at the end of Chapter 1, "Getting Acquainted.") Similarly, many other programs allow you to save files in formats that can be imported into Excel.

- If you want to exchange data with a program that runs under Microsoft Windows, you can copy the data into the Clipboard from one program, activate the other program, and then paste the data from the Clipboard.

- If you want to exchange data with a program that supports Dynamic Data Exchange (DDE), you can create links between documents so that if the data in the supporting document changes, the data in the dependent document is updated accordingly.

The details of these three methods of data transfer are beyond the scope of this book. To explore these possibilities further, see the Microsoft Excel documentation for more information.

USING A WORKGROUP

With Microsoft Excel, you can create a *workgroup*, which allows you to edit a group of related worksheets by editing only one worksheet of the group. Using a workgroup saves you time and enhances accuracy.

Creating a Workgroup

To tell Microsoft Excel that you want the four worksheets you have created to be treated as a workgroup, follow these steps:

1. With the *TOTALS* worksheet active, choose Workgroup from the Window menu. The following dialog box appears:

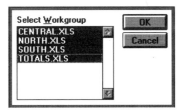

2. Choose which of the open worksheets you want to include in the workgroup. If you have no other worksheets open, click OK, or press Enter, to accept the default selection (in this case, all four

worksheets). If you have other worksheets open, hold down the Shift key while clicking each of the four Balloon City Co. worksheet names, and then click OK or press Enter.

Your screen now looks like Figure 5-5.

Microsoft Excel	
File Edit Formula Format Data Options Macro Window Help	
Normal	
E1	

CENTRAL.XLS [Workgroup]

	A	B	C	D
1		Balloon City Co.		
2	Sales Summary—Central Region			
3				
4	Blue	180		
5	Red	200		
6	Yellow	100		
7	Green	130		
8				
9				

NORTH.XLS [Workgroup]

	A	B	C	D
1		Balloon City Co.		
2	Sales Summary—North Region			
3				
4	Blue	180		
5	Red	200		
6	Yellow	100		
7	Green	130		
8				
9				

TOTALS.XLS [Workgroup]

	A	B	C	D
1		Balloon City Co.		
2	Sales Summary—Company Totals			
3				
4	Blue	540		
5	Red	600		
6	Yellow	300		
7	Green	390		
8				

SOUTH.XLS [Workgroup]

	A	B	C	D
1		Balloon City Co.		
2	Sales Summary—South Region			
3				
4	Blue	180		
5	Red	200		
6	Yellow	100		
7	Green	130		
8				
9				

Ready

FIGURE 5-5. *The Balloon City Co. worksheets after you choose the Workgroup command.*

If you are not sure which worksheets are part of a workgroup, check the title bar for the [Workgroup] *indicator. Or you can pull down the Window menu. The names of the worksheets included in the workgroup are preceded by a check mark.*

Editing a Workgroup

Having created the workgroup, you can now complete the worksheets. To show the sales totals, select cell B9 in the *TOTALS* worksheet, and enter the following formula

```
=SUM(B4:B7)
```

146

Your worksheet now looks like Figure 5-6.

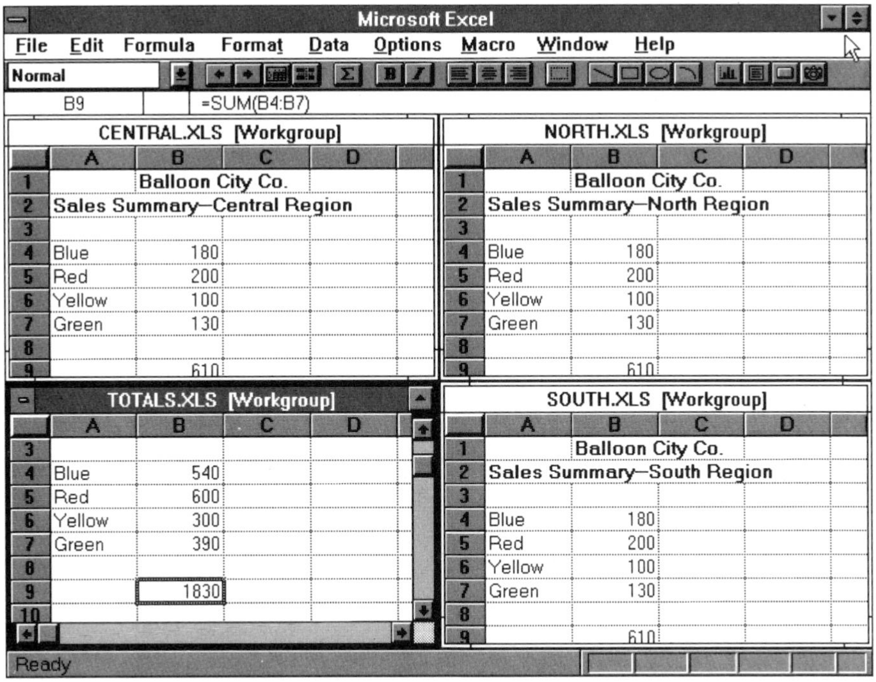

FIGURE 5-6. *The Balloon City Co. worksheets after you enter a formula in cell B9 of the* TOTALS *worksheet.*

If you activate any worksheet other than the one that was active when you created the workgroup, the workgroup is dissolved, and you will have to re-create it. Workgroups are temporary associations of worksheets that remain intact only until you move to a different worksheet.

Notice that, because you created a workgroup, entering the formula in cell B9 of the *TOTALS* worksheet has entered the formula in cell B9 of each worksheet in the group. Now try formatting the same cell, as follows:

1. Be sure that cell B9 in the *TOTALS* worksheet is selected.

2. Choose the Border command from the Format menu.

3. Select the Bottom option, and click OK to underline cell B9 in all four worksheets.

Dissolving a Workgroup

As we mentioned earlier, a workgroup remains in effect only as long as you work in the worksheet that was active when you created the workgroup. To see how this works, follow these steps:

1. Select the *NORTH* worksheet.

2. Choose the Border command from the Format menu.

3. Click the double-underline and Bottom options.

4. Click OK.

This time, the formatting is applied only to the active worksheet. Notice that the word *Workgroup* no longer appears in any of the title bars.

The reason Microsoft Excel dissolves the workgroup is quite simple. As you fine-tune your worksheets, you will often need to make changes that affect only one worksheet. To use workgroups effectively, you must plan ahead. Many of Excel's commands, including most editing and formatting commands, can be applied to workgroups. Plan either to create the workgroup and make all group changes before dissolving the workgroup and making changes to individual worksheets, or plan to make changes to the individual worksheets before creating the workgroup and making the group changes.

Arranging a Workgroup on the Screen

If you have open worksheets that are not a part of the workgroup, they can get in your way at times. To eliminate the clutter on your screen, use the Arrange Workgroup command on the Window menu.

To see how the Arrange Workgroup command works, open two new worksheets by choosing the New command from the File menu twice. Then follow these steps:

1. Choose Arrange All from the Window menu. Microsoft Excel arranges all six worksheets neatly on the screen, as shown in the following screen.

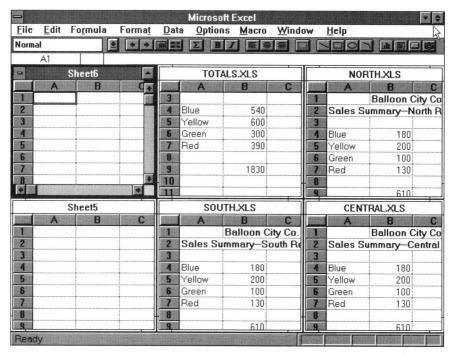

2. Choose Workgroup from the Window menu. A dialog box listing all the open worksheets appears.

3. If the four Balloon City Co. worksheets are not selected, hold down the Shift key while clicking each of the four worksheet names. The dialog box now looks something like this:

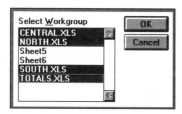

4. Press Enter.

5. Choose Arrange Workgroup from the Window menu. Your screen now looks like this:

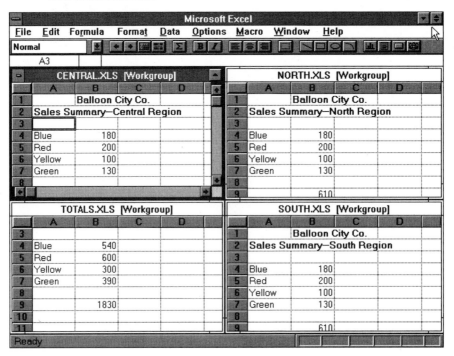

USING WORKSPACES

When you have created a group of linked worksheets, opening the worksheets one by one can be tedious. To save time, Microsoft Excel allows you to save a group of related files as a *workspace* so that later you can open all the worksheets at one time.

Remember that a workspace *is different from a* workgroup. *A workgroup is a temporary association of worksheets that is dissolved when you change the active worksheet. A workspace is simply a way of retrieving a set of worksheets quickly. You can have only one workgroup, whereas you can save as many workspaces as you need.*

Creating a Workspace

To save the current set of linked worksheets as a workspace, simply follow these steps:

1. If you have opened any worksheets other than the four related Balloon City Co. worksheets, close them.

2. Choose Save Workspace from the File menu.

3. Type *BALLOONS*, and press Enter.

4. When Microsoft Excel prompts you to save the changes you made to the individual worksheets, click Yes.

To close all the worksheets at one time, first choose the Workgroup command and press Enter, and then choose the Close command from the File menu. (If you don't choose the Workgroup command, the Close command closes only the active worksheet.) Alternatively, hold down the Shift key, pull down the File menu, and choose the Close All command. (Holding down the Shift key changes the Close command to Close All.)

Opening the Worksheets in a Workspace

Choosing the Save Workspace command creates a file on your disk with the extension .XLW. This file contains a list of all worksheets that were open when you chose Save Workspace. It also records the window positions and dimensions at the time you saved the workspace.

To open the Balloon City Co. files with one command, follow these steps:

1. Choose the Open command from the File menu. A dialog box similar to this one appears:

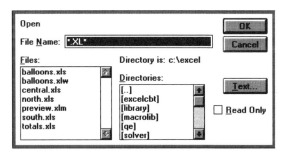

2. Select the BALLOONS.XLW file from the Files list box, and then click OK.

CONSOLIDATING DATA

You saw earlier in this chapter how you can link one worksheet to another in such a way that Microsoft Excel can update the information in a dependent worksheet if the information in a supporting worksheet changes. Excel's new consolidation feature is similar to its linking feature, in that you can obtain similar items of information from several worksheets and then summarize them on a separate worksheet. However, the Consolidate command on the Data menu, which you use to implement consolidation, offers additional flexibility and error protection.

To see how the Consolidate command works, we'll use the worksheets you defined as a workspace in the previous section. Follow these steps:

1. The *BALLOONS.XLW* workspace should be open on your screen, which should be divided into four worksheet windows.

2. Select and delete the entries from the range B4:B7 in the TOTALS.XLS worksheet.

3. Select cell B4 in the TOTALS.XLS worksheet.

4. Choose the Consolidate command from the Data menu. The following dialog box appears:

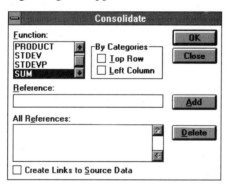

Notice that in the Function list box, the SUM function is selected by default.

5. Select the range B4:B7 in the CENTRAL.XLS worksheet, and then click the Add button to the right of the Reference box. The reference \EXCEL\CENTRAL.XLS!$B$4:$B$7 appears in the Reference box and in the All References box.

6. Select the range B4:B7 in the NORTH.XLS worksheet, and click the Add button.

7. Select the range B4:B7 in the SOUTH.XLS worksheet, and click the Add button again.

To make the selection in the NORTH.XLS worksheet, you might have to move the Consolidate dialog box. Simply drag its title bar until you can see the range you want to select.

The dialog box now looks like this:

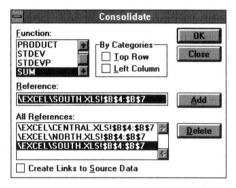

8. Click OK, or press Enter, to carry out the command.

Excel adds the values in the supporting worksheets for the Blue category, then for the Red category, and so forth, entering the totals as numeric values in the TOTALS worksheet.

The results of using consolidation are the same as those you achieved when you used a linking formula earlier. However, instead of storing the instructions for summarizing the data in the form of a formula on the worksheet and recalculating the formula every time you change the worksheet, Excel stores the instructions in the Consolidate dialog box. You can update the totals at any time by rechoosing Consolidate. You can even create links between the dependent worksheet and the supporting worksheets by turning on the Create Links To Source Data check box before you click OK or press Enter in the Consolidate dialog box.

Consolidation is especially useful for creating summary reports of periodic information that is not likely to change. Creating linking formulas is the best approach when the data in the supporting documents changes frequently. By experimenting with both approaches, you'll soon get a feel for which method to use when.

CONCLUSION

Linking offers a number of advantages if used wisely. As you have seen, you can break down large worksheets into a series of small worksheets and open only the section that you need. Opening a small worksheet also conserves memory, allowing Microsoft Excel to work faster. You've also seen how using workgroups and workspaces can increase your efficiency by allowing you to work with sets of worksheets. In the next chapter, you'll see that producing useful reports can be easier with a series of small linked worksheets than with one large worksheet.

Chapter 6

Printing Microsoft Excel Documents

Printing a Microsoft Excel worksheet is simple enough in concept, but when you begin to deal with actual data and reports, you have to make several decisions. For example, how do you want the worksheet to be oriented on the page? What part of the worksheet do you want to print? How many copies do you need? Excel provides many options that make it simple to tailor the printed copy to your needs. This chapter helps you understand these options so that you can make decisions quickly when you're ready to print a worksheet.

SETTING UP YOUR PRINTER

The most effective way to learn how to print is to practice with real data, so first, open the *ALSPORTS* worksheet.

Before you can print a worksheet, you need to set several options for your printer. Choose the Printer Setup command from the File menu to display the dialog box shown in Figure 6-1. This dialog box lists the printers you have installed—either by specifying them when you first set up Microsoft Windows or by using the Windows Control Panel.

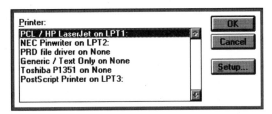

FIGURE 6-1. *The Printer Setup dialog box.*

The Printer Setup dialog box lists your printers and the ports through which they are connected to your computer (LPT1 for the first parallel port, COM1 for the first serial port, and so on). In most cases, you simply select the printer you want to use and press Enter. If the printer you want is not listed in the dialog box, you can use the Microsoft Windows Control Panel to install a different printer. For detailed information about how to use the Control Panel, see the Microsoft Windows documentation.

 This chapter focuses on printing worksheets, but the principles also apply to printing macro sheets and databases. Printing charts is another matter, however; we'll show you how to print charts in Chapter 7, "Plotting Charts."

PREVIEWING THE PRINTED PAGE

Before printing a worksheet, you will usually want to see how it will look when printed. Previewing is particularly useful when you're printing long or heavily formatted worksheets. Without actually printing a copy, you can see the portion of the worksheet that will be printed and see how the worksheet will be positioned on the printed page(s).

To preview the *ALSPORTS* worksheet, choose the Print Preview command from the File menu. Your screen now looks like Figure 6-2. (In Chapter 4, "Enhancing Your Worksheets," you probably saved the *ALSPORTS* worksheet before applying fancy formatting so that you could return to it at any time. If you saved the fancy *ALSPORTS* worksheet without changing its name, the document in your Preview window will have shading and patterns.)

As you can see, Print Preview presents a bird's-eye view of the worksheet. To examine a particular part of the worksheet in more detail, point to the worksheet. The pointer changes shape from an arrow to a magnifying glass. Move the magnifying glass over the part of the worksheet that you want to examine, and then click. Microsoft Excel *zooms in* on that area so you can see the area in detail. To return to normal page preview, click any part of the worksheet.

 You can also click the Zoom button to examine the worksheet. Excel zooms in on the top-left corner of the current page. Use the scroll bars to view different areas. Click Zoom again to return to normal page preview.

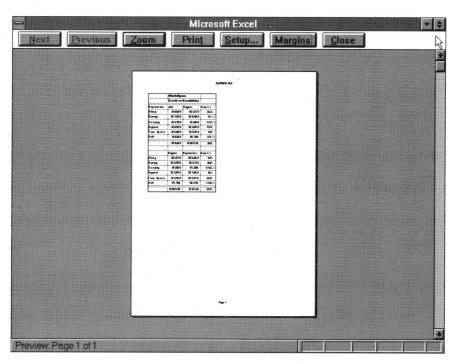

FIGURE 6-2. *Previewing a worksheet before printing.*

As you saw in Figure 6-2, the *ALSPORTS* worksheet will print on only one page, and the Next and Previous buttons are dimmed. For worksheets longer than one page, click the Next button at the top of the Preview window to display the next page of the worksheet. Click the Previous button to display the previous page.

If you're satisfied with the worksheet at this point, you can click the Print button at the top of the screen to print the worksheet. But before you print the *ALSPORTS* worksheet now, let's look at the changes you can make from the Preview window.

Suppose you want to adjust the margins. First, click the Margins button at the top of the window. Your screen now resembles the one in Figure 6-3.

The margins are marked by dotted lines, and the worksheet has margin and column handles that can be moved in the same manner as row and column handles in worksheets. Drag the left margin handle to the right, and release the mouse button. The data shifts to the right. You can also change column widths in the Preview window in a similar manner. (You cannot, however, change row heights in the Preview window.)

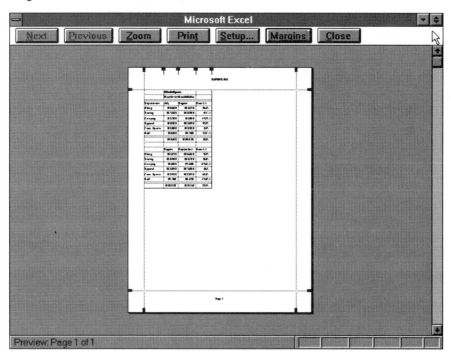

FIGURE 6-3. *The Preview window after you click the Margins button.*

If you do not have a mouse, you can press Alt-M to display the margins in the Preview window. However, you need a mouse to change the margins in the Preview window.

You can also change printing options from the Preview window by clicking the Setup button. (We'll show you these options later in this chapter when we cover the Page Setup command. For now, simply remember than you can change these options from the Preview window.)

If you need to make any other type of revisions to your worksheet (such as deleting unnecessary rows), you can return to the document window by clicking the Close button.

PRINTING THE WORKSHEET

To print your worksheet from the Preview window, simply click the Print button at the top of the Preview window. If you are not previewing the worksheet, choose the Print command from the File menu. Either way, you see a dialog box similar to the one shown in Figure 6-4.

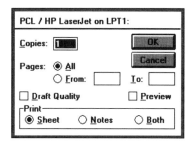

FIGURE 6-4. *The Print dialog box.*

Follow these general steps to print your worksheet:

1. Turn off the Preview option if it's turned on.

2. Specify the number of copies you want to print. For example, to print two copies of your worksheet, type *2* in the Copies text box. By default, Excel prints one copy.

3. Specify which pages to print. By default, Excel prints all the pages. To print only pages 2, 3, and 4 of a six-page worksheet, click the From button, and type *2* in the text box. Then select the To text box, and type *4*.

4. Specify the print quality. For example, to print a worksheet at high speed but with low resolution, select Draft Quality. (This option is dimmed if it is not available for your printer.)

5. Specify whether to print the worksheet only (Sheet), the cell notes only (Notes), or both, by clicking the corresponding button.

6. Click OK, or press Enter.

Excel then prints the worksheet using the options you specified. For the *ALSPORTS* worksheet, simply accept the defaults in the dialog box, and press Enter. Your printed worksheet should look like the one in Figure 6-5. (If your worksheet doesn't print, see ''Resolving Printer Problems'' at the end of this chapter.)

ALSPORTS.XLS

	Alan's Sports		
	Month–to–Month Sales		
Department	July	August	Gain (%)
Skiing	$15,600	$21,270	36.3%
Hunting	$27,280	$25,900	(5.1%)
Camping	$13,750	$11,085	(19.4%)
Apparel	$15,920	$23,540	47.9%
Team Sports	$12,500	$13,930	11.4%
Golf	$10,100	$9,705	(3.9%)
	$95,150	$105,430	10.8%
	August	September	Gain (%)
Skiing	$21,270	$36,560	71.9%
Hunting	$25,900	$28,710	10.8%
Camping	$11,085	$7,250	(34.6%)
Apparel	$23,540	$27,800	18.1%
Team Sports	$13,930	$22,570	62.0%
Golf	$9,705	$8,270	(14.8%)
	$105,430	$131,160	24.4%

FIGURE 6-5. *The printed* ALSPORTS *worksheet.*

Take a look at the printed *ALSPORTS* worksheet. Along with the cell entries, Excel has printed the following:

■ Gridlines

■ The filename of the worksheet as a *header* at the top of the page

■ The page number as a *footer* at the bottom of the page

Later in this chapter, we'll show you how to change these options by using the Page Setup command.

PRINTING PART OF A WORKSHEET

Unless you specify otherwise, Microsoft Excel prints the entire worksheet. To print only a portion of a worksheet, you must specify the *print area* by using the Set Print Area command on the Options menu, or by specifying in the Print dialog box that only specific pages be printed.

To set the print area, follow these steps:

1. Select the range of cells that you want to print.

2. Choose the Set Print Area command from the File menu. The range you selected is set off by dashed lines.

3. Choose the Print command from the File menu, and follow the steps described earlier for previewing and printing your worksheet.

When Excel sets the print area, it assigns the name *Print_Area* to the selected range. When you print the worksheet, Excel prints only the area to which this name is assigned. You can redefine the print area at any time. For example, to reset the print area to encompass two discontinuous blocks of cells, you select the first block, hold down the Ctrl key while you select the second block, and then choose Set Print Area from the Options menu. If you choose Print from the File menu, Excel will print each discontinuous block on a separate page. (If you display the discontinuous blocks in the Preview window, each block is shown on a separate page. The footer reflects the number of the block, not the number of the page from which the block is taken.)

To reset the print area to the entire worksheet, follow these steps:

1. Choose the Define Name command from the Formula menu. A dialog box appears, listing all the currently defined names.

2. Select *Print_Area* from the Names In Sheet list box.

3. Click the Delete button. The name disappears from the list, but the dialog box remains on the screen so you can delete other names.

4. Click OK, or press Enter.

The next time you choose Print, Excel prints the entire worksheet.

 You can also reset the print area by selecting the entire worksheet and choosing the Remove Print Area command from the Options menu. To select the entire worksheet, click the top-left corner of the worksheet at the junction of the row and column headers.

PRINTING LARGE WORKSHEETS

To demonstrate how to print worksheets longer than a single page, we'll use a new example—one with more data than the *ALSPORTS* worksheet—for the rest of this chapter. To work through the examples, you must create a worksheet like the one in Figure 6-6. However, you don't have to painstakingly enter

		Jan-90	Feb-90	Mar-90	Apr-90	May-90	Jun-90	Jul-90	Aug
				Sales by Region and Product					
Northeast									
	Hoisin sauce	$14,583	$15,511	$16,077	$16,028	$16,613	$17,260	$18,131	$18,
	Black beans	9,082	8,923	8,747	9,319	9,598	9,726	9,856	9,
	Sesame oil	13,861	13,621	13,675	13,730	13,493	13,547	13,601	13,
	Bean curd	18,753	18,859	18,547	18,959	18,641	18,692	18,152	18,
	Dried squid	2,673	2,718	2,837	2,805	2,799	2,765	2,795	2,
Southeast									
	Hoisin sauce	17,914	17,751	17,940	18,288	18,122	18,474	18,833	19,
	Black beans	9,565	9,876	10,210	10,620	11,119	11,454	11,799	12,
	Sesame oil	16,788	16,842	16,906	16,972	17,038	16,717	16,402	16,
	Bean curd	18,622	18,131	17,653	17,188	16,735	16,296	15,867	15,
	Dried squid	5,248	5,426	5,610	5,802	6,001	6,207	6,421	6,
North Central									
	Hoisin sauce	13,574	13,961	14,359	14,768	15,190	15,623	16,069	16,
	Black beans	9,192	9,377	9,564	9,756	9,950	10,150	10,353	10,
	Sesame oil	10,745	10,811	10,876	10,943	11,360	11,429	11,499	11,
	Bean curd	16,837	16,946	17,055	17,166	17,277	17,389	17,501	17,

FIGURE 6-6. *Data to be copied to create the SALESREG worksheet.*

the exact data that appears in the sample worksheet. Instead, simply make a few entries, and then copy those entries to other parts of the worksheet.

Start by opening a new worksheet and saving it as *SALESREG*. Then make the entries shown in cells A4 and B5:B9 of Figure 6-6. (We'll tell you how to enter the title in row 1 and the dates in row 3 in a minute.)

To complete the *SALESREG* worksheet, follow these steps:

1. Select the range C5:N9.

2. Type *10000*, and press Ctrl-Enter.

3. Select the range B5:N9 (include the product names).

4. Press Ctrl-Ins.

5. Select the following cells, holding down the Ctrl key as you drag to select these multiple ranges:

   B12:N16
   B19:N23
   B26:N30
   B33:N37
   B40:N44
   B47:N51

6. Press Shift-Ins.

7. Type *Southeast*, *North Central*, *Southwest*, *Northwest*, *South Central*, and *Central* in cells A11, A18, A25, A32, A39, and A46, respectively.

To enter the dates in row 3, follow these steps:

1. Select cell C3.

2. Type *Jan-90*, and press Enter.

3. Select the range C3:N3.

4. Choose the Series command from the Data menu. The dialog box shown on the following page appears.

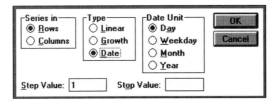

5. Click Month in the Date Unit option box.

6. Press Enter.

If you reduce the width of column A to about 2, enter the title *Sales by Region and Product* in cell F1, and then center the title, you will have a reasonable facsimile of the worksheet used in the remaining examples in this chapter.

Printing Column and Row Labels

When Microsoft Excel prints a long worksheet, it breaks the worksheet into pages and prints them in a specific sequence. Multiple-page worksheets can be difficult to read. For example, the sample worksheet is two screens wide and approximately 51 rows long. The worksheet has labels in columns A and B and in rows 1 and 3. Excel prints this worksheet as four separate pages—printing the first set of columns from top to bottom, until all 51 rows have been printed, and then printing the second set of columns from top to bottom. The resulting printout is somewhat difficult to decipher, as Figure 6-7 shows. Pages 1 and 2 have printed column labels, but pages 3 and 4 don't. Pages 1 and 3 have printed row labels, but pages 2 and 4 don't. Without all the descriptive labels, the reader can't be sure what the numbers on pages 2, 3, and 4 represent.

You can make the printout easier to read by using the Set Print Titles command on the Options menu to repeat the labels on all printed pages.

To print column and row labels on every page, follow these steps:

1. Drag through the headers of the rows whose labels you want to print—in this case, rows 1, 2, and 3.

2. Hold down the Ctrl key while dragging through the headers of the columns you want to print—in this case, columns A and B.

3. Choose the Set Print Titles command from the Options menu.

4. Be sure you set the print area to exclude the print-titles area. (For this example, you would set the print area to C4:N51.) Otherwise, Excel prints the columns and rows with labels twice on some of the pages, as shown in Figure 6-8 on page 166.

Page 1

SALESREG.XLS

Sales by Region and Product	Jan-90	Feb-90	Mar-90	Apr-90	May-90	Jun-90	Jul-90
Northeast							
Hoisin sauce	$14,583	$15,511	$16,077	$16,028	$16,613	$17,260	$18,131
Black beans	9,082	8,923	8,747	9,319	9,598	9,726	9,854
Sesame oil	13,861	13,621	13,675	13,730	13,493	13,547	13,601
Bean curd	18,753	18,859	18,547	18,959	18,641	18,692	18,152
Dried squid	2,673	2,718	2,837	2,805	2,799	2,765	2,795
Southeast							
Hoisin sauce	17,914	17,751	17,940	18,288	18,122	18,474	18,833
Black beans	9,565	9,876	10,210	10,620	11,119	11,454	11,799
Sesame oil	16,788	16,842	16,906	16,972	17,038	16,717	16,402
Bean curd	18,622	18,131	17,653	17,188	16,735	16,296	15,867
Dried squid	5,248	5,426	5,610	5,802	6,001	6,207	6,421
North Central							
Hoisin sauce	13,574	13,961	14,359	14,768	15,190	15,623	16,069
Black beans	9,192	9,377	9,564	9,756	9,950	10,150	10,353
Sesame oil	10,745	10,811	10,876	10,943	11,360	11,429	11,499
Bean curd	16,837	16,946	17,055	17,166	17,277	17,389	17,501
Dried squid	3,738	3,852	3,970	4,090	4,215	4,343	4,475
Southwest							
Hoisin sauce	11,457	11,348	11,393	11,285	11,330	11,222	11,116
Black beans	6,534	6,352	6,705	6,732	6,759	6,786	6,813
Sesame oil	8,640	8,763	8,732	8,600	8,776	8,978	9,185
Bean curd	13,765	13,898	14,402	15,057	14,970	15,480	16,007
Dried squid	2,980	3,055	3,188	3,268	3,237	3,287	3,458
Northwest							
Hoisin sauce	16,875	16,717	16,900	17,238	17,077	17,419	17,767
Black beans	8,769	9,071	9,396	9,794	10,278	10,603	10,938

Page 2

	Jan-90	Feb-90	Mar-90	Apr-90	May-90	Jun-90	Jul-90
Sesame oil	15,782	15,834	15,897	15,961	16,025	15,713	15,407
Bean curd	17,563	17,086	16,622	16,170	15,731	15,304	14,888
Dried squid	4,578	4,751	4,930	5,116	5,309	5,509	5,717
South Central							
Hoisin sauce	8,146	8,388	8,794	9,066	9,535	9,486	10,045
Black beans	6,571	6,604	6,564	6,846	7,136	7,362	7,595
Sesame oil	7,936	7,968	8,000	8,032	7,876	8,201	8,041
Bean curd	9,847	9,995	10,145	9,869	9,908	10,156	10,477
Dried squid	1,984	2,013	3,043	2,077	2,107	2,088	2,119
Central							
Hoisin sauce	11,568	11,898	12,237	12,586	12,945	13,314	13,694
Black beans	7,834	7,991	8,151	8,314	8,480	8,650	8,823
Sesame oil	9,157	9,213	9,269	9,326	9,681	9,740	9,800
Bean curd	14,349	14,442	14,535	14,629	14,724	14,819	14,915
Dried squid	3,186	3,283	3,383	3,486	3,592	3,701	3,814

Page 3

SALESREG.XLS

	Aug-90	Sep-90	Oct-90	Nov-90	Dec-90
	$18,286	$18,969	$19,367	$20,513	$20,742
	9,987	10,120	10,255	10,392	10,531
	13,655	13,710	13,765	13,820	13,875
	18,235	18,670	18,973	18,764	18,424
	2,881	2,878	3,005	3,143	3,083
	19,198	19,571	19,952	20,340	20,737
	12,155	12,523	12,902	13,293	13,697
	16,093	15,790	15,492	15,201	14,915
	15,450	15,044	14,650	14,267	13,894
	6,644	6,874	7,113	7,361	7,619
	16,527	16,999	17,484	17,982	18,495
	10,559	10,771	10,987	11,206	11,430
	11,570	11,640	11,712	11,783	11,855
	17,615	17,729	17,844	17,959	18,075
	4,611	4,752	4,897	5,046	5,199
	11,011	10,907	10,804	10,701	10,599
	6,840	6,867	6,894	6,922	6,950
	9,397	9,614	9,836	10,063	10,295
	16,552	17,116	17,699	18,302	18,925
	3,485	3,519	3,531	3,693	3,673
	18,122	18,484	18,854	19,231	19,616
	11,284	11,641	12,009	12,389	12,781

Page 4

SALESREG.XLS

	Aug-90	Sep-90	Oct-90	Nov-90	Dec-90
	15,107	14,813	14,524	14,241	13,964
	14,483	14,089	13,706	13,334	12,972
	5,933	6,157	6,389	6,630	6,880
	10,354	10,721	11,003	11,536	11,470
	7,835	8,083	8,339	8,603	8,875
	7,982	7,590	7,364	7,061	6,923
	10,808	10,367	10,695	11,033	11,430
	2,150	2,182	2,214	2,246	2,199
	14,085	14,487	14,900	15,325	15,762
	8,999	9,179	9,363	9,550	9,741
	9,860	9,920	9,981	10,042	10,103
	15,012	15,109	15,207	15,305	15,404
	3,930	4,050	4,173	4,300	4,431

FIGURE 6-7. *A four-page worksheet printed without column and row labels.*

SALESREG.XLS

				Sales by Region and Prod			
			Jan-90	Feb-90	Mar-90	Apr-90	May-90
				Sales by Region and Prod			
			Jan-90	Feb-90	Mar-90	Apr-90	May-90
Northeast	Northeast						
Hoisin sauce	Hoisin sauce		$14,583	$15,511	$16,077	$16,028	$16,613
Black beans	Black beans		9,082	8,923	8,747	9,319	9,598
Sesame oil	Sesame oil		13,861	13,621	13,675	13,730	13,493
Bean curd	Bean curd		18,753	18,859	18,547	18,959	18,641
Dried squid	Dried squid		2,673	2,718	2,837	2,805	2,799
Southeast	Southeast						
Hoisin sauce	Hoisin sauce		17,914	17,751	17,940	18,288	18,122
Black beans	Black beans		9,565	9,876	10,210	10,620	11,119
Sesame oil	Sesame oil		16,788	16,842	16,906	16,972	17,038
Bean curd	Bean curd		18,622	18,131	17,653	17,188	16,735
Dried squid	Dried squid		5,248	5,426	5,610	5,802	6,001
North Central	North Central						
Hoisin sauce	Hoisin sauce		13,574	13,961	14,359	14,768	15,190
Black beans	Black beans		9,192	9,377	9,564	9,756	9,950
Sesame oil	Sesame oil		10,745	10,811	10,876	10,943	11,360
Bean curd	Bean curd		16,837	16,946	17,055	17,166	17,277
Dried squid	Dried squid		3,738	3,852	3,970	4,090	4,215
Southwest	Southwest						
Hoisin sauce	Hoisin sauce		11,457	11,348	11,393	11,285	11,330
Black beans	Black beans		6,534	6,352	6,705	6,732	6,759
Sesame oil	Sesame oil		8,640	8,763	8,732	8,600	8,776
Bean curd	Bean curd		13,765	13,898	14,402	15,057	14,970
Dried squid	Dried squid		2,980	3,055	3,188	3,268	3,237

Page 1

FIGURE 6-8. *A printout with duplicate title and column labels, produced by overlapping print and print-titles areas.*

166

Although titles are usually located at the top and far left of a worksheet, they can be placed anywhere in the worksheet. The only restriction is that titles must be one or more entire columns or one or more entire rows; the Set Print Titles command does not accept partial rows or columns.

CHANGING THE PAGE SETUP

We've shown you how to preview and print, and how to print large documents. Now we show you how to control the overall appearance of the pages you print by using the Page Setup command on the File menu. When you choose this command, the dialog box shown in Figure 6-9 appears. (Recall that you can also access this dialog box from the Preview window by clicking the Setup button.) Let's look at each of the Page Setup options.

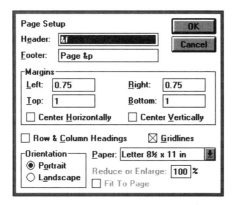

FIGURE 6-9. *The Page Setup dialog box.*

Using Headers and Footers

When you print your worksheets, you may want to add descriptive *headers* and *footers* to the pages. You can include single lines of text at the top and bottom of each page by typing text in the Header and Footer text boxes of the Page Setup dialog box. Headers and footers are different from titles in that they don't appear in the worksheet on the screen—they are part of the printing information that is saved with your worksheet, and they appear only when printed (or in the Preview window). You might want to enter a title or description as a header. Footers are useful for displaying page numbers. However, you can include any information you want in both headers and footers, as long as it fits on one line.

Microsoft Excel provides several codes that specify header and footer content. You can use these codes separately or in combination with each other or with text. Table 6-1 summarizes these header and footer codes. The default entry in the Header text box is *&f*, which tells Excel to print the filename of your worksheet at the top of every page. The default entry in the Footer text box is *Page &p*, which tells Excel to print the word *Page*, followed by a space and the page number, at the bottom of every page.

Code	Display
&d	System date
&t	System time
&f	Filename
&p	Page number
&p+*number*	Page number plus *number*
&p–*number*	Page number minus *number*
&n	Total number of pages in the worksheet (useful for printing the annotation *Page* n *of* nn)
&&	Single ampersand (&)

TABLE 6-1. *Header and footer content codes.*

Excel also provides codes that format the text in headers and footers. Table 6-2 lists the text-formatting codes and their effects. Note that the alignment codes affect only text that *follows* them—up to the next alignment code. The

Code	Effect
&l	Left-aligns the characters that follow.
&c	Centers the characters that follow.
&r	Right-aligns the characters that follow.
&b	Prints the characters that follow in bold.
&i	Prints the characters that follow in italic.
&u	Underlines the characters that follow.
&s	Strikes through the characters that follow.
&"fontname"	Prints in the font you specify.
&nn	Prints in the font size you specify.

TABLE 6-2. *Header and footer text-formatting codes.*

codes relating to fonts affect all text within the same alignment section of the header. For example, *&c&14Marketing Department* centers the title in 14-point type, as does *&cMarketing &14Department.*

To practice using headers, type the following codes in the Header text box (omit *"Tms Rmn"* if your printer can't print the Times Roman font):

```
&l&d&c&b&"Tms Rmn"&14Marketing Department Budget&rPage &p
```

Now preview your worksheet. If you print the worksheet, the header will look like the example in Figure 6-10.

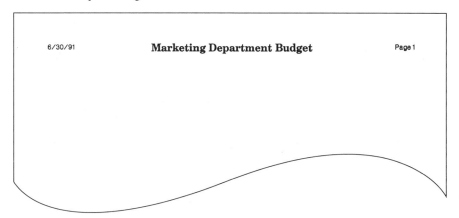

6/30/91   **Marketing Department Budget**   Page 1

FIGURE 6-10. *Printout of the header defined in the Page Setup dialog box.*

Using Other Page Setup Options

Microsoft Excel specifies the left, right, top, and bottom margins in inches. As you saw in Figure 6-9, Excel accepts decimal fractions. By changing margin specifications in the Page Setup dialog box (shown earlier), you can reposition your worksheet on the printed page (just as you did earlier by dragging the margin handle in the Preview window). Try setting different margins now by using the Page Setup command and then previewing your worksheet.

 If a worksheet won't quite print on one page, you might be able to squeeze it onto a single page by reducing the margins or column widths. You can also use the Reduce Or Enlarge or Fit To Page options in the Page Setup dialog box.

Unless you change the default print settings, Excel prints gridlines when it prints your worksheet. Printing gridlines can slow down printing and may make the worksheet harder to read. You can eliminate the gridlines from the final printout by turning off the Gridlines option in the Page Setup dialog box.

Similarly, you can print your worksheet with or without the row and column headers (A, B, 1, 2, and so on). Simply click the Row And Column Headings check box to turn this option on and off. (It is turned off by default.)

Orienting Worksheets on the Printed Page

Many printers supported by Microsoft Excel allow you to choose the way your worksheet is oriented on the page. The standard orientation, called *portrait mode*, is vertical; that is, the page is taller than it is wide. This book is printed in portrait mode. Sometimes printing your worksheet horizontally makes information more readable. This orientation is called *landscape mode*.

Many of the printers supported by Excel allow you to select portrait or landscape mode on a worksheet-by-worksheet basis. If you have the choice of printing modes, the Portrait and Landscape buttons are available in the Page Setup dialog box, as they were in the example in Figure 6-9.

CONTROLLING PRINTING

Now that you've mastered the basics of printing your Microsoft Excel worksheets, let's look at some of the additional options Excel offers for controlling the appearance of your printed pages.

In the following examples, we'll use the Epson 24-pin and Hewlett-Packard LaserJet families of printers. If you are using a different printer, your dialog boxes may look slightly different, but you will still be able to understand the examples.

Choosing Printer Fonts

Few printers can faithfully reproduce all the Microsoft Excel screen fonts, so Excel maintains a separate set of *printer fonts* for each printer it supports. (We discussed fonts in Chapter 4, "Enhancing Your Worksheets.")

To find out which fonts are available for your printer, follow these steps:

1. Choose the Font command from the Format menu. The Font dialog box appears.

2. Turn on the Printer Fonts option by clicking its check box. In the Font list box, Excel lists the fonts available for the current printer:

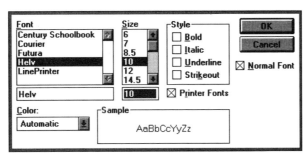

3. Select a font. The sizes available for the selected font appear in the Size list box.

4. Click the Cancel button, or press Esc, to return to your worksheet without selecting a printer font.

Formatting your worksheets entirely with printer fonts can simplify the printing process. The only disadvantage is that some of the printer fonts available for your printer may not be as readable on the screen as the screens fonts.

Spend some time experimenting with printer fonts, referring to Chapter 4, "Enhancing Your Worksheets," to find the most satisfactory and efficient solutions for printing your worksheets.

Changing Page Breaks

As we explained earlier, Microsoft Excel breaks worksheets into printed pages in a specific way, taking into account the page dimensions and margins you specify. With long worksheets, you might want to override Excel's automatic page breaks and establish your own. You can insert your own page breaks in order to print less of the worksheet on a page than Excel's automatic page breaks allow; you cannot increase the size of the print area.

You can set vertical page breaks, horizontal page breaks, or both. To set new page breaks, follow these steps:

1. Select the entire row or column at which you want the page to break. (Excel will break the page *above* the selected row or to the *left* of the selected column.)

2. Choose the Set Page Break command from the Options menu.

SECTION I: WORKSHEETS

Excel displays a dashed line in the worksheet to mark the break. Both manual and automatic page breaks are indicated by dashed lines. Manual breaks are distinguished from automatic breaks by larger dashes, as shown between columns J and K in Figure 6-11.

	D	E	F	G	H	I	J	K	L
31									
32									
33	16,717	16,900	17,238	17,077	17,419	17,767	18,122	18,484	18,85
34	9,071	9,396	9,794	10,278	10,603	10,938	11,284	11,641	12,00
35	15,834	15,897	15,961	16,025	15,713	15,407	15,107	14,813	14,52
36	17,086	16,622	16,170	15,731	15,304	14,888	14,483	14,089	13,70
37	4,751	4,930	5,116	5,309	5,509	5,717	5,933	6,157	6,38
38									
39									
40	8,388	8,794	9,066	9,535	9,486	10,045	10,354	10,721	11,00
41	6,604	6,564	6,846	7,136	7,362	7,595	7,835	8,083	8,33
42	7,968	8,000	8,032	7,876	8,201	8,041	7,982	7,590	7,36
43	9,995	10,145	9,869	9,908	10,156	10,477	10,808	10,367	10,69
44	2,013	2,043	2,077	2,107	2,088	2,119	2,150	2,182	2,21
45									
46									
47	11,898	12,237	12,586	12,945	13,314	13,694	14,085	14,487	14,90
48	7,991	8,151	8,314	8,480	8,650	8,823	8,999	9,179	9,36
49	9,213	9,269	9,326	9,681	9,740	9,800	9,860	9,920	9,98

FIGURE 6-11. *An automatic page break (small vertical dashes between columns I and J) and a page break set using the Set Page Break command (large vertical dashes between columns J and K).*

To set both vertical and horizontal breaks at one time, follow these steps:

1. Select the cell immediately below and to the right of the position where you want the horizontal and vertical breaks to cross. (In this example, select cell G24.)

2. Choose the Set Page Break command from the Options menu.

Your worksheet now looks similar to Figure 6-12.

172

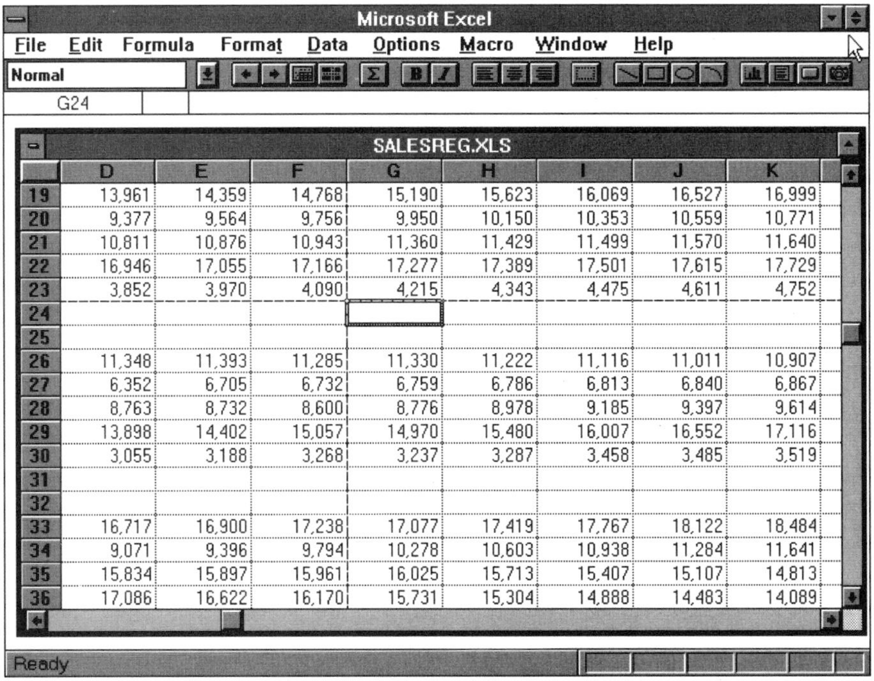

FIGURE 6-12. *A worksheet in which vertical and horizontal manual page breaks were set with a single command.*

If your worksheet contains more than one page following a manual page break, Excel resumes its normal automatic page-breaking routine for the remaining pages (unless it encounters another manual page break).

To remove a manual page break, follow these steps:

1. Select any cell directly below a horizontal manual page break or directly to the right of a vertical manual page break.

2. Choose the Remove Page Break command from the Options menu.

You can remove intersecting horizontal and vertical breaks with one command. Follow these steps:

1. Select the cell below and to the right of the intersection of the horizontal and vertical page breaks.

2. Choose the Remove Page Break command from the Options menu.

RESOLVING PRINTER PROBLEMS

Even experienced Microsoft Excel users can occasionally run into printing difficulties. Sooner or later, you'll choose the Print command and get either odd-looking output or nothing at all. The problem is usually simple and easily corrected. To identify the problem, check the following:

- Be sure the printer is turned on and properly connected to your computer. A good test is to try printing something else with another program. If that doesn't work properly, run the self-test routine for your printer, or consult your printer manual for guidance.

- If the printer itself is working correctly, check to see whether you configured your printer properly when setting up Microsoft Windows. (To check the settings, double-click the Printers icon in the Windows Control Panel).

- If you still haven't found the problem, you may be using the wrong printer driver. Your version of Microsoft Excel or Microsoft Windows may not supply drivers for some of the latest-model printers. If you suspect that this is the problem, contact the technical support group at Microsoft or the printer manufacturer for assistance.

CONCLUSION

You've learned how to preview documents before printing them, how to print documents, how to format your printouts with headers and footers, and how to control page breaks. These are the basics of working with Microsoft Excel worksheets. In the next chapter, we introduce you to charting, another important Excel feature.

SECTION II

Charts

Chapter 7

Plotting Charts

Ultimately, the goal of a worksheet is to provide information that will help you and other people make better decisions. You might even want your worksheets to persuade others to take a certain point of view. To accomplish these goals, you will often need to do more than simply lay out words and numbers—you'll want to *show* the information. Charts and graphs breathe life into your worksheet data. With Microsoft Excel, you can display charts side by side with the related worksheet, create multiple charts to display the same data in different ways, and even set up your charts so that they change dynamically to reflect changes in the data.

CHART BASICS

Microsoft Excel provides seven two-dimensional chart types: column, bar, line, area, and pie charts; scatter diagrams; and combination charts (a combination of any two of the six basic types). Excel also provides four three-dimensional (3-D) chart types: column, line, area, and pie charts. What's more, Excel offers a wide range of variations within each type, gives you complete control over dozens of chart elements, and provides a large selection of fonts, colors, borders, and patterns. In this chapter and the next, you'll learn how to use Excel's powerful charting capabilities.

Until now, you have dealt with only one type of Excel document: worksheets. Excel charts are an entirely different type of document. Charts are made up of a collection of on-screen *objects*. Although some chart objects can be moved around and formatted independently, most are dependent on the other objects in the same chart. The unique characteristics of charts require unique command menus. Whenever you select a chart as the active document, a special chart menu bar appears. Some of the commands on the chart menu bar are the same as their counterparts on the worksheet menu bar; others are unique to the chart environment. We'll discuss the commands later in this chapter and in Chapter 8, "More Advanced Charting Techniques."

Creating a Chart

Although a chart document is different from a worksheet document, the chart is usually linked to worksheet data through external cell references that enable Microsoft Excel to automatically update the information in the chart. Because of this link, you create a chart by starting with worksheet data.

Follow along with an example. Create some sample data for a company called Waterbug Pool Service. Open a new worksheet, and enter this data:

Cell	Entry	Cell	Entry
D1	Waterbug Pool Service	G4	6/91
D2	Sales Analysis— First Half, 1991	A5	Sales
		B5	25916
B4	1/91	C5	28374
C4	2/91	D5	31416
D4	3/91	E5	30958
E4	4/91	F5	38014
F4	5/91	G5	43138

When creating this sample worksheet, you might want to use the Series command for the dates in B4:G4, as you did when you entered a series of dates in the example in Chapter 6, "Printing Microsoft Excel Documents."

Notice that the dates appear in the default mmm-yy format. To change this format, select the range B4:G4, and choose the Number command from the Format menu. In the Format text box, select the default entry, and overwrite it by typing the format *mmm*. This eliminates the year from the dates in the worksheet. (We also applied bold formatting to the title and headings and centered the title, but this formatting is not critical to the task of creating the chart, so you can skip these steps if you want.) When you have finished, choose the Save As command from the File menu, and give the new worksheet the name *WATERBUG*.

Now create a chart depicting the sales figures from the *WATERBUG* worksheet. Follow these steps:

1. Select the range A4:G5.

2. Choose the New command from the File Menu. The following dialog box appears:

3. Select the Chart option.

4. Click OK, or press Enter, to carry out the command.

Your screen now displays a column chart like the one shown in Figure 7-1 on the next page.

 If your chart looks different from the one in Figure 7-1, the default "preferred" chart type has been changed. To change the chart to the Column type, refer to the section entitled "Using Other Types of Charts," later in this chapter.

Behind the scenes, Microsoft Excel determines how to place the chart elements. First, Excel sets the sizes of the columns, called the *data-series markers*, according to the numeric values in the worksheet cells you selected. Notice in

179

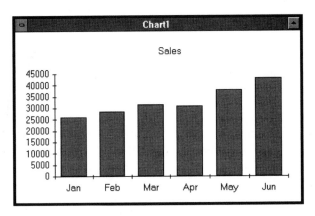

FIGURE 7-1. *A simple Microsoft Excel column chart.*

Figure 7-1 that Excel uses the dates in row 4 of the worksheet as labels along the *x* axis and uses the word *Sales* from cell A5 as the chart's title. Excel's assumptions about the relationship between worksheets and charts are usually on target, but sometimes you must change these assumptions. You'll learn how later in this chapter and in Chapter 8, ''More Advanced Charting Techniques.''

 On IBM enhanced keyboards, the keyboard shortcut for choosing the New command from the File menu and selecting Chart from the New dialog box is F11. On keyboards with only 10 function keys, the keyboard shortcut is Alt-F1.

Each chart is *dynamically linked* to the worksheet that is active when you choose the New command from the File menu and select the Chart option. If both the chart and the worksheet are open, when you make a change to the contents of a worksheet cell whose value is plotted in the chart, the chart immediately reflects the change. Excel uses a SERIES function to link the chart to its associated worksheet data by means of a special type of external cell reference. You will learn more about SERIES functions in Chapter 8, ''More Advanced Charting Techniques.''

A Tour of the Chart Window

As you can see, when you create a chart by selecting Chart from the New dialog box, Microsoft Excel displays the chart in its own window. You can manipulate chart windows as you do other types of Excel windows. Move the chart window now so that you can view both the chart and the worksheet data at the same time, as shown in Figure 7-2.

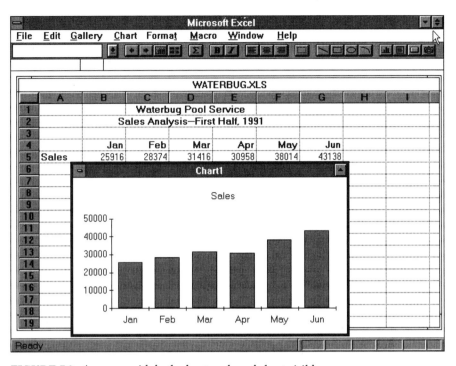

FIGURE 7-2. *A screen with both chart and worksheet visible.*

To move the chart, follow these steps:

1. Point to the title bar of the chart window.

2. Drag the chart window down and to the right until you can see the worksheet's row 5 above the top of the chart.

The entire chart always appears in the chart window, eliminating the need for scroll bars. When you shrink or expand the window, Excel shrinks or expands the chart proportionally.

As we've already mentioned, when a chart window is active Excel displays a chart menu bar that differs from a worksheet menu bar in the following ways:

- Although the File, Macro, Window, and Help menus generally contain the same commands as their worksheet counterparts, some commands work a little differently. For example, the chart-environment Print command is different. (You'll learn more about Print in Chapter 8, "More Advanced Charting Techniques.")

■ Some familiar worksheet commands are missing from the chart-environment menus. For example, the row-and-column oriented Edit-menu commands (Delete, Insert, Fill Right, and Fill Down) are missing from the chart Edit menu.

■ The chart-environment Format menu is entirely different from its worksheet-environment counterpart, because formatting charts requires different capabilities from formatting data.

■ The Chart and Gallery menus are unique to the chart menu bar.

You'll learn about the new commands contained in the Format, Chart, and Gallery menus later in this chapter and in the next.

Saving and Retrieving Charts

Microsoft Excel names the first chart you create in a session *Chart1*, the second chart *Chart2*, and so on. You can rename the charts by choosing the Save As command from the File menu. The procedure for saving a chart is identical to the procedure for saving a worksheet, except that Excel attaches the extension *.XLC* (rather than *.XLS*) to the name. Choose Save As now to save *Chart1* with the name *WATERBUG.XLC*.

As you may have gathered, charts are in some ways similar to dependent worksheets: They are linked to a supporting worksheet and take their values from the supporting worksheet, even if that worksheet is closed. When you open an existing chart, it appears with the values it had when you last saved it. Excel displays the message shown in Figure 7-3, asking whether you want to update the references to the supporting worksheet.

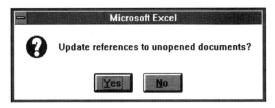

FIGURE 7-3. *The Microsoft Excel "update references" message.*

To see how updating works, follow these steps:

1. Close the *WATERBUG* chart by choosing Close from the File menu.

2. Change one of the values in the plotted range of the worksheet. For example, change the value in cell G5 from 43138 to 13138.

3. Close the *WATERBUG* worksheet by choosing the Close command from the File menu again.

4. Click Yes to save your changes.

5. Choose the Open command from the File menu.

6. Select *WATERBUG.XLC* in the File list box.

7. Click OK, or press Enter.

8. When the message box appears, click the Yes button, or press Enter, to update the chart.

Microsoft Excel updates the chart to reflect the new value in the worksheet (it reduces the height of the rightmost column). Now open WATERBUG.XLS, and restore the value in cell G5 to 43138.

CREATING AN EMBEDDED CHART

In the current example, the chart is a separate document from the worksheet, making it impossible to print a report that includes both the chart and the worksheet data on the same page. For those times when you want to be able to include the data and the chart side by side in a printed report, Microsoft Excel lets you create charts that are actually embedded in the worksheet. To see how, follow these steps:

1. Make WATERBUG.XLS the active window.

2. Be sure the chart data—A4:G5—is still selected.

3. Click the chart button, the leftmost icon in the group of four icons at the right end of the tool bar. The chart button looks like this:

4. Point to the location on the worksheet where you want the chart to appear, hold down the mouse button, and drag to create a rectangle the size you want the chart to be. Then release the mouse button.

Excel plots the data in the selected range of the worksheet within the rectangle. Your screen now looks like Figure 7-4 on the next page.

You can move an embedded chart by clicking anywhere within its rectangle and dragging, and you can size the chart by dragging one of the small black handles that appear along its border when you click it.

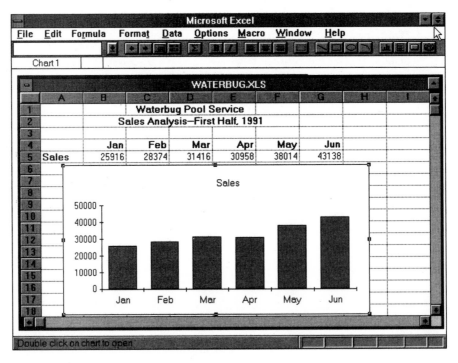

FIGURE 7-4. *A chart embedded in a worksheet.*

When you save the worksheet, the embedded chart is also saved. You cannot save an embedded chart as a separate document. However, you can transform an embedded chart into a full-fledged chart document at any time simply by double-clicking it. You can then save the chart in the usual manner. Conversely, Excel lets you copy a fully formatted chart from its own window and paste it into a worksheet as an embedded chart.

DESIGNING CHARTS

Creating a chart with Microsoft Excel is a breeze, but getting just the right look—making the chart show the information exactly the way you want it—requires considerable skill. You can format a chart in thousands of different ways, and you can modify a variety of chart elements, such as data-series markers, titles, and legends. In this section, we'll apply some of these elements to the *WATERBUG* column chart, and then we'll take a look at Excel's other basic chart types. We'll return to these topics again in Chapter 8, ''More Advanced Charting Techinques.''

To follow along with the examples in this section, you need to add more data to the *WATERBUG* worksheet you created earlier. Enter this data:

Cell	Entry	Cell	Entry
A6	Cost of sales	D6	16649
A8	Gross profit	E6	18487
B6	12426	F6	21067
B8	=B5–B6	G6	25580
C6	14321		

Then copy the formula in cell B8 to the range C8:G8 by selecting B8:G8 and choosing the Fill Right command from the Edit menu.

To create a chart that includes the cost-of-sales data, select the range A4:G6, and then press F11. The resulting chart looks like Figure 7-5. (Many of the chart windows in the remainder of this chapter have been maximized for clarity. As a result, the relative proportions of the plot area and other chart objects in the illustrations may vary from those of the charts on your screen.)

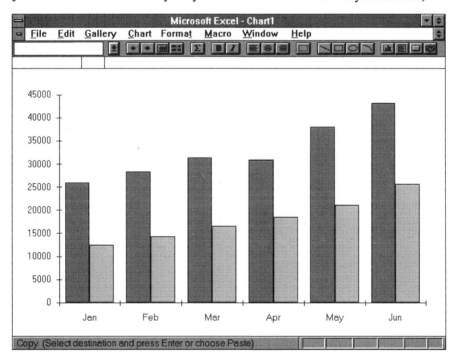

FIGURE 7-5. *A column chart with two data series.*

Working with Chart Objects

To get the most out of charting, Microsoft Excel lets you select individual elements of a chart, called *chart objects*, and change their appearance by using formatting commands.

Identifying chart objects

In Figure 7-6, we identify the various Microsoft Excel chart objects. Not all of these objects are present in all types of charts. Pie charts, for instance, have no axes, so the Axes command on the Chart menu is not available when the active window contains a pie chart. Other commands on the Chart and Format menus are available only when certain chart objects are selected. Table 7-1 describes the various types of chart objects.

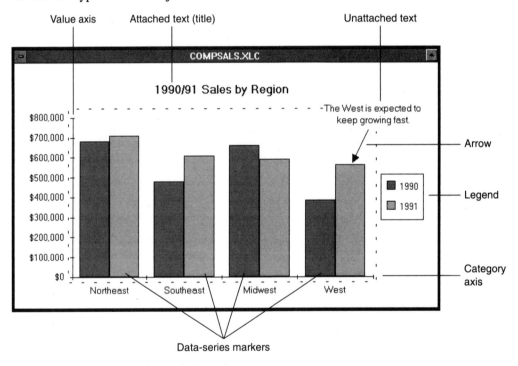

FIGURE 7-6. *The Microsoft Excel chart objects.*

Object type	Description
Chart	The chart as a whole.
Plot area	The rectangular area containing the elements of the chart proper, extending the width of the horizontal axis and the height of the vertical axis.
Axes	The vertical and horizontal lines that indicate amounts, points in time, or categories. Usually, the vertical (value) axis indicates amounts, and the horizontal (category) axis indicates points in time or categories.
Attached text	Axis labels, category names, or the chart title.
Unattached text	Free text that you add to the chart—usually a subtitle or comments.
Data-series markers	The pictorial representation of values on the chart in the form of bars, lines, dots, or pie sections, depending on the chart type.
Legend	A cross-reference between the series names and the patterns representing them in the chart.
Arrow	An arrow symbol placed on a chart to emphasize a particular item.

TABLE 7-1. *Types of chart objects.*

Selecting chart objects

As with cells and ranges in worksheets, you must select the particular chart object you want to format before you choose the formatting command. To select a chart object, simply point to the object, and then click.

Microsoft Excel marks the currently selected object with white or black squares. (Black squares indicate that an object can be moved.) As shown in Figure 7-7 on the next page, sometimes the squares surround the object. Sometimes they appear in the midst of objects. If you select an axis, the squares appear at the ends of the axis.

The name of the currently selected object always appears at the left end of the formula bar. The content of the object, which can be text or a SERIES function, always appears on the right side of the formula bar.

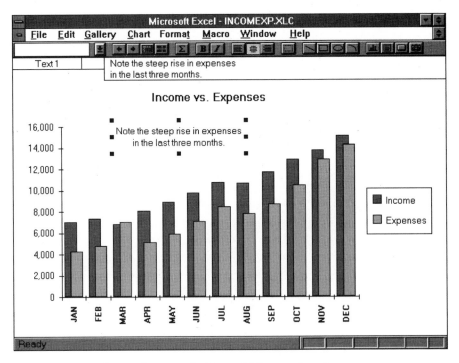

FIGURE 7-7. *A chart with unattached (movable) text selected.*

Adding a Title

Explanatory text is an important part of a chart. You can add titles, labels, and even comments to a Microsoft Excel chart.

To add a title to the two-series column chart you just created, simply follow these steps:

1. Choose the Attach Text command from the Chart menu. The following dialog box appears:

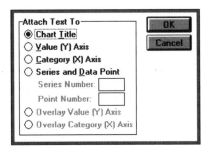

2. Click OK, or press Enter, to select the default option, Chart Title. Excel centers the word *Title* at the top of your chart, surrounded by white squares. This word is a placeholder for the title you're going to add.

3. Type *Waterbug Pool Service*, and press Ctrl-Enter, to move the insertion point to the beginning of the next line in the formula bar.

4. Type *Sales and Cost Analysis*, and press Enter.

5. Click another part of the chart, or press a direction key, to turn off the selection and remove the white squares from the title.

Your chart now looks like Figure 7-8.

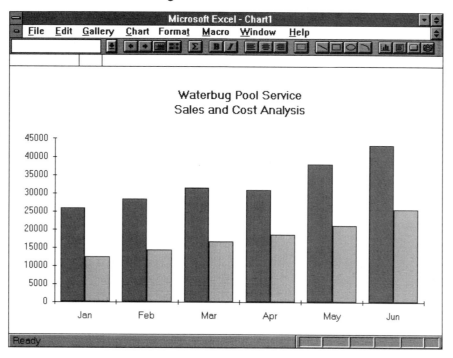

FIGURE 7-8. *The column chart with a title added.*

Adding Axis Labels

As things stand now, anyone reading your chart might wonder what the numbers along the two axes represent. Follow the steps on the next page to add descriptive labels to both axes.

189

1. Choose the Attach Text command from the Chart menu again.

2. Select the Category Axis option.

3. Click OK, or press Enter. A placeholder *X* label appears below the category axis, and the plot area moves up slightly to make room.

4. Replace the placeholder with the word *Period*, and then press Enter.

5. Select a different chart object to remove the white squares from around the axis label.

Adding a Legend

With a two-series chart, a legend can be helpful for identifying each series. To add a legend, simply choose the Add Legend command from the Chart menu. Microsoft Excel creates the legend for you and encloses it in a box. Click a blank area to remove the black squares. Your chart now looks like Figure 7-9.

The text labels in the legend are taken from the entries in cells A5 and A6 in the *WATERBUG* worksheet. Excel "knows" from the position of these text entries that they are the names of the series in the chart.

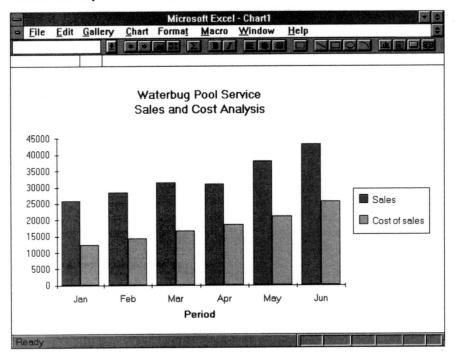

FIGURE 7-9. *The column chart with a legend added.*

Adding Unattached Text

Sometimes you'll want to add notes or comments to a chart. These notes and comments are called *unattached text*, because they are not attached to any specific chart object. In Figure 7-10, the comment *(June figures are preliminary.)* is an example of unattached text.

To add unattached text, follow these steps:

1. Before adding unattached text, be sure that no chart object containing text (such as a title or an axis label) is currently selected.

2. Type *(June figures*, and then press Ctrl-Enter to move the insertion point to the next line in the formula bar.

3. Type *are preliminary.)*, and then press Enter.

The sentence appears in the middle of the chart, surrounded by black squares.

To move the unattached comment to a better location, follow these steps:

1. Point *inside* the rectangle of black squares.

2. Hold down the mouse button. A box replaces the black squares.

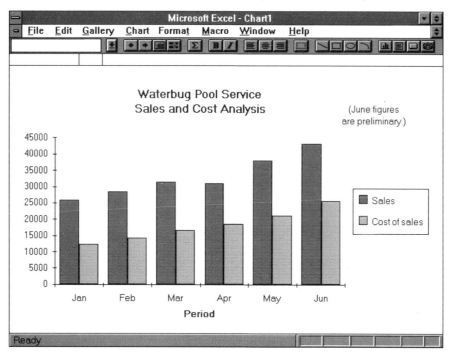

FIGURE 7-10. *The column chart with unattached text added.*

3. Drag the box to the top-right corner of the chart.

4. When the text is in position, release the mouse button. The black squares reappear.

5. Select a different area of the chart to remove the black squares.

Your chart now looks like Figure 7-10.

When the unattached text is selected, the black squares around it indicate the area within which Excel aligns the text. You can resize and reshape this area by dragging any of the black squares.

To protect all the formatting you've applied so far, choose the Save As command from the File menu, and name this chart *WATERBUG*.

Formatting Embedded Charts

Formatting a chart that is embedded in a worksheet requires a roundabout approach, because the worksheet menus don't contain chart formatting commands. First, double-click the embedded chart to create a chart document, which mirrors the embedded chart but is independent of the worksheet. You can then format the chart document using the chart menus. The formatting is applied simultaneously to the embedded chart. When you are done, simply close the chart window without saving the changes.

USING OTHER TYPES OF CHARTS

When you first start creating charts, Microsoft Excel plots your data as a column chart. The Gallery menu, shown in Figure 7-11, allows you to quickly and easily convert the chart into a different chart type.

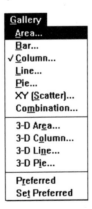

FIGURE 7-11. *The Gallery menu.*

As we already mentioned, Excel provides 11 chart types. The first 6 types listed on the Gallery menu are basic formats for single, two-dimensional charts. Figure 7-12 shows examples of the 6 basic chart types.

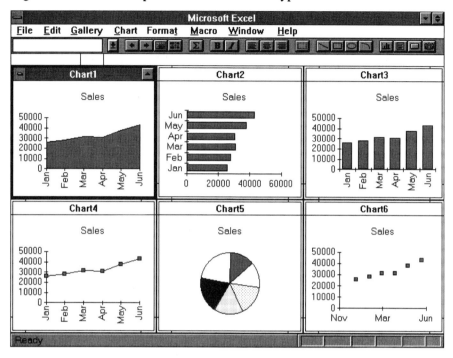

FIGURE 7-12. *Excel's six basic chart types: Area (Chart1); Bar (Chart2); Column (Chart3); Line (Chart4); Pie (Chart5); and Scatter Diagram (Chart6).*

The combination type, as its name suggests, combines two or more of the basic types in one chart. In addition, Excel offers four three-dimensional (3-D) chart types, examples of which are shown in Figure 7-13 on the next page.

Later in this chapter, we discuss each of these chart types and give examples of when to use each type. For now, let's take a look at the available types. Follow these steps:

1. Choose the Area command from the Gallery menu. Excel displays a group of predefined formats for area charts.

2. Click the Next button to view the group of predefined formats for bar charts.

3. Click the Next button until you've viewed the predefined formats of all the chart types.

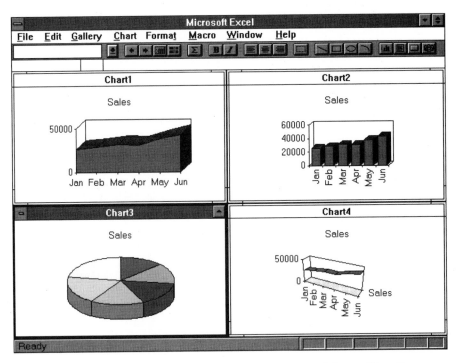

FIGURE 7-13. *Excel's four 3-D chart types: Area* (Chart1); *Column* (Chart2); *Pie* (Chart3); *and Line* (Chart4).

Try changing the *WATERBUG* chart to a variety of other types by selecting formats from the different galleries. Save each type with a different name, and then choose the Arrange All command from the Window menu so that you can compare the charts on the screen.

> *Although you can use the Gallery menu commands at any time to change the chart type, you should avoid doing so after adding formatting to the chart. Most formatting is lost when you change the chart type. To avoid losing formatting, you can change types by choosing the Main Chart command from the Format menu instead of a Gallery-menu command. (We briefly discuss the Main Chart command in Chapter 8, "More Advanced Charting Techniques.")*

Choosing a chart type for a particular situation is often a matter of personal taste, but your choice can be dictated by the nature of the data itself. Certain types of data are best suited for a particular chart type. In the following sections, we offer a few suggestions about when each type is appropriate.

Using Bar Charts

A bar chart is simply a column chart turned on its side. The difference between them is that column charts are useful for illustrating results over time, whereas bar charts are better suited for making comparisons among items.

Figure 7-14 shows how the *WATERBUG* data looks when option 1 of the Bar chart gallery is selected. (We've removed the title, legend, unattached text, and axis label to display a larger chart.)

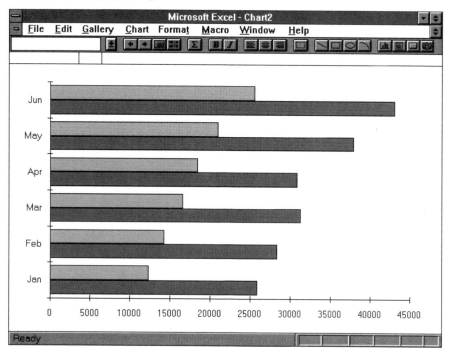

FIGURE 7-14. *A bar chart of the* WATERBUG *data.*

Using Line Charts

A line chart plots the points in a series and connects them with lines. Line charts draw attention to rates of change over time.

Figure 7-15 on the next page shows the *WATERBUG* data when option 1 of the Line chart gallery is selected.

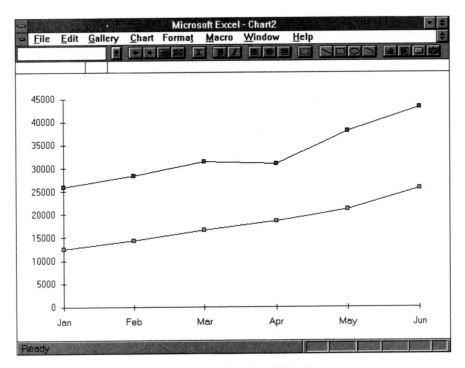

FIGURE 7-15. *A simple line chart of the* WATERBUG *data.*

Using Area Charts

An area chart connects the values in the data series with lines and fills in the areas below the lines with shading or coloring. You might think of an area chart as a colorful line chart. When you're charting a large number of data points, area charts are preferable to column charts because when you have 15 or more data points, the columns get too narrow. Area charts are also better than column charts at highlighting the relative trends of two data series.

Figure 7-16 shows how the *WATERBUG* data looks if you select ranges A4:G4 and A6:G8 (the Cost of sales and Gross profit series), create a new chart, and then select option 1 from the Area chart gallery. Notice that this area chart is cumulative, accentuating the relationship between Cost of sales, Gross profits, and Sales (Cost of sales plus Gross profits) over time.

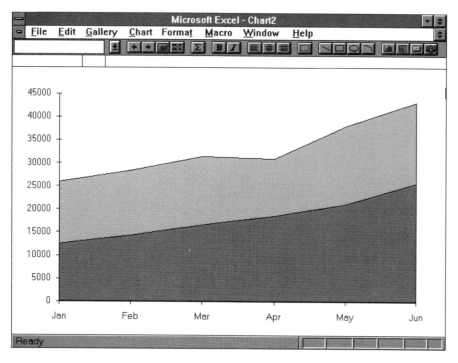

FIGURE 7-16. *An area chart of the Cost of sales and Gross profits series of the* WATERBUG *data.*

Using Pie Charts

A pie chart is a good choice for times when you want to show relative portions of a total. Each slice of the pie represents a single value, and Microsoft Excel sizes the slice in proportion to its share of the total value. The nature of pie charts restricts them to one data series. If several series are selected when the chart is created, Excel uses only the first series to create the pie chart. Note, however, that if you change the chart type to something other than a pie chart, the additional data series reappear in the chart.

Figure 7-17 on the next page shows the Sales series of the *WATERBUG* data when option 1 of the Pie chart gallery is selected. Each slice of the pie is a different color or, if you have a monochrome display, a different pattern. You can *explode* a pie slice by dragging it out from the center with the mouse. When you explode the chart, the pie becomes smaller.

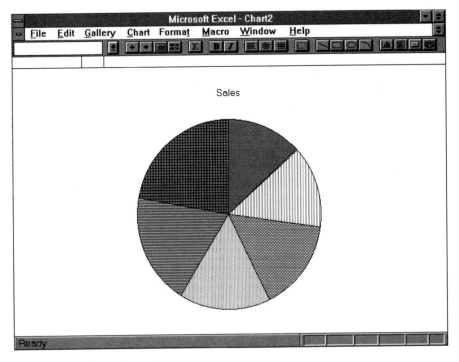

FIGURE 7-17. *A pie chart of the* WATERBUG *data.*

Using Scatter Diagrams (XY Charts)

Scatter diagrams (XY charts) seem to be little more than line charts without the lines, but they are really quite different from line charts. Scatter diagrams don't represent results over time, and they don't use the labels from a worksheet as categories. Instead, they use values on both axes to plot the data points on an XY grid, illustrating the correlation between two variables.

Creating a scatter diagram requires one more step than creating other types of charts. To create a scatter diagram, follow these steps:

1. Open a new worksheet, and enter the following data.

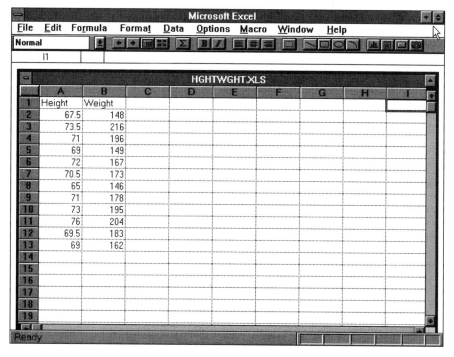

2. In the worksheet, select the pairs of values to be reflected in the chart—in this case, the range A1:B13.

3. Press F11, the keyboard shortcut for selecting Chart from the New dialog box. (Press Alt-F1 if you don't have an IBM extended keyboard.) The following dialog box appears:

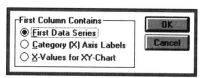

4. Select the X-Values For XY-Chart option, and press Enter. This option tells Excel that you are plotting two series of values on an XY chart.

5. Click OK, or press Enter.

Your chart now looks like Figure 7-18 on the next page. From this scatter diagram, you can visually judge whether a correlation exists between a person's height and weight.

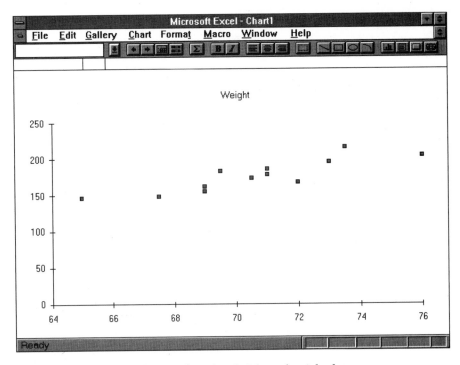

FIGURE 7-18. *A scatter diagram based on height and weight data.*

Using Combination Charts

With multiple-series worksheets, you can combine certain chart types into one chart. When you create a combination chart, Microsoft Excel divides the data series evenly between the *main chart* and the *overlay chart*. If the number of data series is uneven, Excel assigns the odd series to the main chart. The first set of data series is plotted on the main chart, the second set on the overlay chart. Take a few minutes now to experiment with combination charts for your *WATERBUG* worksheet.

You can change the type of the main chart by choosing the Main Chart command from the Format menu. You can change the type of the overlay chart by choosing the Overlay command, also from the Format menu. (We cover these commands in Chapter 8, "More Advanced Charting Techniques.")

CHOOSING A DEFAULT FORMAT

When you install Microsoft Excel, the default, or *preferred*, chart format is the first predefined format shown in the gallery displayed when you choose Column from the Gallery menu. All newly created charts appear in the preferred format. If you would rather that Excel use a different format when you choose Chart from the New dialog box to plot a new chart, use the Set Preferred command on the Gallery menu to make that format the preferred type.

To change the preferred chart format, you simply create a chart in the format you prefer and, with that chart open, you choose the Set Preferred command from the Gallery menu. The next time you create a new chart, the chart will have the format you assigned using the Set Preferred command.

If you have changed the type or format of a chart and you want to quickly return it to the preferred format, you simply select the chart, and then choose the Preferred command from the Gallery menu. If you have more than one chart window open, the Preferred command affects only the active chart.

CONCLUSION

In this chapter, you've learned the basics of creating charts with Microsoft Excel. In the next chapter, you'll get a chance to work more extensively with combination and 3-D charts, when we explain Excel's sophisticated chart formatting capabilities.

Chapter 8

More Advanced Charting Techniques

In addition to basic chart types, Microsoft Excel offers two other types of visually interesting charts—3-D and picture charts—which we discuss in this chapter. Because Excel provides so many predefined chart formats, you can usually choose a chart type and select a format that meets your needs. For those times when none of the predefined formats will do, we show you how to create custom formats. Excel's charting capabilities are extensive, but this chapter provides enough background for you to experiment with advanced techniques on your own.

CREATING 3-D CHARTS

Microsoft Excel offers four 3-D (three-dimensional) chart types—bar, column, line, and pie—which are variations of the chart types we examined in Chapter 7, "Plotting Charts." If the *WATERBUG* chart is not already displayed on your screen, open it, and then follow these steps to create a 3-D chart:

1. Choose 3-D Column from the Gallery menu.

2. Select the fifth option from the gallery, and press Enter.

The resulting chart looks like Figure 8-1.

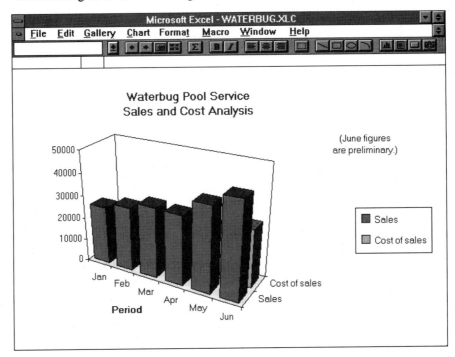

FIGURE 8-1. *A 3-D column chart.*

Changing the View

To emphasize certain aspects of the data in the chart, you can change the angle at which the chart is viewed. Choose the 3-D View command from the Format menu to display the dialog box shown in Figure 8-2. To change the Elevation option, which controls the vertical viewing angle, click the up and down arrow buttons above the option. To change the Rotation option, which controls the lateral viewing angle, click the clockwise and counterclockwise icons to the right of the option. To change the Perspective option, which controls the relative sizes of data markers at the front and back of the chart and gives a sense of distance, click the up and down arrow buttons above the option. Clicking the buttons changes the viewing angle incrementally. You can also enter new values directly into the option text boxes. Because describing the effects of these options well enough for you to visualize them is difficult, we suggest that you experiment with these options, observing the effects of different settings on the sample chart displayed in the middle of the dialog box.

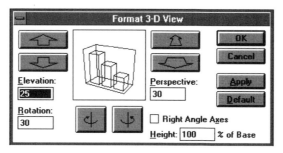

FIGURE 8-2. *The Format 3-D View dialog box.*

Changing the Plot Order

As you saw in Figure 8-1, the data markers in the front of the chart (which indicate sales) are larger than and consequently obscure most of the markers in the back (which indicate cost of sales). To remedy this problem, you must change the *plot order* of the data series. Follow these steps:

1. Click one of the markers for the Sales data series. White squares appear at the top of the first and last columns to indicate that the whole series is selected.

2. Choose the Edit Series command from the Chart menu. The following dialog box appears:

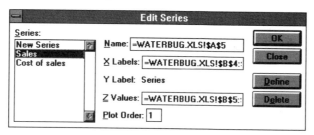

3. In the Plot Order box, change the value from 1 to 2.

4. Click OK, or press Enter.

Your chart now resembles Figure 8-3. The relationship between sales and cost of sales is now much clearer.

Now select the Cost of Sales data series, and choose Edit Series from the Chart menu. Notice that the Plot Order box indicates that Microsoft Excel now plots this series first. For the remaining examples in this chapter, change the value in the Plot Order box from 1 to 2, and click OK or press Enter.

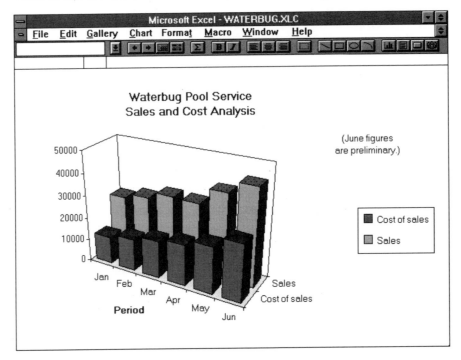

FIGURE 8-3. *Changing the plot order makes the relationship between the series clearer.*

CREATING PICTURE CHARTS

When you want to create a fancy chart for a special occasion or add a touch of whimsy to your presentations, Microsoft Excel allows you to specify your own data-series markers. You can use any graphic that can be imported into Excel to create markers for your charts. Figure 8-4 shows a column chart whose columns are made up of stacked images representing dot-matrix printers.

Detailed instructions for creating picture charts are beyond the scope of this book. For information about how to create them, see the Microsoft Excel documentation.

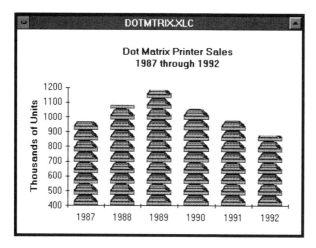

FIGURE 8-4. *A chart that uses imported graphics as data-series markers.*

FORMATTING CHART OBJECTS

With charts, the term *formatting* covers a lot of ground. For example, you can format chart text much the same way as you format worksheet text. In addition, you can emphasize any chart object by adding borders, colors, and patterns.

Before you practice using Microsoft Excel's many chart-formatting options, choose the Column command from the Gallery menu, and select the first option to change *WATERBUG* to a simple column chart.

Adding Boxes

Putting a box around chart text emphasizes the text and gives the chart a more polished look. You can put a box around any text in your chart. To put a shadowed box around the chart title, follow these steps:

1. Select the title.

2. Choose the Patterns command from the Format menu. The following dialog box appears:

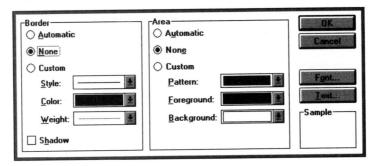

 You can display the Patterns dialog box for an object at any time by simply double-clicking the object. This one action both selects the object and chooses the Patterns command.

3. The Border options control the appearance of the box frame. From the Color drop-down list, select the dark blue color. (If you have a monochrome monitor, the colors appear as shades of gray. Pick any one of the gray shades.) Excel changes the sample lines in the Style and Weight groups to the color you select.

4. Pull down the Weight list box, and select the heaviest line.

5. Turn on the Shadow option by clicking its check box.

6. Click OK, or press Enter.

Your chart now looks like Figure 8-5.

Changing the Pattern and Color

The Patterns command from the Format menu provides an outlet for your artistic impulses. You can use any two colors from the basic palette of 16 colors and apply them to any one of 18 patterns. Many of the patterns are so finely drawn that the two colors visually combine to create a new color.

 As we explained in Chapter 4, "Enhancing Your Worksheets," patterns are made up of combinations of foreground and background colors. For example, an even gray pattern might have an equal number of black foreground dots and white background dots. If you change the foreground and background colors to red and blue, the visual result is solid purple.

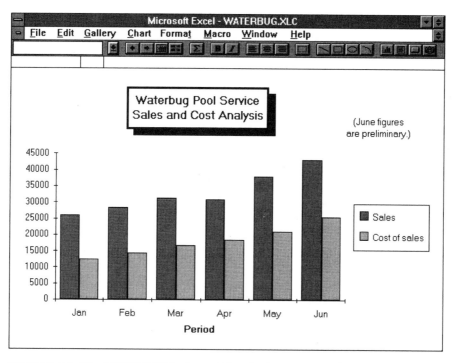

FIGURE 8-5. *The* WATERBUG *chart with a shadowed box around the title.*

To add a pattern to the title box, follow these steps:

1. Select the title box.

2. Choose the Patterns command from the Format menu.

3. Experiment with various color combinations by making selections from the Foreground and Background list boxes, and then view the effects of the colors on different patterns. (We suggest that you use combinations of light colors so that the title is still readable against the pattern.) The Sample box in the Patterns dialog box shows you how the currently selected pattern will appear on the chart.

4. When you have made the selections you want, press Enter to view the result.

Your chart title now looks something like Figure 8-6. You can follow the same basic procedure to add patterns to chart legends, labels, and unattached text.

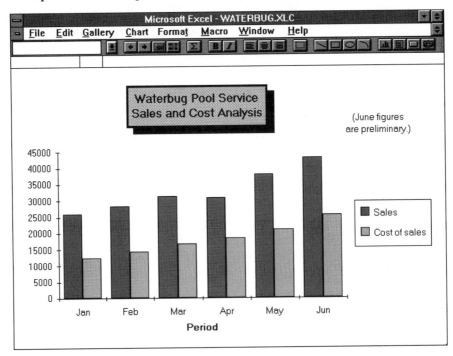

FIGURE 8-6. *The* WATERBUG *chart with the title formatted.*

Formatting Axes

In addition to formatting text, you can format axes and their labels. Microsoft Excel gives you many options, including how to scale the axes, whether to display tick marks along them, and whether to display labels.

To format the axes on your chart, follow these steps:

1. Click the horizontal axis.

2. Choose the Patterns command from the Format menu. The following dialog box appears.

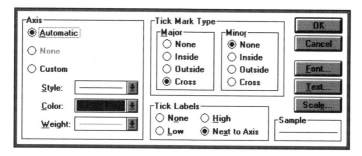

3. In the Weight drop-down list, select one of the thicker weights for the axis, and then press Enter. The horizontal axis and its tick marks now appear as thick lines.

4. Click the vertical axis.

5. Choose the Patterns command from the Format menu. The dialog box appears again.

6. Click the Scale button at the right of the dialog box. The Value (Y) Axis Scale dialog box appears:

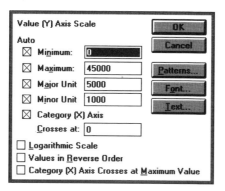

7. Change the Major Unit amount from 5000 to 10000, and then press Enter.

Your chart now looks like Figure 8-7 on the next page. Notice that every 10,000 unit now has a tick mark, instead of every 5000 unit.

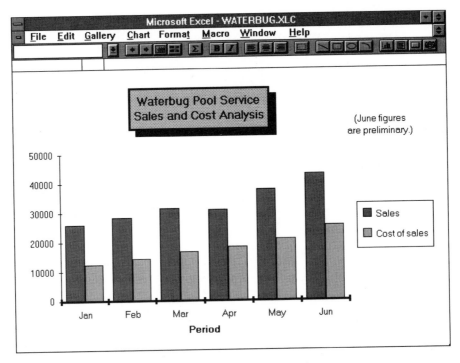

FIGURE 8-7. *The* WATERBUG *chart after formatting the axes.*

Formatting Chart Text

Microsoft Excel gives you as much control over chart text as over worksheet text. You can align and orient chart text in a variety of ways, and you can use fonts and colors to emphasize and enhance it.

Positioning text

Let's look at some ways you can position various types of text in your charts. Note that not all of the positioning commands work with all text objects.

To position the title, select the title box, and then choose the Text command from the Format menu. The dialog box shown in Figure 8-8 appears.

The choices in the Text Alignment option group are self-explanatory. The options in the Horizontal group work basically the same way as their counterparts in the worksheet Alignment dialog box: They center, right-align, or left-align the text within the text-box area. The options in the Vertical group work in the same general fashion. Experiment by changing the Alignment settings for the title, returning it to its centered position when you are done.

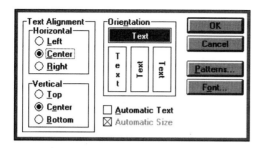

FIGURE 8-8. *The Text dialog box.*

The Orientation option group offers four possible text alignments. Each option button shows the effect clicking the button has on the chart. Obviously, horizontal text is most appropriate for title boxes. But vertical text can be useful for labels along the value (vertical) axis. To see how vertical text looks, follow these steps:

1. If the Text dialog box is still displayed, click Cancel, or press Esc, to remove the dialog box from the screen.

2. Click the vertical axis.

3. Choose the Attach Text command from the Chart menu. Click OK, or press Enter, to confirm the default selection, Value Axis.

4. Replace the placeholder, *Y,* with the word *Dollars.*

5. Click OK, or press Enter.

6. Choose the Text command from the Format menu. Notice that the middle orientation option (reading sideways from bottom to top) is selected by default.

7. Select the first vertical Text button in the Orientation option group.

8. Click OK, or press Enter.

The *Dollars* label is now oriented vertically with the letters one on top of the other from top to bottom. Although this format can be useful at times, it is somewhat difficult to read. For clarity, you will probably want to change it back to the sideways/bottom-to-top format.

Changing the font

The shadowed box adds interest to the title, but the title text itself still looks like all the other text in the chart. Now add more emphasis by changing the text font to Roman 18-point bold. Follow these steps:

1. Select the title again.

2. Choose the Font command from the Format menu. The following dialog box appears (the fonts available depend on the printer you have installed):

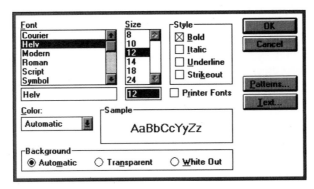

3. Select Roman in the Font list box.

4. Select 18 in the Size list box.

5. If the Bold option is not selected in the Style group, click it.

6. If you have a color monitor, select red in the Color drop-down list.

7. Click OK, or press Enter.

 As you may have noticed, the dialog boxes available through the Format menu contain buttons that link you to other related dialog boxes. From the Font dialog box, for example, you can go directly to the Patterns or Text dialog boxes.

FORMATTING THE CHART ITSELF

The quickest way to format the chart as a whole is to select the chart type you want by using the commands on the Gallery menu. Microsoft Excel then formats the chart for you. If you want something other than Excel's predefined formats, you can make changes to the entire chart just as you have done with individual chart objects.

Adding Borders and Patterns

The Patterns command on the Format menu also lets you format the chart background. To customize the background of your chart, follow these steps:

1. Choose the Select Chart command from the Chart menu to select the entire chart.

2. Choose the Patterns command from the Format menu.

3. Create a border around the chart by using the options in the Border group of the Patterns dialog box. Select the solid line style, the blue color (if you have a color monitor), and the medium line weight. Then turn on the Shadow option by clicking its check box.

4. Create a background pattern for the whole chart by using the options in the Area group. Select a pattern and new foreground and background colors.

5. Click OK, or press Enter.

Your chart now looks something like Figure 8-9.

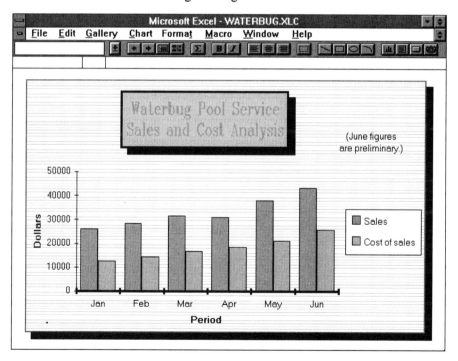

FIGURE 8-9. *The chart after adding a background pattern.*

You'll probably spend quite a bit of time experimenting with formatting patterns, so if you come up with a pattern you particularly like, be sure to save the chart so you can reuse the pattern later.

Changing Fonts

Earlier we showed you how to use the Font command on the Format menu to format text chart objects. You can also use the Font command to change all the chart text. To apply a single font to all text objects, follow these steps:

1. Choose the Select Chart command from the Chart menu to select the entire chart.

2. Choose the Font command from the Format menu.

3. Select Helv (Helvetica) in the Font list box and 10 in the Size list box. Turn on the Italic option in the Style option group.

4. Click OK, or press Enter, to carry out the command.

Your chart now looks like Figure 8-10.

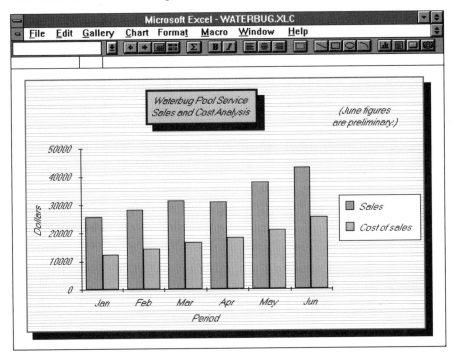

FIGURE 8-10. *The results of assigning a different font to the* WATERBUG *chart.*

Notice that the title box has lost its special font, but not its background and border. To restore the title box's special font, select the title box, and choose the Font command from the Format menu. Select the red, Roman, 18-point, and Bold options.

Formatting the Data-Series Markers

The data-series markers are the heart and soul of the chart. No matter what else you do to the chart, you'll want to ensure that these markers display the data in the most easy-to-understand way. Now we show you how to format the markers for an entire series and how to format a single marker.

Formatting an entire series

Microsoft Excel assigns colors to series in charts in a specific order. If you have a color monitor, the first series markers are red, the second are green, the third are blue, and so on. However, you can change the color of any series by using the Patterns command on the Format menu.

Because the Waterbug Pool Service chart contains only two data series, Excel uses red and green. To try out different effects, follow these steps:

1. Select a series by clicking one of the markers in that series.

2. Choose the Patterns command from the Format menu. This Patterns dialog box appears:

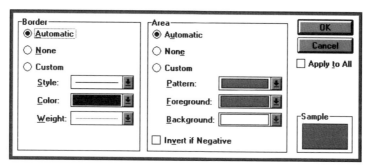

3. Select a different pattern and foreground and background colors from the Area option group.

4. Select the color, style, and weight of the marker borders from the Border option group.

5. Click OK, or press Enter, to see the effect.

6. Repeat the procedure with the other data series.

When you find an effect you like, save the chart to preserve its format.

Formatting a single marker

Sometimes it's handy to format a single marker. For example, if you are creating a chart that includes historical and projected data, you might want to highlight the information for the current year to mark the boundary between what happened in the past and what you think will happen in the future.

To select a single data-series marker, hold down the Ctrl key while you click the marker. Any changes you make with the Patterns command will then affect only the selected marker. Try this now, and then choose the Undo command from the Edit menu.

Usually when you are working with a column or bar chart that plots only one series, Microsoft Excel assigns the same color and pattern to every marker. You can tell Excel to assign each marker a different pattern, by choosing Main Chart from the Format menu and turning on the Vary by Category option in the Format area of the Main Chart dialog box.

When you are working with a line chart, you can control the style and color of each data-series marker by selecting options from the Patterns dialog box for line charts, shown in Figure 8-11. You can also control the weight, style, and color of the connecting lines. (If you want to work with only one data-series marker, remember to select the marker before you choose the Patterns command from the Format menu; otherwise, your changes will affect all the data-series markers in the series.)

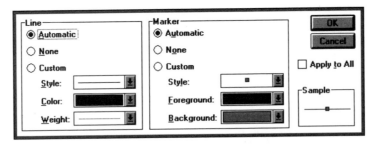

FIGURE 8-11. *The Patterns dialog box for line charts.*

DECIDING ON A CHART FORMAT

We've shown you several different chart formats, but there's more to creating interesting charts than fancy formatting. The most important goal is to present data accurately and in an easy-to-understand form. You must decide what type of chart to use, and you must decide what data to include in the chart.

In this section, we use the data in Figure 8-12 (an expanded version of the Waterbug Pool Service worksheet) to explore the decisions you must make when creating a chart for presentation.

	A	B	C	D	E	F	G
	Microsoft Excel - WATERBUG.XLS						
	File Edit Formula Format Data Options Macro Window Help						
	Normal						
	H1						
1	Waterbug Pool Service, Inc.						
2	Sales Analysis—First Half, 1991						
3							
4		Jan	Feb	Mar	Apr	May	Jun
5	Sales	25916	28374	31416	30958	38014	43138
6	Cost of sales	12426	14321	16649	18487	21067	25580
7							
8	Gross profit	13490	14053	14767	12471	16947	17558
9	Selling and general expenses	10357	10573	10984	10348	12627	12943
10							
11	Net income	3133	3480	3783	2123	4320	4615
12							
13	Profit margin	12.09%	12.26%	12.04%	6.86%	11.36%	10.70%
14							
15							
16							
17							
18							
19							
20							
21							
22							

FIGURE 8-12. *Sales, expense, and profit data for Waterbug Pool Service.*

First, add the new information in Figure 8-12 to your worksheet. Then follow these steps:

1. Enter the new labels in cells A9, A11, and A13.

2. Enter the amounts in cells B9 through G9.

3. Enter the following formula in cell B11:

   =B8-B9

4. Copy the formula in cell B11 to the range C11:G11. (You might want to use the Fill Right command on the Edit menu.)

5. Enter the following formula in cell B13:

   =B11/B5

6. Copy the formula in cell B13 to the range C13:G13.

7. Apply the 0.00% format to row 13.

8. Widen column A to completely display the labels.

Now suppose you've been asked to make a presentation at a management meeting, highlighting significant aspects of the company's performance in the first half of 1991. You see immediately that the revised worksheet contains too much information to present in one chart; you must decide which information is most important for your presentation.

The *WATERBUG* chart you produced earlier shows that business seems to be going well. Sales are increasing briskly, and the cost of sales appears to be appropriate. Row 11 in the worksheet indicates that net income shows a general upward trend. But something in the worksheet strikes a sour note. Notice that net income as a *percentage* of total sales (profit margin) has declined over the six-month period. You're aware of the reasons behind the severe drop in April, but you still think the overall downward trend should be discussed at the meeting. How can you call attention to this trend in a chart?

The answer is with a combination chart. To contrast the good news (steady sales growth) with the bad news (lagging profit margins), you can create a chart with the sales data series plotted on a main chart and the profit margin data series plotted on an overlay chart. Combining two different chart types will highlight the divergent trends in the two data series. For this example, use a column chart for sales and a line chart for profit margin. Follow these steps:

1. Select the range A4:G5, and then hold down the Ctrl key and select A13:G13.

2. Press F11 or Alt-F1.

Your chart looks like Figure 8-13. Only the sales figures appear in this chart. Because the value axis is scaled in increments of 5000, the percentage values are too small to show up.

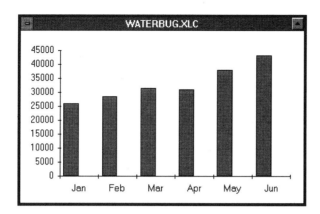

FIGURE 8-13. *A column chart of the* WATERBUG *sales data.*

To show the percentage values, choose the Combination command from the Gallery menu, and select the second option (which shows a second value axis on the right). Excel redraws the chart so that it now depicts the contrast between the sales trends on the main column chart and the profit-margin trends on the overlay line chart, as shown in Figure 8-14.

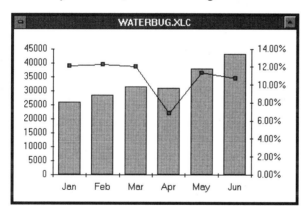

FIGURE 8-14. *A combination chart of the* WATERBUG *sales vs. profit-margin data with two value axes.*

Notice that the scale of the axis on the right causes Excel to plot the profit-margin data toward the top of the chart. You can dramatize the profit-margin trend by overriding the automatic scaling of the percentage axis.

To change the scaling, follow these steps:

1. Select the axis on the right.

2. Choose the Scale command from the Format menu. The following dialog box, which you saw in an earlier example, appears:

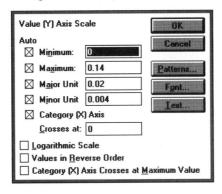

3. Change the value for the Minimum option to *0.06* to make 6 percent the lowest value on the scale.

4. Click OK, or press Enter.

Because the vertical range of the overlay chart is now from 6.00% to 13.00%, Excel redraws the overlay chart so that it accentuates April's downward trend, as shown in Figure 8-15.

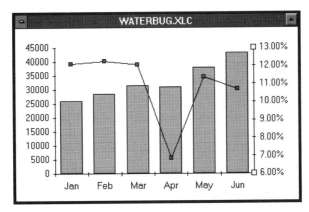

FIGURE 8-15. *The combination chart from Figure 8-14 after adjusting the scale of the percentage-value axis.*

The previous example demonstrates how you can bring some creativity to bear on business data. Microsoft Excel can point out troublesome trends before they become big problems. On the other hand, you can easily go overboard if you're not careful. For example, it's possible to make an insignificant trend look overly important by severely narrowing the range of an axis.

Changing the Combination Chart Layout

You learned earlier in this chapter how to format a chart as a whole. You have yet to learn how to change the chart type while preserving the formatting. If you have added formatting to such items as series markers and axes, that formatting generally disappears when you change the chart type with the Gallery command. To preserve all your formatting, choose the Main Chart command from the Format menu. Excel then displays the dialog box shown in Figure 8-16.

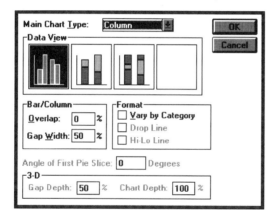

FIGURE 8-16. *The Main Chart dialog box.*

The Main Chart Type box allows you to change the chart type by selecting the desired type from the drop-down list. The graphical examples shown in the Data View group change dynamically when you change the chart type. Together, these two option groups provide most of the capability of the Gallery menu.

The other options in the dialog box provide a number of global options relating to data-series markers. You learned how to use the Vary By Category option a few minutes ago. Explanation of the other options is beyond the scope of this book. For more information, see the Microsoft Excel documentation.

Choosing the Overlay command from the Format menu brings up a similar dialog box that allows you to format the overlay part of a combination chart.

CHANGING MICROSOFT EXCEL CHARTING CONVENTIONS

Before we leave the subject of charting, we need to cover a few technical topics. In general, Microsoft Excel can do most of the work of plotting data for you. Occasionally, though, you may want to alter Excel's charting conventions, and you will need to understand some of Excel's internal mechanisms so that you can achieve the results you want.

Overriding Category and Series Assumptions

When you create a chart, Microsoft Excel assumes that the chart has more categories than series. For example, if your worksheet data tracks the sales of Product A and Product B over a 12-month period, when you select the data and instruct Excel to create a chart, Excel assumes that the two products are data series and the 12 months are categories. If you are plotting a column chart, Excel groups a marker from the Product A data series with the corresponding marker from the Product B data series to create 12 clusters of markers, one for each month category. You can then compare the sales of the products for each month.

Suppose you want Excel to plot a chart in which the 12 months are data series and the two products are categories. You want Excel to group corresponding markers from each of the 12 data series to create two clusters of markers, one for each product category. You can then compare month-to-month sales for each product. To create such a chart, you need to override Excel's assumption that a chart should have more categories than data series.

Let's work through an example to see how you can override Excel's charting conventions. In a new worksheet, enter the data shown in Figure 8-17, and then follow these steps:

1. Select the range A1:C5.

2. Choose the New command from the File menu, select the Chart option, and then click OK, or press Enter, to create a new chart in the preferred format.

Unless you have changed the preferred chart type, your chart now looks like Figure 8-18.

This chart design calls attention to the change in sales volume from last year to this year. But suppose you want to look at the data from a different perspective by grouping all the series markers for each year so that you can

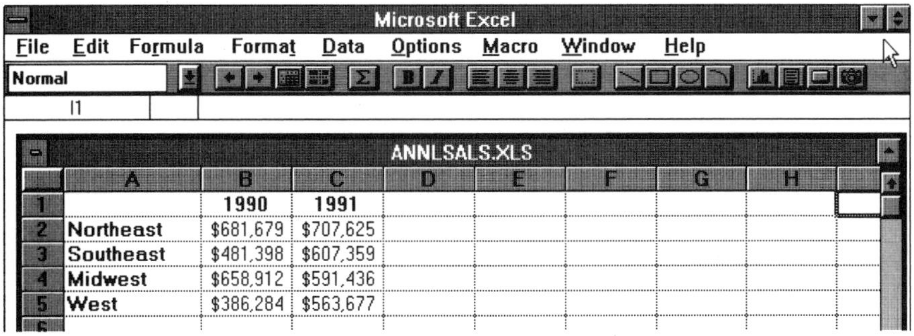

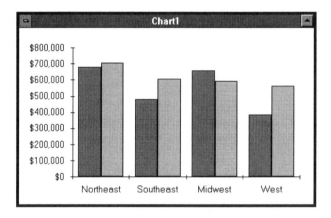

FIGURE 8-17. *Regional sales data for 1990 and 1991.*

FIGURE 8-18. *The data from Figure 8-17 plotted as a simple column chart in the usual way.*

compare regional sales by year. In other words, instead of using the regions as categories and the years as data series, you want to use the years as categories and the regions as data series. To achieve this effect, you must create the chart in a different way. Follow these steps:.

1. In the worksheet, select the range A1:C5 as you did before.

2. Choose the Copy command from the Edit menu.

3. Choose the New command from the File menu, and select the Chart option. Then click OK, or press Enter. Instead of creating a chart, Excel opens an empty chart window.

On IBM extended keyboards, instead of choosing New, selecting Chart, and then clicking OK, you can simply press F11. On other keyboards, press Alt-F1.

4. Choose the Paste Special command from the Edit menu. The following Paste Special dialog box appears:

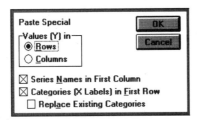

5. At this point, you can specify how you want your data plotted. Select the Rows option in the Values (Y) In group to tell Excel that you want each row to be a data series.

6. Click OK, or press Enter.

7. To distinguish the regional data series, choose the Add Legend command from the Chart menu.

Your chart now looks like Figure 8-19. As you can see, the emphasis of the new chart is quite different from the previous one. It highlights the relative importance of the regions rather than year-to-year growth. The key concept here is that Excel is flexible when you need to diverge from its conventions.

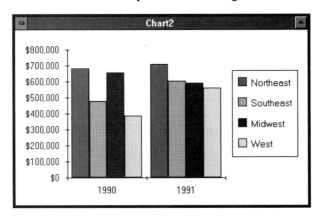

FIGURE 8-19. *The data from Figure 8-18, plotted with the years as categories and the regions as data series.*

226

Understanding SERIES Functions

You may have noticed that whenever you select series markers in a chart window, long SERIES functions appear in the formula bar. Microsoft Excel uses these functions to link charts to worksheets. Table 8-1 explains the various arguments that appear in SERIES functions. The argument numbers in the table correspond to the sequence in which they appear in the function.

Argument number	Contents
1	Location of series name in the worksheet
2	Location of category labels in the worksheet
3	Location of values in the worksheet
4	Position of the series in the sequence of series in the chart

TABLE 8-1. *SERIES function arguments.*

You can edit SERIES functions to change the way Excel plots the chart, either by making changes directly in the formula bar or by using the Edit Series command on the Format menu. Details about when and how you edit these functions are beyond the scope of this book, so consult the Microsoft Excel documentation for more information.

PRINTING CHARTS

You usually print charts in the same way you print worksheets. However, you must make a few additional decisions when you print charts. The dialog box that appears when you select a chart and choose Page Setup from the File menu has three options—Screen Size, Fit To Page, and Full Page—not found in its worksheet counterpart. Table 8-2 explains these options.

Option	Dimensions of printed chart
Screen Size	Identical to size on screen
Fit To Page	Expanded as large as possible while retaining the height-to-width proportions shown on the screen (the default)
Full Page	Expanded to fill the entire page, regardless of effect on chart's proportions

TABLE 8-2. *Page-setup options and their effects on charts.*

The Row & Column Headings and Gridlines options have no meaning for charts, so they are omitted from the Page Setup dialog box when you're printing a chart.

Having made your selections in the Page Setup dialog box, choose the Print command to print your chart. The Print dialog box for charts is similar to the one for worksheets, except that the options for printing worksheets, notes, or both are omitted. However, the Preview option is available and operates in much the same way as it does for worksheets.

CONCLUSION

Microsoft Excel provides a wide variety of chart design options. In Chapters 7 and 8, we've explained only those that have the broadest use. Fortunately, most aspects of charting with Excel are easy to learn by experimenting, and you will have fun trying out all the options.

In the next section, we move on from worksheets and charts to databases, starting with the basics and then covering more advanced database topics.

SECTION III

Databases

Chapter 9

Using Databases

Now that you've learned how to create and use Microsoft Excel worksheets and charts, we move on to the third major Excel component— databases. A database is a set of related data items that is stored on a worksheet and structured so that individual items can be efficiently located and summarized. You are already familiar with databases that exist outside of computers—printed listings such as the telephone book. This chapter explains the basics of working with Excel databases.

UNDERSTANDING DATABASES

As an example, consider a typical address file made up of cards like the one pictured in Figure 9-1. Each card shows a name, company, address, and telephone number. The fact that each card contains the same type of information is what makes the address file a database.

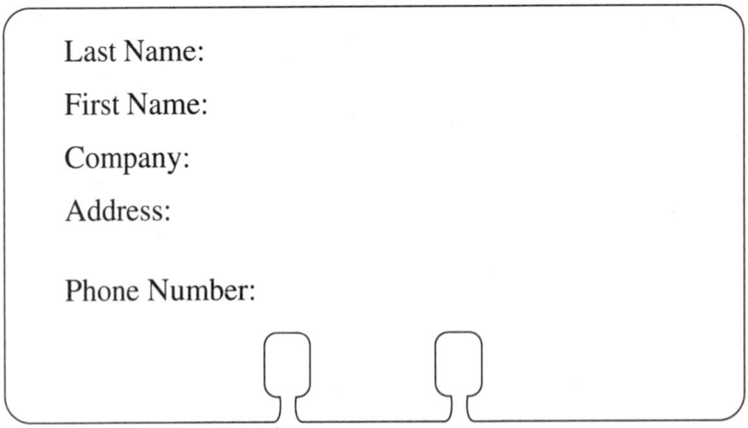

Last Name:

First Name:

Company:

Address:

Phone Number:

FIGURE 9-1. *A Rolodex card—one record in a database.*

Figure 9-2 shows how the address database might look in a Microsoft Excel worksheet. The column headings, called *field names*, serve the same purpose as the printed categories on each card. Each row, called a *record*, is equivalent to one card. For example, the information in row 2 of the database is equivalent to the information you might record on a Rolodex card for Harrison Small. Each column, called a *field*, is equivalent to one of the categories that appears on all the cards.

Storing this kind of data electronically provides capabilities that you don't have with telephone books and address files. Using commands on the Data menu, you can have Excel find all the records that meet specific conditions. This is much quicker than flipping through your file cards. You can also tell Excel to sort the records, rearranging the database records in whatever order you specify.

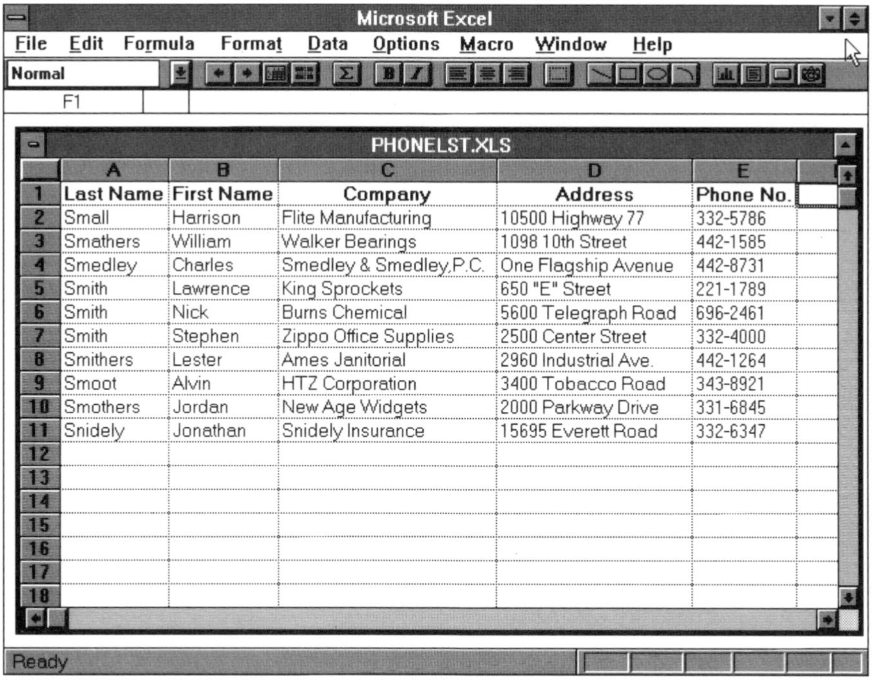

	A	B	C	D	E
1	Last Name	First Name	Company	Address	Phone No.
2	Small	Harrison	Flite Manufacturing	10500 Highway 77	332-5786
3	Smathers	William	Walker Bearings	1098 10th Street	442-1585
4	Smedley	Charles	Smedley & Smedley,P.C.	One Flagship Avenue	442-8731
5	Smith	Lawrence	King Sprockets	650 "E" Street	221-1789
6	Smith	Nick	Burns Chemical	5600 Telegraph Road	696-2461
7	Smith	Stephen	Zippo Office Supplies	2500 Center Street	332-4000
8	Smithers	Lester	Ames Janitorial	2960 Industrial Ave.	442-1264
9	Smoot	Alvin	HTZ Corporation	3400 Tobacco Road	343-8921
10	Smothers	Jordan	New Age Widgets	2000 Parkway Drive	331-6845
11	Snidely	Jonathan	Snidely Insurance	15695 Everett Road	332-6347
12					
13					
14					
15					
16					
17					
18					

FIGURE 9-2. *Part of an address database in a Microsoft Excel worksheet.*

CREATING A DATABASE

For the examples in this chapter, suppose you are a stockbroker and you want to use Microsoft Excel to maintain information on each of your clients. To begin, you must create a database containing the following client information:

- Last name
- First name
- Account balance
- Commissions generated in 1990
- Commissions generated to date in 1991
- Total commissions generated in 1990 and 1991
- Date you last met with the client

These items will be the fields in your database. For reasons we explain later in Chapter 10, "Manipulating Records," it's best to leave some blank rows at the top of the worksheet, so you will enter the field names in row 6 of your worksheet.

To create the sample database, follow these steps:

1. Open a new, blank worksheet.

2. Type the following field names in the specified cells:

Cell	Field name
A6	Last Name
B6	First Name
C6	Account Balance
D6	1990 Commissions
E6	1991 Commissions
F6	Total Commissions
G6	Last Meeting

Note that field names must be text entries; numeric entries and formulas are not allowed.

3. Click the row 6 header to select the entire row, and then choose the Alignment command from the Format menu.

4. Select the Center and Wrap Text options in the Alignment dialog box, and then click OK or press Enter.

5. Click the Bold button in the tool bar.

6. Adjust the column widths and row heights as needed, so that all field names are visible.

7. Enter the first record in row 7, using the following data:

Cell	Entry
A7	Walton
B7	Wilbur
C7	43870
D7	916
E7	159
F7	=D7+E7
G7	1/11/91

8. Choose the Save As command from the File menu, and name the worksheet *CLIENTS*.

Take a minute now to format the cells of your database. For example, you might assign all the fields that contain numbers the #,##0 format. If you want to adjust the horizontal alignment of headings, as we have in cell A6 of Figure 9-3, click an insertion point before *Last Name*, and press Alt-Enter to push the field name to the second line.

Notice that, although field names must be text entries, the data itself can contain formulas. Fields that contain formulas are called *computed fields*. In Figure 9-3, the formula bar shows the computed field in F7. (We have scrolled the worksheet so that the five blank rows at the top are no longer visible.) The formula =D7+E7 adds the values in the 1990 Commissions and 1991 Commissions fields (D7 and E7) and returns the sum in cell F7.

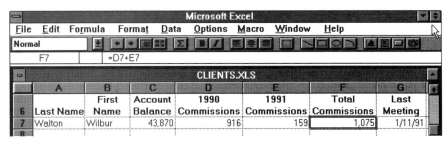

FIGURE 9-3. *The first record in the* CLIENTS *database, showing the computed field in cell F7.*

Setting the Database

To carry out most of the commands on the Data menu, Microsoft Excel needs to know which part of the worksheet contains the active database. Although you can have several databases on a worksheet, only one of them can be active at a time. Designating the active database is called *setting the database*.

To set the database you have just created, follow these steps:

1. Select the range A6:G8.

2. Choose the Set Database command from the Data menu.

Although nothing appears to happen, behind the scenes Excel assigns the name *Database* to the selected range. Excel recognizes only the range A6:G8 as a database, unless you select a new range and choose Set Database, or you choose Define Name from the Formula menu and delete the name *Database*, or you choose Define Name and assign that name to a different range.

You might have noticed that the range you defined contains three rows: the field names in row 6, the record in row 7, and the blank row 8. Including at least one blank row at the end of the database makes it easier to add new records. For example, if you want to add a second record to the example database, all you have to do is select the blank row 8 below the existing record in row 7, choose the Insert command from the Edit menu, and enter the information for the new record in the new row 8 that Excel inserts above the selected blank row. Excel extends the range defined with the name *Database* so that it continues to include the blank row, which is now row 9. If you don't include a blank row at the end of the database when you use the Set Database command and you later need to add a new record, you will have to set the database again, to tell Excel that the new record is part of the database.

USING THE DATA FORM

To help you create and edit your databases, Microsoft Excel provides a special kind of dialog box, called a *data form*. You can use the data form to add entries to your database, change entries, and view specific entries. Choose the Form command from the Data menu to see the default data form, shown in Figure 9-4.

The *title bar* at the top of the data form displays the name of the worksheet that contains the active database. The *record indicator* at the top right shows the sequence number of the record displayed in the database (or the phrase *New*

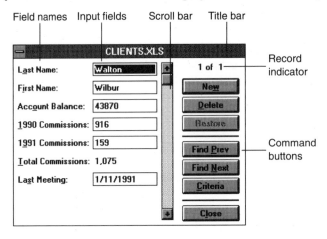

FIGURE 9-4. *The Microsoft Excel default data form.*

Record if a blank record is displayed). Excel does not count blank rows at the end of the database in determining the total number of records in the database.

The *scroll bar* is similar to the worksheet scroll bars. You can move among the records in the database by clicking the scroll-bar arrows or by dragging the scroll box. You can move through the database ten records at a time by clicking above or below the scroll box.

You can carry out several commands from within the data form by clicking the appropriate *command button*. In a moment, we'll look at these buttons in more detail. Right now, you can take advantage of one of the data form's main benefits—streamlined data entry.

Using Input Fields

The data form displays the field names in text boxes called *input fields*. To enter or revise a record, you simply select an input field and type or edit the information for that field, using ordinary mouse or keyboard methods. (You cannot edit the Total Commissions field, however, because that entry is the result of a calculation.)

When you choose the Form command from the Data menu, Excel displays the record located in the first row of the database. Some of the buttons at the right of the data form let you move to other records in the database. (The button is dimmed if its option is not available.)

At the moment, we're not interested in examining the database records. We simply want to enter a new record with the following data:

Field name	*Entry*
Last Name	Miller
First Name	Herman
Account Balance	6960
1990 Commissions	459
1991 Commissions	55
Last Meeting	3/30/91

Follow these steps to create this record:

1. Click the New command button at the top right of the data form (or press Alt-W). The data form's input fields are now blank, and the position indicator displays *New Record*.

2. Type the last name in the Last Name text box.

3. Press the Tab key to move to the next field (First Name), and type the first name.

4. Type the rest of the data, pressing the Tab key to move through the remaining input fields.

5. Press Enter when you're ready to add the record to the database.

Excel uses the information you enter in the 1990 Commissions and 1991 Commissions fields to calculate the value for the Total Commissions field.

 To move back to the previous field in the data form, press Shift-Tab. If you accidentally move to a different record by pressing Enter instead of the Tab key while you're entering data, you can move back to the correct record by clicking the Find Prev button or by pressing Shift-Enter.

Now use the data form to enter the following data for the remaining 13 records in the sample database:

Last Name	First Name	Account Balance	1990 Commissions	1991 Commissions	Last Meeting
Williams	Oliver	10940	137	73	8/12/90
Hendricks	Margaret	48750	1014	387	10/1/90
Smith	Jeffrey	62550	1718	299	8/7/90
Johnson	Johnny	57248	1101	296	5/9/91
Baker	Abel	55080	1386	379	7/15/91
Devine	Dennis	112300	2712	553	6/13/91
Spencer	David	8145	121	0	10/13/90
Terry	Florence	74640	1236	294	2/20/91
Green	Scott	36460	867	224	3/27/91
Moser	L.Y.	54153	770	346	12/8/90
Smith	Harvey	12690	190	122	5/5/91
Wilson	Harry	29240	439	249	5/10/91
Nevin	John	90890	868	391	6/28/91

Using the data form to add a new record automatically extends the database range to include the new record, provided that blank rows are available immediately below the existing database range. Excel extends the range regardless of whether or not you included a blank row in the selected range when you set the database. In fact, Excel fills in the blank row with information from the data form so that the *Database* range no longer includes a blank row.

When you've finished adding records, save the worksheet again.

Performing Operations Within the Data Form

As we mentioned earlier, the data form's command buttons enable you to do much more with the data form than simply enter data. Table 9-1 describes the effects of these buttons.

Command button	Effect
New	Creates blank fields for a new record and puts the data after the last row in the database.
Delete	Removes the currently displayed record from the database.
Restore	Undoes all current edits to the displayed record.
Find Prev	Searches upward in the database and displays the first previous record that meets the criteria defined by the Criteria command. If no criteria are defined, displays the immediately preceding record in the database.
Find Next	Searches down in the database and displays the next record that meets the criteria defined by the Criteria command. If no criteria are defined, displays the next record in the database.
Criteria	Determines the criteria to be used in searching for specific records.
Close	Removes the data form from the screen and reactivates the worksheet proper.

TABLE 9-1. *The effects of the data-form command buttons.*

You've already learned how to use the data form to add new records. Now we'll show you some other useful operations.

Finding records

Some databases, such as address files, are relatively static—you'll rarely need to update records. Other databases are more dynamic, changing frequently, sometimes daily. For example, suppose today is October 1, 1991, and you've just had lunch with Scott Green, one of your clients. You need to update your database to reflect this meeting. To find Green's record, follow these steps:

1. Choose the Form command from the Data menu.

2. Click the Criteria button. The data form's input fields go blank, as shown in the following data form:

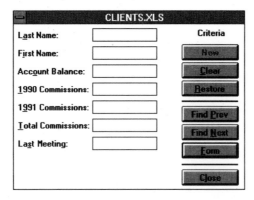

3. Type *Green* in the Last Name input field.

4. Click the Find Next button.

The Scott Green record is now displayed in the form, as shown in Figure 9-5.

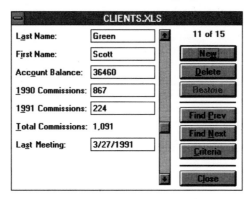

FIGURE 9-5. *The data form displayed when you instruct Excel to find the record that has* Green *in its Last Name field.*

240

By filling in more input fields, you can be even more specific about the record you want to locate. For example, to locate the record for Harvey Smith, not Jeffrey Smith, you would type *Harvey* in the First Name input field as well as *Smith* in the Last Name input field.

While you are in Criteria mode, you can edit the Total Commissions field so that you can search for matching records based on the results of this computed field.

Editing records

Using the data form, you can easily revise the data in your database. In the record for Scott Green, the Last Meeting input field currently contains the date 3/27/1991. To edit this entry, follow these steps:

1. Select the Last Meeting field.

2. Type *6/15/91* in the text box.

3. Press Enter.

Microsoft Excel makes the change in the database, and the data form displays the next record.

To make an editing change permanent, press Enter. To make an editing change permanent and remove the data form from the screen with one command, click the Close button.

Deleting records

You can use the data form to quickly delete entire records. For example, to delete the currently displayed record without returning to the database on the worksheet, follow these steps:

1. Click the Delete button. Excel displays the following message asking you to confirm that you want to delete this record:

2. Click OK, or press Enter.

The record vanishes, and the next record in the database appears in its place. On the worksheet, Excel clears the database cells that contained the record you deleted, and then moves subsequent records up to fill the gap. The database range also moves up one row.

Closing the Data Form

When you've finished working with the data form, remove it from the screen by clicking the Close button or by pressing Esc. Excel returns you to the place in the worksheet where you were working when you chose the Form command from the Data menu.

Before continuing, open the *CLIENTS* worksheet again to revert to the version you saved earlier. All subsequent examples in this chapter use this earlier version of the *CLIENTS* worksheet, which contains only the 15 records you originally entered.

SORTING RECORDS

Depending on the nature of the information you store in your databases, you may want to arrange the database in numeric, chronologic, or alphabetic order. *Sorting*, or arranging your data in particular ways, is an important database feature. Microsoft Excel gives you the ability to sort records according to values in particular fields, using up to three *keys*. A key is simply a cell address that indicates which field you want Excel to use as a basis for sorting the records.

You can sort the entire database, or you can sort only a specific range of records. In either case, the Sort command on the Data menu requires that you select the range of cells to be sorted. (Most of the other Data-menu commands use the defined database as the object of the command, regardless of the current selection in the worksheet.)

Figure 9-6 shows how your clients rank, from highest to lowest, in 1990 commissions. To sort by commissions generated, follow these steps:

1. Select the range A7:G21 in the *CLIENTS* worksheet.

 Don't include the field names in the range you select for sorting. If you do include the field names, Excel sorts the names along with the data.

2. Choose the Sort command from the Data menu. The following dialog box appears.

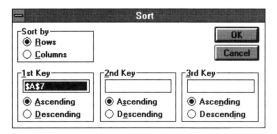

3. Be sure the Rows option in the Sort By group is selected.

4. Select the 1st Key text box, and type *D7* to sort on the basis of the values in the 1990 Commissions field. (You can use the address of any cell in column D.) Ignore the 2nd Key and 3rd Key options.

5. Select the Descending option to sort the database from highest 1990 commission to lowest.

6. Click OK, or press Enter.

	Microsoft Excel						

File Edit Formula Format Data Options Macro Window Help

Normal

H6

CLIENTS.XLS

	A	B	C	D	E	F	G
		First	Account	1990	1991	Total	Last
6	Last Name	Name	Balance	Commissions	Commissions	Commissions	Meeting
7	Devine	Dennis	112,300	2,712	553	3,265	6/13/91
8	Smith	Jeffrey	62,550	1,718	299	2,017	8/7/90
9	Baker	Abel	55,080	1,386	379	1,765	7/15/91
10	Terry	Florence	74,640	1,236	294	1,530	2/20/91
11	Johnson	Johnny	57,248	1,101	296	1,397	5/9/91
12	Hendricks	Margaret	48,750	1,014	387	1,401	10/1/90
13	Walton	Wilbur	43,870	916	159	1,075	1/11/91
14	Nevin	John	90,890	868	391	1,259	6/28/91
15	Green	Scott	36,460	867	224	1,091	6/15/91
16	Moser	L.Y.	54,153	770	346	1,116	12/8/90
17	Miller	Herman	6,960	459	55	514	3/30/91
18	Wilson	Harry	29,240	439	249	688	5/10/91
19	Smith	Harvey	12,690	190	122	312	5/5/91
20	Williams	Oliver	10,940	137	73	210	8/12/90
21	Spencer	David	8,145	121	0	121	10/13/90
22							
23							

Ready

FIGURE 9-6. *The* CLIENTS *database sorted from highest to lowest based on the 1990 Commissions field.*

Excel can also perform sorts based on fields that contain text, because every character that you can enter in a cell has a specific ranking. The lowest-valued text characters are special characters such as @, #, and &. Next come numeric characters that you have entered as text. (Numeric characters entered as numbers are sorted before any text characters.) Next come alphabetic characters. (Because Excel ignores capitalization when sorting, *A* has the same ranking as *a*.) Highest are the logical values TRUE and FALSE and Excel error values. Excel always puts blank cells at the bottom of the sorted range, whether you are sorting in ascending or descending order.

Sorting by More Than One Key

Microsoft Excel lets you specify more than one sort key. For example, suppose you want to sort your client database alphabetically, using last names as the first key and first names as the second key. To create a list that is alphabetized by first name within last name, follow these steps:

1. Select the range A7:G21.

2. Choose the Sort command from the Data menu.

3. Type *A7* in the 1st Key text box. (Column A is the Last Name field.)

4. Type *B7* in the 2nd Key text box. (Column B is the First Name field.)

5. Because you want the list in alphabetical order, leave the Ascending buttons selected for both keys.

6. Click OK, or press Enter.

Your database now looks like the one in Figure 9-7. Notice that, because you entered the cell address B7 in the 2nd Key box, Harvey Smith is listed before Jeffrey Smith.

If you enter a series of sequential numbers in a blank column of the original database, you can sort on that column to re-create the original sequence of the records. Later in this chapter, you'll learn how to use the Series command on the Data menu to quickly generate a sequence number for each record in the database.

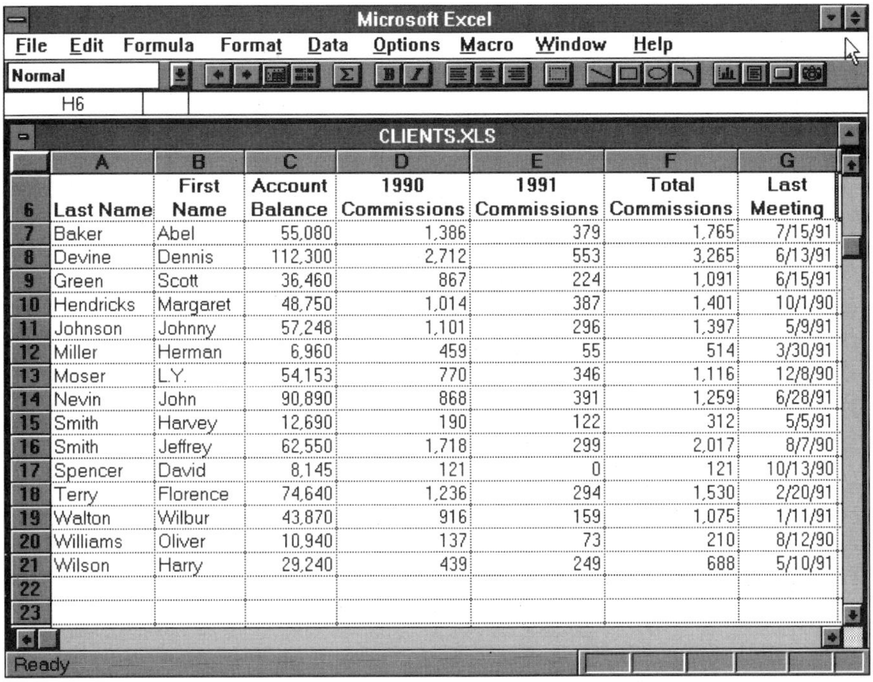

	A	B	C	D	E	F	G
6	Last Name	First Name	Account Balance	1990 Commissions	1991 Commissions	Total Commissions	Last Meeting
7	Baker	Abel	55,080	1,386	379	1,765	7/15/91
8	Devine	Dennis	112,300	2,712	553	3,265	6/13/91
9	Green	Scott	36,460	867	224	1,091	6/15/91
10	Hendricks	Margaret	48,750	1,014	387	1,401	10/1/90
11	Johnson	Johnny	57,248	1,101	296	1,397	5/9/91
12	Miller	Herman	6,960	459	55	514	3/30/91
13	Moser	L.Y.	54,153	770	346	1,116	12/8/90
14	Nevin	John	90,890	868	391	1,259	6/28/91
15	Smith	Harvey	12,690	190	122	312	5/5/91
16	Smith	Jeffrey	62,550	1,718	299	2,017	8/7/90
17	Spencer	David	8,145	121	0	121	10/13/90
18	Terry	Florence	74,640	1,236	294	1,530	2/20/91
19	Walton	Wilbur	43,870	916	159	1,075	1/11/91
20	Williams	Oliver	10,940	137	73	210	8/12/90
21	Wilson	Harry	29,240	439	249	688	5/10/91
22							
23							

FIGURE 9-7. *The* CLIENTS *database sorted by first name within last name.*

Sorting by Columns

Although sorting rows is more common, you may occasionally need to sort columns. For example, Figure 9-8 on the next page contains ratings for several software products. The product data is arranged vertically. To sort columns, you follow the same steps you did to sort rows, except that after you choose Sort from the Data menu, you select the Columns option in the Sort By group.

Take a minute now to open a new worksheet and enter the data shown in Figure 9-8. Then choose the Save As command from the file menu, and name the worksheet *PRODANAL*. To sort the products in the *PRODANAL* database in order of overall performance rating, follow the steps on the next page.

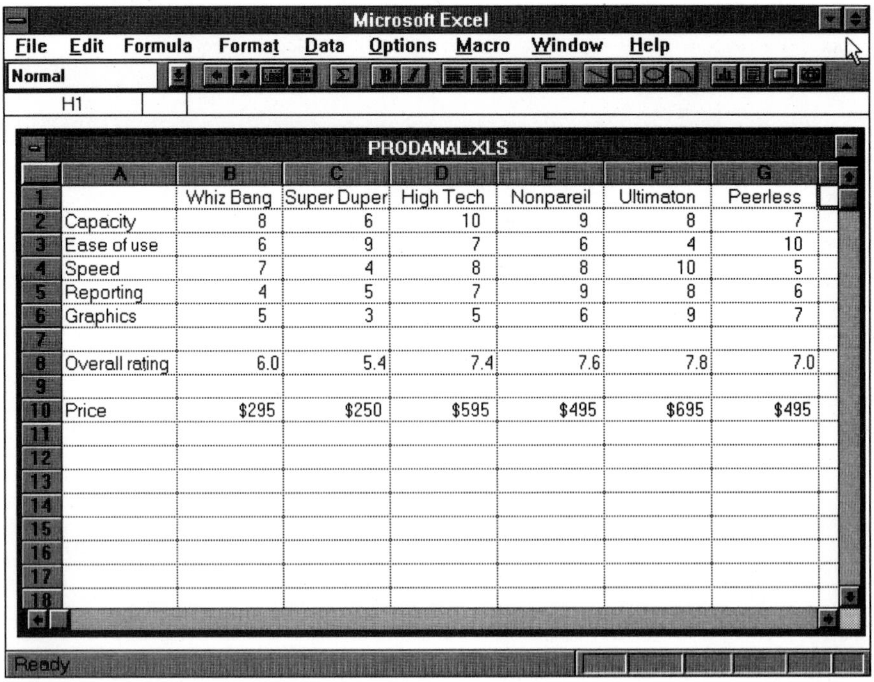

FIGURE 9-8. *A product database with records in columns and fields in rows.*

1. Select the range B1:G10.

2. Choose the Sort command from the Data menu.

3. Select the Columns option in the Sort By group.

4. Type *B8* in the 1st Key text box. (Row 8 is the *Overall rating* field.)

5. Select the Descending option to sort from highest rating to lowest.

6. Click OK, or press Enter.

Your database now looks like Figure 9-9.

Before you move on, choose the Close command from the File menu to close the *CLIENTS* and *PRODANAL* worksheets without saving the changes you have made in the last few examples.

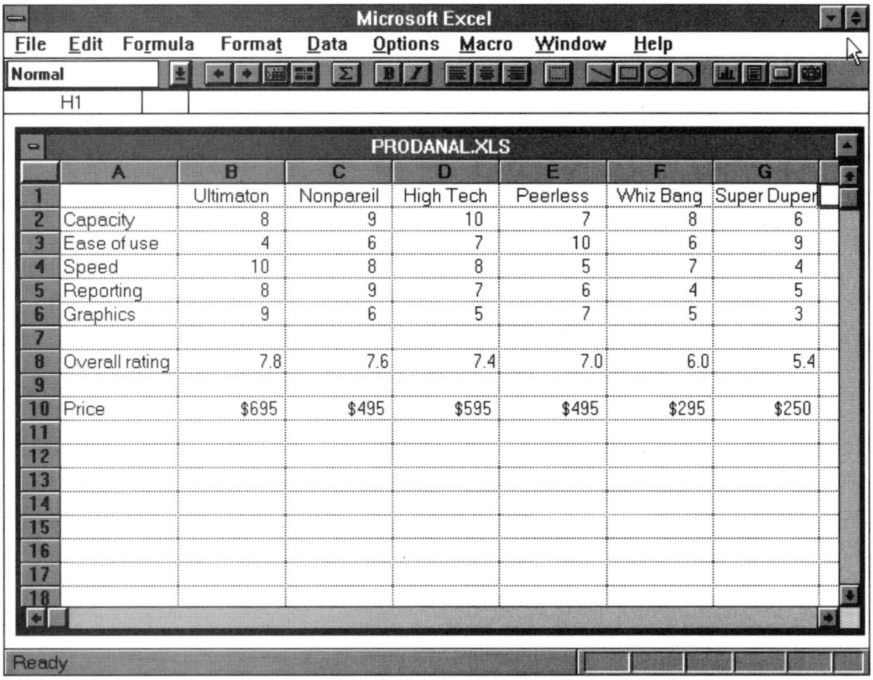

	A	B	C	D	E	F	G
1		Ultimaton	Nonpareil	High Tech	Peerless	Whiz Bang	Super Duper
2	Capacity	8	9	10	7	8	6
3	Ease of use	4	6	7	10	6	9
4	Speed	10	8	8	5	7	4
5	Reporting	8	9	7	6	4	5
6	Graphics	9	6	5	7	5	3
7							
8	Overall rating	7.8	7.6	7.4	7.0	6.0	5.4
9							
10	Price	$695	$495	$595	$495	$295	$250

FIGURE 9-9. *The data in Figure 9-8 sorted by columns, in order of highest overall performance rating.*

FILLING A RANGE WITH A SERIES

Immediately after you sort a database, you can restore the records to their original sequence by choosing the Undo Sort command from the Edit menu. But what if you don't realize until later that you need to put the database records back in their original sequence?

Excel can help you restore the original sequence only if you have planned ahead. You can protect yourself against erroneous sorts by using the Series command on the Data menu, which you learned to use earlier. You can number the records in a database so that you can, if necessary, restore the database to its original order after you have sorted it.

For example, suppose you want to number the records in the *CLIENTS* database. Open the original worksheet, and then follow these steps:

1. Click the column A header, and choose Insert from the Edit menu to insert a new, blank column in front of the Last Name column.

2. Select cell A6, and enter *Number* as a new field name.

3. Enter *1* in cell A7.

4. Select the range A7:A21.

5. Choose the Series command from the Data menu. This dialog box appears:

6. Be sure Columns in the Series In box and Linear in the Type box are selected.

7. Click OK, or press Enter.

Excel then enters a set of sequential numbers from 1 through 15 in the selected range. Now you can sort the database any way you want and return it to its original arrangement simply by sorting in ascending numeric order based on the Number field.

Note that because you added the column at the edge of the *Database* range, Excel did not automatically expand the range to include the new column. If you want column A to be included in the *Database* range, you will have to reset the database. Also note that if you add new records to the database, they are not automatically assigned a sequential number in column A. You must either type in the number or expand the series by selecting a new range that includes the cells in column A adjacent to the new records and using the Series command again.

Because we are not going to sort this database further, delete column A before saving the worksheet and moving on to the next chapter.

CONCLUSION

In this chapter, we have covered some basic database concepts and have created and manipulated a database, both on the worksheet and by using the Microsoft Excel data form. In the next chapter, we continue our discussion of databases by showing you how to select records that meet specific criteria.

Chapter 10

Manipulating Records

You've learned the basics of using the Microsoft
Excel database-management tools. Now it's time
to learn how criteria can help you create useful
subsets of database records and how to extract
specific data. First, you establish *selection criteria*
to tell Excel which records you are interested in
working with. Excel then uses these criteria to
determine which records are affected when you
choose the Find, Extract, and Delete commands
from the Data menu.

ENTERING CRITERIA

The best way to understand selection criteria is to actually walk through an example. Along the way, we'll explain the underlying concepts so that you can apply what you learn to your own work.

Using the *CLIENTS* database that you created in the last chapter, suppose you want Microsoft Excel to list all clients with the last name *Smith*. You need to tell Excel to look for records that match a criterion of *Last Name equals Smith*. You give this instruction by creating a *criteria range*. The top row of the criteria range contains the names of all the database fields that you intend to use for selecting records, so the first step in creating the range is to copy those field names into the area of your worksheet that you plan to use as the criteria range.

 You don't have to include every database field name in the top row of the criteria range. However, doing so allows you to add criteria to the range later without having to add field names. Copying all the database field names also ensures that the database names and the criteria-range names are exactly the same. For clarity and consistency, all the examples in this chapter include all the database field names in the criteria range.

To copy the database field names into the top row of the criteria range, follow these steps:

1. Select the range A6:G6.

2. Choose the Copy command from the Edit menu.

3. Select the range A1:G1.

4. Choose the Paste command from the Edit menu.

5. Adjust the row height so that you can see the field names.

 Now you see why we told you to start entering the database in row 6. Leaving some blank rows at the top of the worksheet for the criteria range makes revising criteria more convenient, because you can easily jump to the top-left corner of the worksheet.

Next you need to specify the actual selection criteria. For this example, you need to enter only one. Simply type the name *smith* in cell A2 (capitalization doesn't matter). Your worksheet now looks like Figure 10-1.

	A	B	C	D	E	F	G
	Last Name	First Name	Account Balance	1990 Commissions	1991 Commissions	Total Commissions	Last Meeting
1							
2	smith						
3							
4							
5							
6	Last Name	First Name	Account Balance	1990 Commissions	1991 Commissions	Total Commissions	Last Meeting
7	Walton	Wilbur	43,870	916	159	1,075	1/11/91
8	Miller	Herman	6,960	459	55	514	3/30/91
9	Williams	Oliver	10,940	137	73	210	8/12/90
10	Hendricks	Margaret	48,750	1,014	387	1,401	10/1/90
11	Smith	Jeffrey	62,550	1,718	299	2,017	8/7/90
12	Johnson	Johnny	57,248	1,101	296	1,397	5/9/91
13	Baker	Abel	55,080	1,386	379	1,765	7/15/91
14	Devine	Dennis	112,300	2,712	553	3,265	6/13/91
15	Spencer	David	8,145	121	0	121	10/13/90
16	Terry	Florence	74,640	1,236	294	1,530	2/20/91
17	Green	Scott	36,460	867	224	1,091	3/27/91

FIGURE 10-1. *The criterion* smith *entered in the Last Name field of the criteria range.*

SETTING THE CRITERIA RANGE

You can enter several different sets of criteria on a worksheet, but only one set can be active at a time. Just as Microsoft Excel needs to know which is the active database, it also needs to know which is the active criteria range. Designating the active criteria range is called *setting the criteria range.*

To set the criteria range for the *CLIENTS* worksheet, follow these steps:

1. Select the range A1:G2.

2. Choose the Set Criteria command from the Data menu.

Although you see no change in the worksheet, Excel has now assigned the name *Criteria* to the range you selected. Unless you select a new range and choose the Set Criteria command again, or you choose the Define Name command from the Formula menu and delete the name *Criteria*, or you choose Define Name and assign that name to a different range, Excel recognizes only the range A1:G2 as a criteria range.

The criteria range must be a single rectangular range. The range you defined for this example contains only two rows, because including blank rows in a criteria range causes Excel to select all records in the database, defeating the purpose of defining criteria. If you later need to add a new criteria row, you will have to reset the criteria range to include that row. (We talk more about using more than one criterion later in this chapter.)

EXTRACTING RECORDS

Now that you have specified a criterion, we can discuss its uses. The process of producing a list of all records that meet this criterion is called *extracting*. To extract records that match the criterion, you use the Extract command on the Data menu. When you choose Extract from the Data menu, Microsoft Excel checks the criteria range, identifies all matching records, and then copies the matching records to an area of the worksheet called the *extract range*.

Defining the Extract Range

Before extracting records from your database, Microsoft Excel needs to know where to put the matching records. The first step in designating the extract range is to copy the field names to an empty area of the worksheet. You don't have to include every field name. For example, if you aren't interested in displaying the first names in the selected records, you could omit the First Name field from the extract range. (As with the criteria range, for clarity and consistency the examples in this chapter include all the database field names in the extract range.)

To define an extract range, follow these steps:

1. Copy the field names in row 1 of the worksheet to row 25.

2. Select the range A25:G25.

3. Adjust the row height so that you can see the field names.

4. Choose the Set Extract command from the Data menu.

Extracting the Data

After you've defined the criteria and extract ranges, you simply choose the Extract command from the Data menu to tell Microsoft Excel to extract the matching records. To extract the records for *Smith* in the *CLIENTS* database, follow these steps.

1. Choose the Extract command from the Data menu. The following dialog box appears:

2. Turn on the Unique Records Only option. Excel includes this option because you can sometimes erroneously enter records into the database twice. Selecting Unique Records Only eliminates exact duplicates from the extract range. The *CLIENTS* database doesn't contain any completely identical records, so you don't really need to use this option, but it's a good habit to get into.

3. Click OK, or press Enter.

Your worksheet now looks like Figure 10-2. Excel has copied the records of both Jeffrey Smith and Harvey Smith, in the order in which they appear in the database, below the field names in the extract range.

	Microsoft Excel							
File	Edit	Formula	Format	Data	Options	Macro	Window	Help

Normal

H20

CLIENTS.XLS

	A	B	C	D	E	F	G
20	Wilson	Harry	29,240	439	249	688	5/10/91
21	Nevin	John	90,890	868	391	1,259	6/28/91
22							
23							
24							
25	Last Name	First Name	Account Balance	1990 Commissions	1991 Commissions	Total Commissions	Last Meeting
26	Smith	Jeffrey	62,550	1,718	299	2,017	8/7/90
27	Smith	Harvey	12,690	190	122	312	5/5/91
28							
29							
30							
31							
32							
33							
34							
35							
36							
37							

Ready

FIGURE 10-2. *The records extracted using the criterion* smith.

If the top row of your extract range contains anything other than field names, Excel displays the message shown in Figure 10-3 when you choose the Extract command from the Data menu. If this message appears, click OK, or press Enter, to close the message box; then define a valid extract range, and choose the Extract command again.

FIGURE 10-3. *The invalid-extract-range message.*

Using a Limited Extract Range

In the preceding example, Microsoft Excel found only 2 matching records. But suppose that, while working with a large database, Excel extracted 100 records. If valuable data was stored anywhere in the 100 rows below the field names of the extract range, the data would be lost, because extracted records always overwrite any existing data. You can avoid inadvertently overwriting data by always putting the extract range below (or to the side of) all the data in the worksheet. Or you can limit the extract range by selecting a specific number of blank rows when you define the extract range. (In the previous example, your extract rage included only the field names so that Excel would *not* limit the numbers of records extracted.) Keep in mind, however, that because you generally will not know how many records match the criteria, you should specify a large extract range.

For example, suppose you select a range containing 10 blank rows (in this example, the range A25:G35), and then choose the Set Extract command from the Data menu. When Excel has extracted 10 matching records, the next matching record causes Excel to stop extracting and display an *Extract range is full* message telling you that Excel has stopped the operation prematurely and that the database may contain more criteria-matching records than were extracted.

To see how this works on a small scale, follow these steps, using the criteria from the previous example:

1. Select the range A26:G27.

2. Choose the Clear command from the Edit command to remove any data from rows 26 and 27.

3. Select the range A25:G26 (the field names and the blank row below them).

4. Choose the Set Extract command from the Data menu.

5. Choose the Extract command from the Data menu.

6. When the Extract dialog box appears, click OK, or press Enter. Excel displays the message shown here:

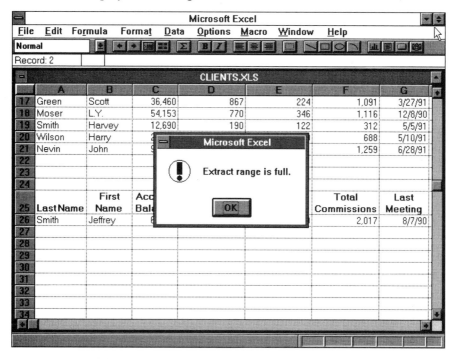

7. Click OK to remove the message from the screen.

You can then scan the extract range to see how much larger you should make it, set the extract range again, and choose Extract to repeat the extraction.

 If you want to preserve a group of extracted records intact, you must move them to another part of the worksheet. Otherwise, the next time you use the Extract command, Excel overwrites the previously extracted records.

USING CRITERIA TO BEST ADVANTAGE

You can search text and numeric fields in ingenious ways, and you can mix and match criteria to produce useful subsets of the overall database. Let's look now at some of the fine points of defining criteria.

Searching for Text

In the preceding examples, you knew exactly how to spell the last names of the clients you were searching for, but you won't always be so fortunate. Suppose you have several hundred clients and you want to contact one of them about a special investment opportunity. The trouble is, you can't remember the particular client's name—it's something like Wilson or Wellman. How can you find the client's record?

With Microsoft Excel, the solution is simple. Excel can extract records using your "best guess" about selection criteria. First, delete all entries in the criteria range (cells A2:G2). Then follow these steps to extract the records of all clients whose last names begin with the letter *W*:

1. Enter *w* in cell A2.

2. Define A25:G25 as the extract range.

3. Choose the Extract command from the Data menu.

4. When the Extract dialog box appears, click OK, or press Enter.

The extract range now includes the records of the three clients whose last names begin with *W*, as shown in Figure 10-4.

You can further control the selection by using *wildcard characters* in the criteria you specify. An asterisk (*) substitutes for any number of characters in whatever position it occupies in the criterion. In the preceding example, if you enter *w*n* instead of *w* as your criterion, Excel would extract only names beginning with *W* and ending with *n*, such as Walton and Wilson. If records with last names of Winn, Wilkinson, Waterman, and Williamson were included in the database, Excel would also extract those records.

For even greater precision, you can use a question mark (?), which substitutes for a single character in a criterion. For example, the criterion *w????n* limits the extraction to records with six-letter names beginning with *W* and ending with *n*, such as Walton and Wilson. Excel would not extract records such as Winn, Wilkinson, Waterman, and Williamson with this criterion.

256

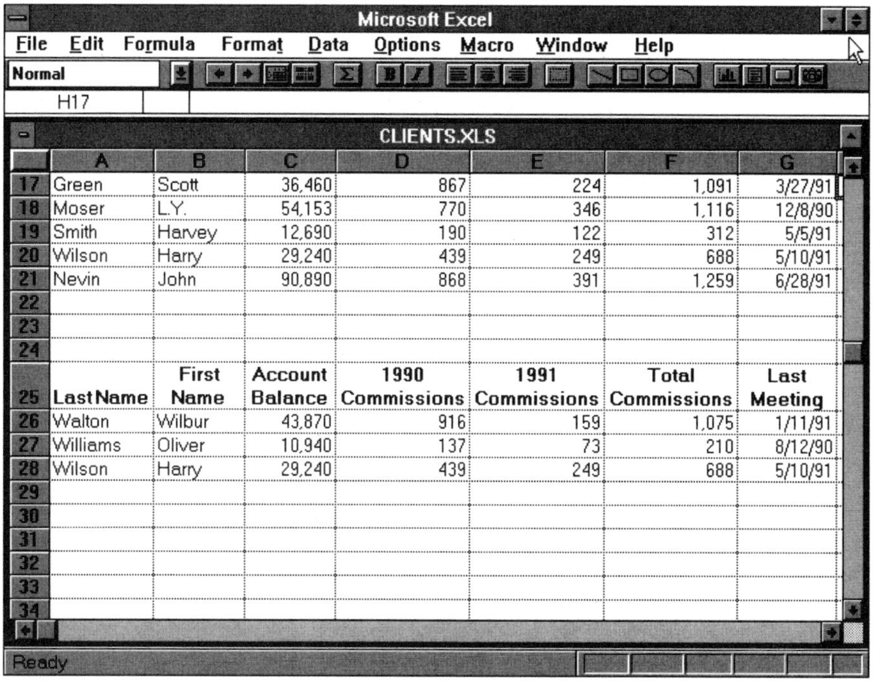

	A	B	C	D	E	F	G
17	Green	Scott	36,460	867	224	1,091	3/27/91
18	Moser	L.Y.	54,153	770	346	1,116	12/8/90
19	Smith	Harvey	12,690	190	122	312	5/5/91
20	Wilson	Harry	29,240	439	249	688	5/10/91
21	Nevin	John	90,890	868	391	1,259	6/28/91
22							
23							
24							
25	Last Name	First Name	Account Balance	1990 Commissions	1991 Commissions	Total Commissions	Last Meeting
26	Walton	Wilbur	43,870	916	159	1,075	1/11/91
27	Williams	Oliver	10,940	137	73	210	8/12/90
28	Wilson	Harry	29,240	439	249	688	5/10/91
29							
30							
31							
32							
33							
34							

FIGURE 10-4. *The records of all clients whose last names begin with* W.

Using Comparison Criteria

You'll often need to find records with values that fall within a certain range in a given field. To limit the extraction in this way, you can enter a criterion that consists of a numeric value preceded by a comparison operator—for example, = (equal to), < (less than), or > (greater than).

For example, suppose you want a list of all clients whose account balances exceed $40,000. To extract this list from the database, follow these steps:

1. Delete the entry in cell A2.

2. Enter *>40000* in cell C2. The criteria range should now look like the screen on the next page.

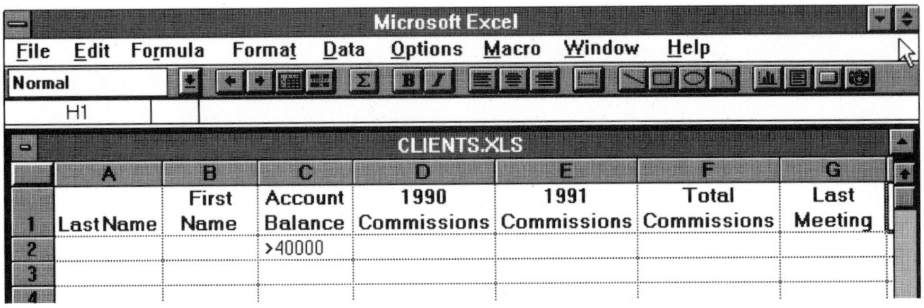

3. Choose the Extract command from the Data menu.

4. When the Extract dialog box appears, click OK, or press Enter.

Your worksheet now looks like Figure 10-5.

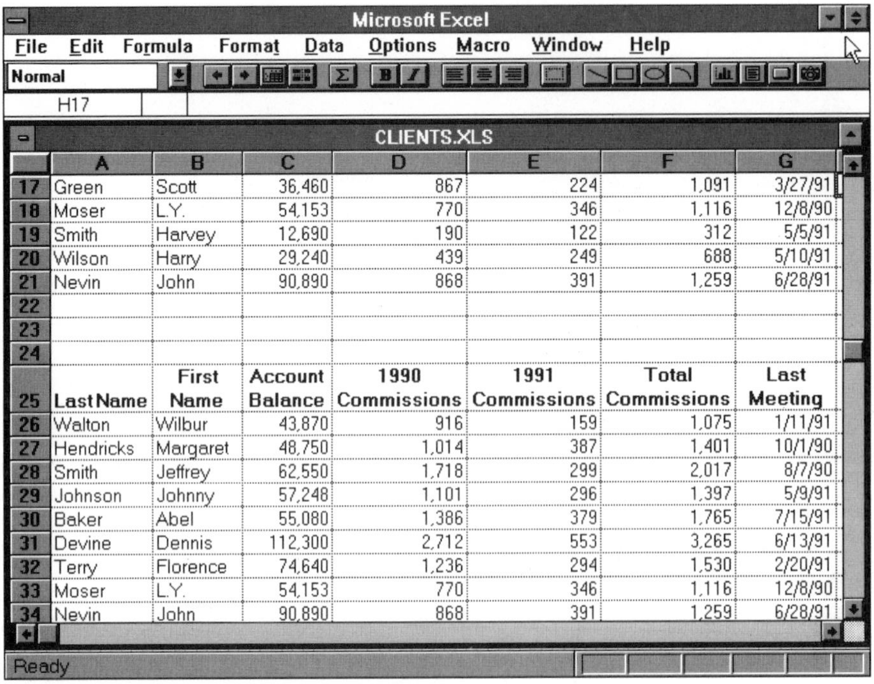

FIGURE 10-5. *The records of all clients who have account balances greater than $40,000.*

To produce a list of clients who have account balances *greater than or equal to* $40,000, you can use the >= operator. Microsoft Excel also accepts the <= (less than or equal to) operator and the <> (not equal to) operator.

Combining Criteria

Suppose that, despite your best efforts to keep in close touch with your most important clients, you have a feeling you haven't met with a few of them in quite a while. You decide to print a list of all clients about whom *both* of the following statements are true:

- The client's account balance exceeds $50,000.

- You haven't met with the client since February, 1991.

Such criteria are called *AND criteria*, because both the first *and* the second criterion must be matched for a record to be selected. Microsoft Excel requires you to enter both these criteria *in the same row* in the criteria range.

To extract the records that meet both criteria, follow these steps:

1. Enter *>50000* in cell C2.

2. Enter *<3/1/91* in cell G2 (meaning *before March 1, 1991*).

3. Choose the Extract command from the Data menu.

4. When the Extract dialog box appears, click OK, or press Enter.

Your worksheet looks like Figure 10-6. Now all you have to do is pick up the telephone and set up meetings with these "neglected" clients.

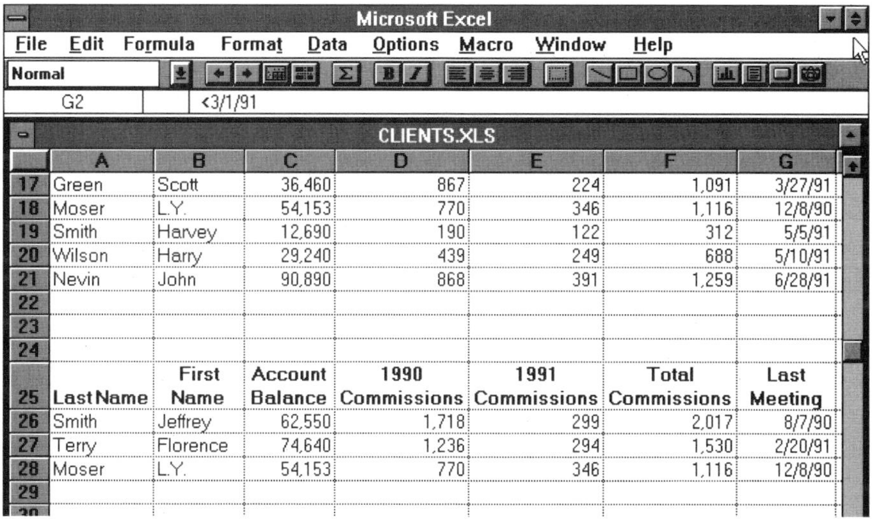

FIGURE 10-6. *Important clients you need to meet with soon.*

You can also define two AND criteria for the same field. For example, to extract the records of clients with account balances between $50,000 and $60,000, follow these steps:

1. Copy the field name *Account Balance* to cell H1.

2. Select the new criteria range (cells A1:H2).

3. Choose the Set Criteria command from the Data menu to redefine the criteria range.

4. Delete the criterion from cell G2.

5. Enter *<60000* in cell H2.

6. Choose the Extract command from the Data menu.

7. When the Extract dialog box appears, click OK, or press Enter.

As you can see in Figure 10-7, three clients have account balances between $50,000 and $60,000. Now before you continue with this chapter, delete the entries in cells H1 and H2.

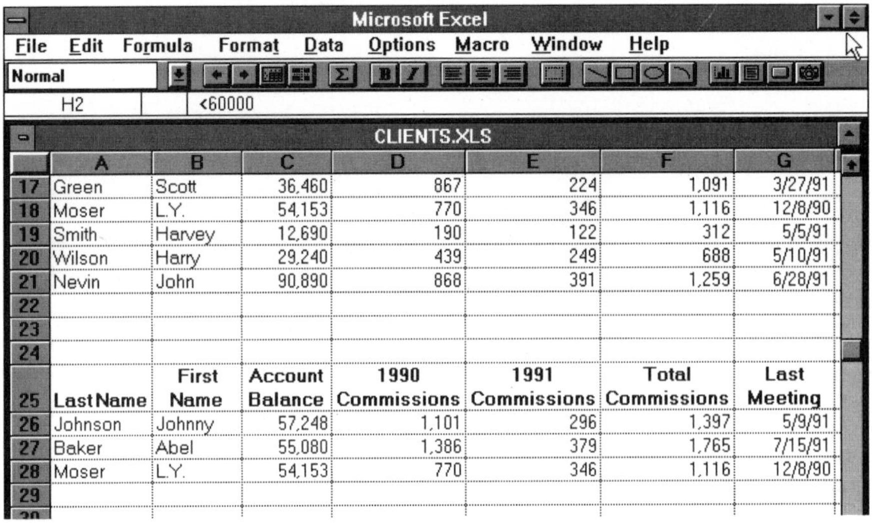

	Microsoft Excel					
File Edit Formula Format Data Options Macro Window Help						
Normal						
H2	<60000					

CLIENTS.XLS

	A	B	C	D	E	F	G
17	Green	Scott	36,460	867	224	1,091	3/27/91
18	Moser	L.Y.	54,153	770	346	1,116	12/8/90
19	Smith	Harvey	12,690	190	122	312	5/5/91
20	Wilson	Harry	29,240	439	249	688	5/10/91
21	Nevin	John	90,890	868	391	1,259	6/28/91
22							
23							
24							
25	Last Name	First Name	Account Balance	1990 Commissions	1991 Commissions	Total Commissions	Last Meeting
26	Johnson	Johnny	57,248	1,101	296	1,397	5/9/91
27	Baker	Abel	55,080	1,386	379	1,765	7/15/91
28	Moser	L.Y.	54,153	770	346	1,116	12/8/90
29							

FIGURE 10-7. *The records of all clients that meet two AND criteria in the same field.*

Using Alternative Criteria

Sometimes you'll want to select records that meet either, but not necessarily both, of two criteria. Such criteria are called *OR criteria*. They must be entered *on separate rows* in the criteria range.

In the example in Figure 10-5, you extracted records of clients with account balances exceeding $40,000. Suppose you've decided to send a mailing to clients who have balances over $60,000 and to clients whose accounts generated more than $1,000 in commissions in 1990, regardless of their current balances.

To extract the records that meet either (or both) of these criteria, follow these steps:

1. Select the range A1:G3.

2. Choose the Set Criteria command from the Data menu to extend the criteria range to include row 3.

3. Enter the criterion *>60000* in cell C2.

4. Enter the criterion *>1000* in cell D3. Your criterion range now looks like this:

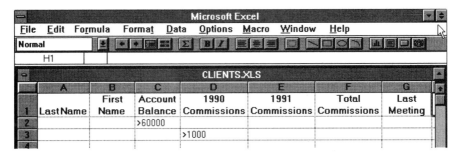

5. Choose the Extract command from the Data menu.

6. When the Extract dialog box appears, click OK, or press Enter.

Figure 10-8 on the next page shows the results of this extraction. Because rows 2 and 3 contain OR criteria, the extract range includes three clients who have account balances of less than $60,000 but 1990 commissions of more than $1,000 (Margaret Hendricks, Johnny Johnson, and Abel Baker) and one client who has an account balance of more than $60,000 but 1990 commissions of less than $1,000 (John Nevin). In addition, the range include three clients who have both account balances of more than $60,000 *and* 1990 commissions of more than $1,000 (Jeffrey Smith, Dennis Devine, and Florence Terry).

	Microsoft Excel								
File	Edit	Formula	Format	Data	Options	Macro	Window	Help	

Normal | H17

CLIENTS.XLS

	A	B	C	D	E	F	G
17	Green	Scott	36,460	867	224	1,091	3/27/91
18	Moser	L.Y.	54,153	770	346	1,116	12/8/90
19	Smith	Harvey	12,690	190	122	312	5/5/91
20	Wilson	Harry	29,240	439	249	688	5/10/91
21	Nevin	John	90,890	868	391	1,259	6/28/91
22							
23							
24							
25	**Last Name**	**First Name**	**Account Balance**	**1990 Commissions**	**1991 Commissions**	**Total Commissions**	**Last Meeting**
26	Hendricks	Margaret	48,750	1,014	387	1,401	10/1/90
27	Smith	Jeffrey	62,550	1,718	299	2,017	8/7/90
28	Johnson	Johnny	57,248	1,101	296	1,397	5/9/91
29	Baker	Abel	55,080	1,386	379	1,765	7/15/91
30	Devine	Dennis	112,300	2,712	553	3,265	6/13/91
31	Terry	Florence	74,640	1,236	294	1,530	2/20/91
32	Nevin	John	90,890	868	391	1,259	6/28/91
33							
34							

Ready

FIGURE 10-8. *The records of all clients whose accounts generated more than $1,000 in commissions in 1990 or who have account balances greater than $60,000.*

You can combine AND and OR criteria. In the example criteria range shown below, row 2 contains AND criteria and rows 2 and 3 constitute an OR criterion. For example, these criteria instruct Excel to find records with account balances between $40,000 AND $70,000 OR with total commissions greater than or equal to $600:

	Microsoft Excel								
File	Edit	Formula	Format	Data	Options	Macro	Window	Help	

Normal | J1

CLIENTS.XLS

	A	B	C	D	E	F	G	H	I
1		**Last name**	**First name**	**Account Balance**	**1990 Commissions**	**1991 Commissions**	**Total Commissions**	**Last meeting**	**Account Balance**
2				>40000					<70000
3							>=600		
4									

If you later perform another search with only one row of criteria, you must redefine the criteria range to two rows (the field-name row and the criteria row), even if you delete all the entries in the second criteria row. Remember, a blank row in a criteria range causes Microsoft Excel to select all records in the database.

Using Computed Criteria

Sometimes you'll want to select records based on how the values in a specific field compare with other values. Such criteria are called *computed criteria* because to extract this information, you must enter in the criteria range a comparison formula that includes a computed value.

For example, suppose you want to consult with clients who have had a low level of trading activity since the beginning of 1990. You decide to limit your contacts to clients whose accounts have generated 1990 and 1991 commissions totaling less than 2 percent of the value of the account.

To create a list of these clients, follow these steps:

1. Delete all existing criteria from the criteria range.

2. Type the name *Activity* (short for the formula that measures trading activity) in cell H1.

3. Enter the following formula in cell H2:

   `=F7/C7<2%`

   The formula returns the logical value FALSE because the record in row 7 doesn't meet the criterion set by the formula. However, this result doesn't affect the extraction process, because Excel calculates the value of an equivalent formula for every record in the database and selects only the records for which the result of the formula is TRUE.

4. Set A1:H2 as the criteria range.

5. Choose the Extract command from the Data menu.

6. When the Extract dialog box appears, click OK, or press Enter.

Figure 10-9 on the next page shows the records of the clients who may need your advice in updating their investment portfolios.

	A	B	C	D	E	F	G
17	Green	Scott	36,460	867	224	1,091	3/27/91
18	Moser	L.Y.	54,153	770	346	1,116	12/8/90
19	Smith	Harvey	12,690	190	122	312	5/5/91
20	Wilson	Harry	29,240	439	249	688	5/10/91
21	Nevin	John	90,890	868	391	1,259	6/28/91
22							
23							
24							
25	**Last Name**	**First Name**	**Account Balance**	**1990 Commissions**	**1991 Commissions**	**Total Commissions**	**Last Meeting**
26	Williams	Oliver	10,940	137	73	210	8/12/90
27	Spencer	David	8,145	121	0	121	10/13/90
28	Nevin	John	90,890	868	391	1,259	6/28/91
29							
30							
31							
32							
33							
34							

FIGURE 10-9. *A list of clients whose accounts generated commissions totaling less than 2 percent of the value of the account.*

FINDING RECORDS QUICKLY

The Extract command on the Data menu helps you create subsets of your database. Sometimes, though, you may simply want a "quick read" of the records that meet specific criteria. That's where using the Find command on the Data menu is handy. The Find command allows you to look at matching records one at a time, without copying them to another part of your worksheet.

To see how the Extract and Find commands differ, follow these steps:

1. Keeping the criteria you used in the preceding example, choose the Find command from the Data menu. Excel highlights the record of Oliver Williams, the first client in the database who meets the current criteria. The scroll-bar pattern becomes striped, and the status bar indicates that the program is in Find mode. Your screen now looks like the following.

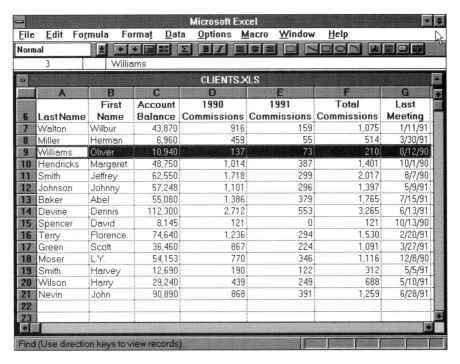

	A	B	C	D	E	F	G
		First	Account	1990	1991	Total	Last
6	LastName	Name	Balance	Commissions	Commissions	Commissions	Meeting
7	Walton	Wilbur	43,870	916	159	1,075	1/11/91
8	Miller	Herman	6,960	459	55	514	3/30/91
9	Williams	Oliver	10,940	137	73	210	8/12/90
10	Hendricks	Margaret	48,750	1,014	387	1,401	10/1/90
11	Smith	Jeffrey	62,550	1,718	299	2,017	8/7/90
12	Johnson	Johnny	57,248	1,101	296	1,397	5/9/91
13	Baker	Abel	55,080	1,386	379	1,765	7/15/91
14	Devine	Dennis	112,300	2,712	553	3,265	6/13/91
15	Spencer	David	8,145	121	0	121	10/13/90
16	Terry	Florence	74,640	1,236	294	1,530	2/20/91
17	Green	Scott	36,460	867	224	1,091	3/27/91
18	Moser	L.Y.	54,153	770	346	1,116	12/8/90
19	Smith	Harvey	12,690	190	122	312	5/5/91
20	Wilson	Harry	29,240	439	249	688	5/10/91
21	Nevin	John	90,890	868	391	1,259	6/28/91
22							
23							

2. Click the down arrow in the vertical scroll bar, or press the Up and Down direction keys, to move among the matching records. Excel skips over nonmatching records.

3. When you are finished, choose the Exit Find command from the Data menu, or press Esc, to turn off Find mode.

If you want to print a list of the matching records, you must choose the Extract command from the Data menu, and then print the extract range.

Using Criteria in the Data Form

You can also search quickly through your database by setting criteria within the data form. To use the data-form method, follow these steps:

1. Choose the Form command from the Data menu.

2. Click the Criteria button to turn on Criteria mode and display the criteria form.

3. Enter *>60000* in the Account Balance field.

4. Enter *>1000* in the 1990 Commissions field. Your criteria form now looks like this:

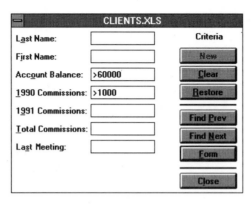

5. Click the Find Next button. The data form now displays the first matching record (Jeffrey Smith).

6. Click the Find Next button to move forward through the matching records; click the Find Prev button to move backward.

7. Click the Close button, or press Esc, to return to the worksheet.

If you change your mind about the criteria you want to use and the criteria form is still on your screen, you can click the Clear button to remove all criteria from the form. To return to the data form without carrying out the search, choose the Form button.

If you've moved partway through your database with previous searches and haven't closed the data form before you set new criteria, Microsoft Excel begins searching the database for matching records from the most recent position in the data form. Consequently, you shouldn't assume that the first matching record displayed is the first matching record in the database.

The data-form criteria are completely independent of those in the criteria range of the worksheet. After you remove the data form, all Find and Extract operations revert to using the worksheet criteria range.

You can use wildcards in criteria in a data form. However, because the data form contains only one input field for each field name, you can't specify OR criteria or computed criteria in the form, nor can you specify two criteria for a single field as you did in the example in Figure 10-7 on page 260.

DELETING RECORDS

You may want to delete certain records from your database. You can use criteria to find the records and then use the Delete command from the Data menu to remove from the database all records matching the criteria in the criteria range.

When you choose the Delete command, Microsoft Excel displays the warning message shown in Figure 10-10. Always take this warning seriously, because using the Delete command can be risky. For example, if you accidentally include a blank row in the criteria range, *all* records in the database are matching records and will be destroyed if you click OK or press Enter to tell Excel to go ahead with the Delete command.

FIGURE 10-10. *The data-deletion warning message.*

To avoid losing data, be sure to double-check the criteria range before you choose Delete. To quickly determine which range is currently assigned the name *Criteria*, follow these steps:

1. Choose Goto from the Formula menu (or press F5).

2. Select Criteria from the Goto list box.

3. Click OK, or press Enter.

Excel highlights the criteria range. When you're certain nothing in the criteria range will cause Excel to destroy important records, choose the Delete command from the Data menu. After deleting the matching records, Excel reduces the range defined with the name *Database* accordingly.

 As an added precaution, you might want to use the Extract command to extract the criteria-matching records. You can then review them before choosing Delete. If the extract range contains records you don't want to delete, you can modify the criteria and repeat the process until you are sure the Delete command won't eradicate records you want to retain.

ADVANCED DATABASE TOOLS

Microsoft Excel offers powerful statistical functions that help you analyze data. For example, you can compute totals, averages, and variances for matching records only or for the entire database. You can also create a table that displays results based on the use of different values for a specified argument in a formula. For more information about these advanced topics, consult the Microsoft Excel documentation.

CONCLUSION

This chapter concludes our discussion of Microsoft Excel's database features. You've learned enough to begin using databases to keep track of important data and to extract information when you need it. In the next section, we move on to discuss another powerful Excel feature: macros.

Macros

Chapter 11

Creating Macros

Now that you're getting used to Microsoft Excel, you're probably starting to depend on it in your daily work. You may have noticed that you're using certain commands over and over again, and you may also be spending a great deal of time entering and formatting data. That's where *macros* come in: They can save time and reduce errors by automating routine worksheet tasks. In this chapter, you'll learn how to create, edit, and correct errors in macros, and we take a brief look at the macro language.

RECORDING AND RUNNING MACROS

The best way to gain an understanding of both the mechanics of macros and the concepts behind them is to actually create one. Microsoft Excel offers an easy way to get started with macros. By using the *macro recorder*, you can create a macro simply by typing and carrying out commands. After you finish recording, you can run, or "play back," the macro and have it perform the recorded actions.

Turning On the Macro Recorder

We'll start by recording a very simple formatting macro. Open a new, blank worksheet, and move the cursor to cell A1. Then follow these steps:

1. Choose the Record command from the Macro menu. The following dialog box appears:

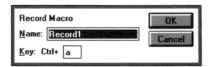

2. In the Name text box, replace the name *Record1* with a name that will remind you later of what the macro does. The macro you're about to record applies a pattern to the current selection in the worksheet, so for this example, use the name *Pattern1*.

3. In the Key text box, specify a shortcut key that you can use later (in conjunction with the Ctrl key) to run the macro. In this case, *p* for *Pattern1* is probably the easiest key to remember.

 Be sure to enter a lowercase p *in the Key text box. Excel recognizes capitalization in macro shortcut keys, so you can assign* p *to this macro and still use* P *for another macro.*

4. Click OK, or press Enter, to turn on the macro recorder.

When the dialog box disappears, things seem to be back to normal. But behind the scenes, Excel has opened a macro sheet, an Excel document that resembles a worksheet but that is used exclusively for storing macros.

Recording Macros

From the moment you click OK or press Enter to carry out the Record command, Microsoft Excel translates the commands you choose into its *macro language* and records them in the macro sheet. The *Recording* message in the status bar at the bottom of your screen alerts you to the fact that your keystrokes and mouse actions are being recorded. As Excel records your actions, it also carries them out in the worksheet.

To record the commands for the *Pattern1* macro, follow these steps:

1. Choose the Patterns command from the Format menu. The Patterns dialog box appears.

 The macro recorder allows you to correct some keystroke or mouse errors while recording. For example, if you accidentally choose the Font command instead of the Patterns command while the recorder is turned on, you can click Cancel and then choose the correct command without recording the erroneous Font command.

2. Display the following Pattern drop-down list by clicking the arrow to the right of the box:

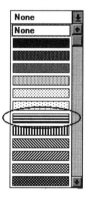

3. Select the seventh pattern from the top (circled above).

4. Display the Foreground drop-down list, and select yellow as the foreground color. (For those of you who do not have a color monitor, yellow is the sixth color from the top.)

5. Click OK, or press Enter, to carry out the Patterns command.

6. Choose the Stop Recorder command to turn off the macro recorder. (When you started the macro recorder, Excel changed the Record command in the Macro menu to Stop Recorder.)

Your worksheet now looks like Figure 11-1 on the next page. Excel has applied the new pattern and color to cell A1. On a color monitor, cell A1 is pale yellow. On a monochrome monitor, it is shaded.

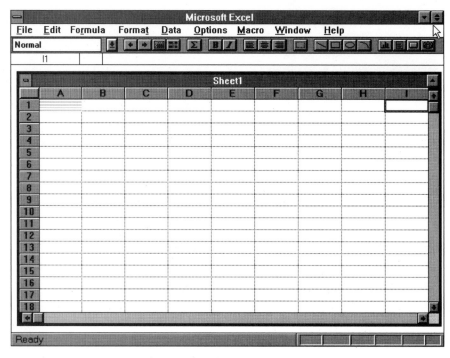

FIGURE 11-1. *The worksheet after the* Pattern1 *macro is created.*

Running Macros

To use the *Pattern1* macro in another location in your worksheet, simply follow these steps:

1. Select the range C3:F6.

2. Choose the Run command from the Macro menu. The following dialog box appears:

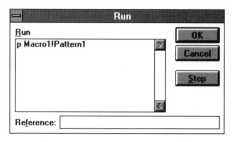

If the dialog box doesn't appear, you may have forgotten to turn off the macro recorder. Check whether the Recording *message is still displayed in the status bar. If it is, close the macro sheet, open a new one, and then record the macro again. Be sure to turn off the recorder when you're done.*

3. The Run list box displays the names of all the macros in the currently open macro sheets. Select the *Pattern1* macro.

4. Click OK, or press Enter.

Your worksheet now looks like Figure 11-2.

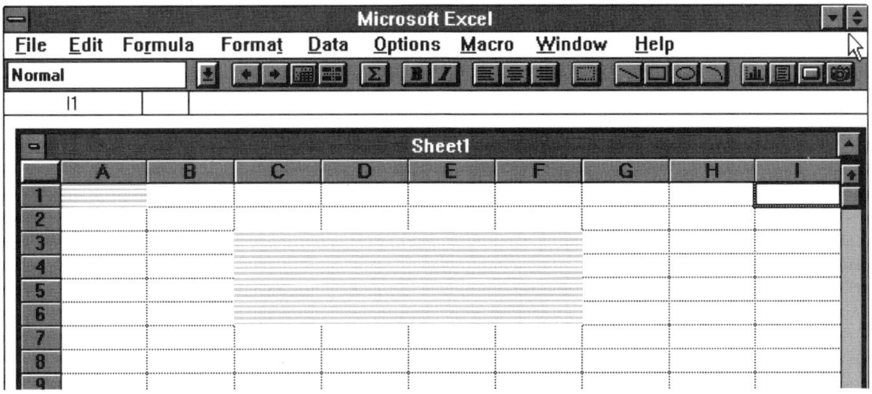

FIGURE 11-2. *The worksheet after the* Pattern1 *macro is run with the range C3:F6 selected.*

Now choose another range of cells, and then run the *Pattern1* macro again, a different way. Simply press Ctrl-p, the shortcut key you assigned when you recorded the macro. Microsoft Excel applies the pattern and color to the selected range.

Creating a Macro That Enters Column Headings

Creating the *Pattern1* macro was a simple way of demonstrating some basic macro techniques, but let's now try something that may be more useful in your day-to-day work. Suppose you work in the accounting department of a chain of retail stores. You need to prepare schedules that summarize financial results by month. You repeatedly use the Data Series command to produce column headings for the time periods in your worksheets. To create a macro to auto-mate this process, open a new, blank worksheet, and follow these steps:

1. Select cell B1, and enter *1/1/91*.

2. Choose the Record command from the Macro menu. The Record Macro dialog box appears.

3. Type *Topdates* in the Name text box.

4. Type *D* (be sure it's a capital *D*) in the Key text box.

5. Click OK, or press Enter.

6. Select the range B1:G1.

7. Choose the Series command from the Data menu.

8. Select the Month option in the Date Unit group.

9. Click OK, or press Enter.

10. Choose the Number command from the Format menu, and select the mmm-yy format.

11. Click OK, or press Enter.

12. Choose the Stop Recorder command from the Macro menu.

Your worksheet now looks like Figure 11-3. If it doesn't, you may have made a keystroke error when recording the macro. (We show you how to check the macro for errors later in this chapter.)

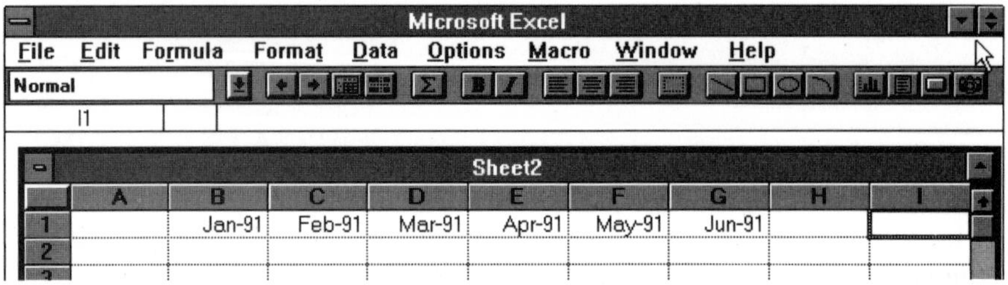

FIGURE 11-3. *The worksheet after the* Topdates *macro is created.*

Before you test the shortcut key for this macro, choose the Clear command from the Edit menu, and select the All option to delete the headings and the for-mats you recorded in the range B1:G1. Then enter *7/91* in cell B1 and run the macro by pressing Ctrl-D; that is, hold down the Ctrl and Shift keys while pressing the d key. Your worksheet now looks like Figure 11-4.

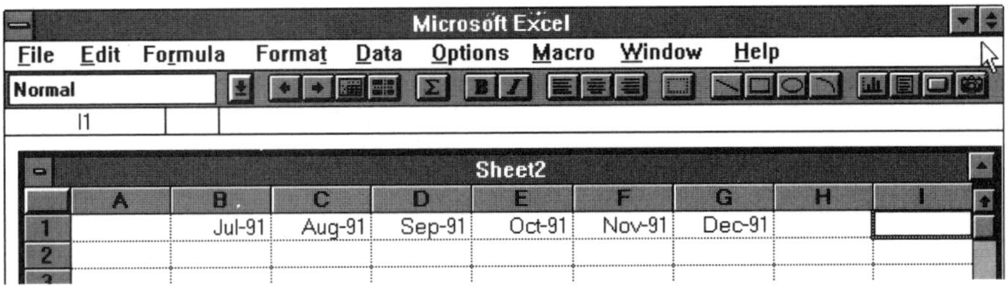

FIGURE 11-4. *The worksheet after the* Topdates *macro is run, beginning with the date 7/91.*

The *Topdates* macro doesn't work unless you've previously entered a value in cell B1. (You'll learn how to remedy this deficiency later.)

You might be wondering whether using a macro is the best way of entering this information. Wouldn't it be easier to simply create a template worksheet with the headings across the top and open that worksheet whenever you need these headings? The answer depends on how you want to use the headings. The primary advantage of using a macro is that you can begin the series with any date. If you simply saved the worksheet pictured in Figure 11-3 as a template, you could use the template only when the period covered in the worksheet began with January 1991.

UNDERSTANDING THE MICROSOFT EXCEL MACRO LANGUAGE

When you record a macro, Microsoft Excel opens a macro sheet and names it *Macro1*. The first macro you record in a session occupies column A of the macro sheet, the second occupies column B, and so on. While the macro recorder is turned on, Excel enters your keyboard and mouse actions in the macro sheet in the form of *macro functions*. Instead of creating a literal record of keystrokes, Excel translates keyboard and mouse actions into a procedural language that can be easily read and understood.

Now let's take a look at Excel's macro language. To examine the macros you've just created, choose the *Macro1* macro sheet from the Window menu and adjust the widths of columns A and B so that you can see all the text in both columns. (You'll almost always find it necessary to widen the macro columns to see their entire contents.) Your screen now looks like Figure 11-5 on the next page.

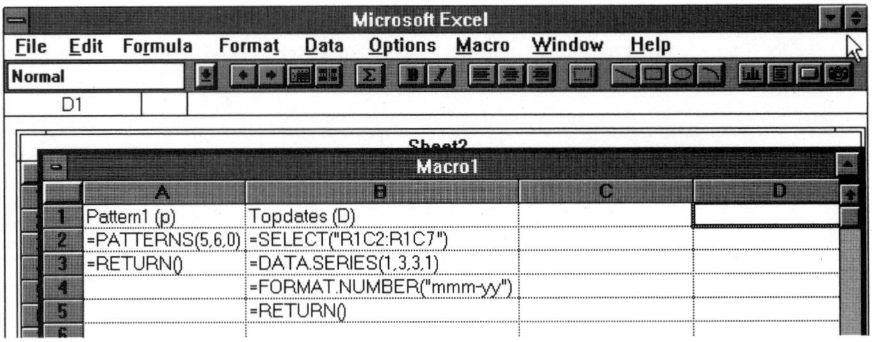

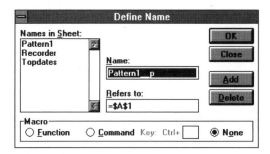

FIGURE 11-5. *The* Pattern1 *and* Topdates *macros as they appear in the* Macro1 *macro sheet.*

Notice that Excel has entered the name of the first macro as a label in cell A1. Excel has also assigned this name to cell A1. To verify this assignment, choose the Define Name command from the Formula menu, and look at the items in the Names In Sheet list box, shown in Figure 11-6. In addition, Excel has assigned the name *Recorder* to column A, and the name *Topdates* to cell B1. When you finish exploring, press Esc to close the dialog box.

FIGURE 11-6. *The Define Name dialog box, displaying the names assigned in* Macro1.

Macro Functions

The Microsoft Excel macro language consists of more than 200 macro functions, which tell Excel to carry out various tasks automatically. (Later in this chapter, we show you how to display a list of all the available functions.) For example, the first command you chose after turning on the macro recorder to record your first macro was the Patterns command. This action generated the PATTERNS function in cell A2 of the macro sheet. The PATTERNS function has three arguments. These arguments correspond to the three list boxes in the Patterns dialog box, and the sequence of the arguments corresponds to the sequence in which the list boxes appear (top to bottom) in the dialog box. In Figure 11-5, the values 5, 6, and 0 indicate which options you chose from each list box when you recorded the macro. Every available option in Excel dialog boxes is assigned an identifying number for purposes of macro recording. When you record macros, you don't have to worry about which number goes with which option, because the macro recorder automatically generates the proper numbers.

Although using the macro recorder insulates you from concerns about macro-function syntax, you may have to address such issues when you try to correct, or debug, macros that are not working as they should. The PATTERNS function is a good example of the way Excel macros represent commands that use dialog boxes. The number of arguments varies with the complexity of the dialog box, but generally the system is logical, allowing you to learn the conventions fairly easily.

The DATA.SERIES function in cell B3 provides an example of the arguments that correspond to a more complex dialog box. When you choose the Series command from the Data menu, you are presented with the Series dialog box, which contains five sets of options: the Series In, Type, and Date Unit option groups, and the Step Value and Stop Value text boxes. When you carried out the Series command while recording the *Topdates* macro, you provided four responses, leaving the Stop Value text box blank. As a result, the DATA.SERIES function in cell B3 of the macro sheet reflects only four responses. The values 1, 3, 3, 1 indicate that you selected the first option (counting from the top) in the first option group (Series In), the third option in the second option group (Type), the third option in the third option group (Date Unit), and that you accepted the default entry, 1, in the Step Value text box.

The DATA.SERIES function also has an optional fifth argument. If, while recording the macro, you had entered a number in the Stop Value text box, it would have appeared as the last argument of the DATA.SERIES function, preceded by a comma.

 Microsoft Excel macro functions that correspond to menu commands usually have names that make the association clear. You should have little trouble figuring out the commands that correspond to specific functions. For example, relating the macro function in cell B4 to the command that generated it is easy. You chose the Number command from the Format menu and selected the mmm-yy format. Excel added the required quotation marks.

R1C1 Notation

As you can see in Figure 11-5 on page 278, the first function in the *Topdates* macro, SELECT, is self-explanatory, but the argument R1C2:R1C7 may not be so obvious. This range reference uses what's known as *R1C1* notation, instead of the A1 notation we have used throughout this book. When you record a macro, Microsoft Excel uses R1C1 notation to specify references.

The number following the *R* is the row number (counting from the top); the number following the *C* is the column number (counting from the left). Thus, the argument R1C2:R1C7 in the formula in cell B2 refers to the range starting with cell B1 and ending with cell G1 (the cells in the first row of columns 2 and 7. The function means *Select the range B1:G1*.

Notice that the argument is enclosed in quotation marks. Text arguments must be enclosed in quotation marks; when you record a macro, Excel inserts the quotation marks automatically.

The RETURN Function

Both the *Patterns1* and *Topdates* macros end with a RETURN function. When you choose Stop Recorder from the Macro menu, Microsoft Excel automatically places a RETURN function (which has no arguments) at the end of the macro. The RETURN function is like a period at the end of a sentence. If a macro doesn't end with either a RETURN or a HALT function, Excel beeps and displays an error message when you try to run the macro. (You'll learn about the HALT function later in this chapter.)

 The Function Reference, *which is part of the Microsoft Excel documentation, provides detailed explanations of every macro-function argument.*

EDITING MACROS

If you change your mind about some of the details in a macro after you've recorded it, you don't have to start over. You can simply edit the macro in the macro sheet. Before we look at an editing example, delete column A from the macro sheet, thereby removing the *Pattern1* macro and leaving *Topdates* in the new column A. Then choose the Save As command from the File menu to save the macro sheet under the name *DATES*.

Suppose you now decide that you want all the date headings created by the *Topdates* macro to be centered. You want to insert this formatting command at the end of the macro, but recording the entire macro again would duplicate work you've already done. To add the command without rerecording the entire macro, follow these steps:

1. Choose *DATES.XLM* from the Window menu.

2. Select cell A5.

3. Choose the Insert command from the Edit menu.

4. In the Insert dialog box, select the Shift Cells Down option to add a new row before the RETURN function.

5. Enter the following function in the new cell A5:

    `=ALIGNMENT(3)`

    The ALIGNMENT function is like the Alignment command on the Format menu, and the value 3 corresponds to the Center option.

Your macro sheet now looks like Figure 11-7.

Now clear the formulas and formats from the first row of your worksheet, enter *1/1/91* in cell B1, and test the edited macro. If it doesn't work, compare your macro with Figure 11-7 to see if you made any typographical errors.

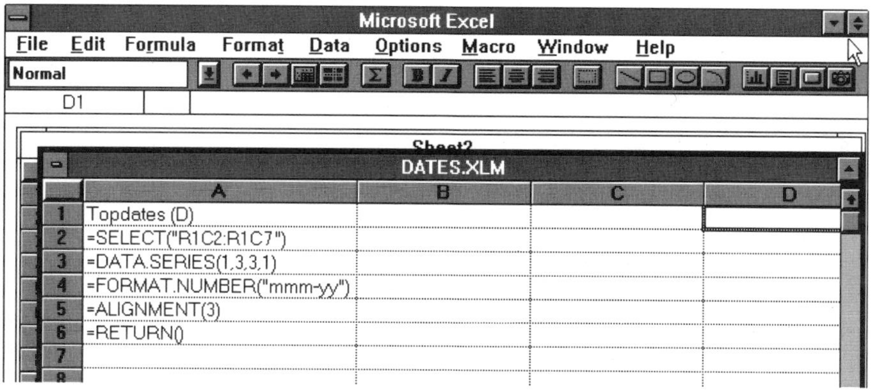

FIGURE 11-7. *The* Topdates *macro with the ALIGNMENT function added.*

UNDERSTANDING MACRO MECHANICS

To get the most out of Microsoft Excel macros, you need to understand their structure and their mechanics. Let's take a few minutes to examine some basic principles.

Macro Sheets vs. Worksheets

A macro sheet resembles a worksheet in several obvious respects:

- It has the same row-and-column structure as a worksheet, and it has a menu bar and a tool bar.

- You revise and manipulate macro-sheet cell entries the same way you do worksheet entries.

- With a few exceptions, menu commands work the same way in macro sheets as they do in worksheets.

But macro sheets and worksheets also differ in important ways. Most notably, macro-sheet columns are wider than their worksheet counterparts, because the Formulas option in the Display dialog box is selected by default for macro sheets. (When you examine a macro, Microsoft Excel assumes that you want to read the formulas rather than view their returned values.) The wider columns make working with macros easier. If you turn off the Formulas option, the macro-sheet column widths return to normal worksheet dimensions.

Another key difference between macro sheets and worksheets is the functions you can use. To view the functions available for use in macros, follow these steps:

1. Choose *DATES.XLM* from the Windows menu.

2. Choose the Paste Function command from the Formula menu. A dialog box appears, listing the available functions, just as it does when you choose Paste Function while working with a worksheet.

3. Scroll through the available functions. The box lists some functions you haven't seen before, because Excel's macro language includes more than 200 functions that are not available in worksheets. Many of the Excel macro functions perform macro operations that have no command equivalents. These functions are particularly useful for passing values from one operation to another and for directing the order in which operations are carried out. (You'll learn how some of these functions operate later in this chapter.)

4. Click Cancel, or press Esc, to remove the Paste Function dialog box from the screen.

Before you continue, save and close the *DATES* macro sheet. You'll use it later in this chapter.

Storing Macros

A single macro sheet can contain several macros, and you can run any macro in any open macro sheet from within any Microsoft Excel document. When you choose the Record command from the Macro menu, Excel records your macro in the first empty column in the macro sheet. (If two or more macro sheets are open, Excel records the macro in the macro sheet that contains the most recently recorded operations.) To store a macro in a specific location in a specific macro sheet, you must *set the recorder range*, which involves opening the macro sheet, selecting the cell in which you want to begin your macro, and then choosing the Set Recorder command from the Macro menu.

Setting the recorder range

To specify the location where you want Microsoft Excel to store a recorded macro, follow these steps:

1. Open the macro sheet you want to use. (For this example, open a new macro sheet.)

2. Select the first cell of the range where you want to record the macro. (Leave an empty cell at the top of the column for the macro name.)

3. Choose the Set Recorder command from the Macro menu.

4. Choose the Start Recorder command from the Macro menu.

5. Record a simple formatting macro.

6. Choose the Stop Recorder command from the Macro menu.

You might find the presence of both the Record and Start Recorder commands on the Macro menu confusing, especially because, whichever way you turn on the recorder, you stop recording by choosing Stop Recorder. However, the two commands differ in subtle ways. The Record command always prompts you to name the macro, and is therefore suitable for creating new macros. The Start Recorder command does not require you to enter a name, because it is designed to help you insert new functions in an already existing macro. The Start Recorder command does, however, require you to decide beforehand where the macro will be stored, because it is available only when you've defined a recorder range.

To assign a name to a macro you have created by using the Start Recorder command, use the Define Name command on the Formula menu. The Define Name dialog box for macro sheets, shown in Figure 11-8, is a bit different from its worksheet counterpart. At the bottom of the dialog box is a Macro option group in which you must indicate the type of macro you've created. Excel offers two types of macros: *function macros* and *command macros*. Function macros are custom worksheet functions that you create to perform specialized calculations. Command macros carry out worksheet operations, just as Excel's built-in commands do. So far, you've created only command macros. (When you use the macro recorder to record a set of commands, the recorded macro is automatically a command macro.) We'll show you how to design function macros later in Chapter 12, "More Advanced Macro Techniques."

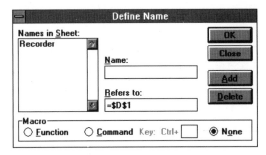

FIGURE 11-8. *The Define Name dialog box for macro sheets.*

To name the formatting macro you just created, follow these steps:

1. Select the empty cell above the recorder range.

2. Enter an appropriate name for the macro.

3. Choose the Define Name command from the Formula menu. When the dialog box appears, be sure the name you entered in the cell above the macro range is displayed in the Name text box.

4. Select the Command option in the Macro group.

5. Type a shortcut-key letter in the Key text box.

6. Click OK, or press Enter.

You can now run this macro in the same way you would run a macro created with the Record command.

More About the Macro Cell-Referencing Scheme

By default, Microsoft Excel macros use fixed (absolute) cell referencing. You can see how this works by running the *Topdates* macro several times in succession, selecting a different starting cell each time. As things stand now, the *Topdates* macro works only if cell B1 contains a date, and the macro always puts the dates in cells B1 through G1.

Suppose you want to be able to put the date headings anywhere in the worksheet. You can create this option by changing the appropriate cell references in the macro from fixed to relative. By default, the macro recorder enters fixed cell references in R1C1 format. In R1C1 notation, you designate a relative cell address by enclosing the numbers in the address in square brackets ([]).

To see how this works, open the *DATES* macro sheet, and then follow these steps:

1. Copy the *Topdates* macro (without the name) to cells B2:B6.

2. Select cell B2. The formula bar displays the following formula:

   `=SELECT("R1C2:R1C7")`

3. Edit the formula in the formula bar to read as follows:

   `=SELECT("R[0]C[0]:R[0]C[5]")`

   The R[0]C[0] address indicates the active cell (zero rows, zero columns from the current position). The R[0]C[5] address indicates the cell in the current row, five columns to the right of the active cell.

 To indicate a reference to a cell above in the same column or to the left in the same row in relative R1C1 format, precede the number within the square brackets with a minus sign.

4. Press Enter.

5. Enter the name *Anydates* in cell B1.

6. Choose the Define Name command from the Formula menu.

7. Accept the default range ($B$1). This assigns the name *Anydates* to the macro.

8. Select the Command option in the Macro group.

9. Type a lowercase *d* in the Key text box to assign a shortcut key to the new macro.

10. Click OK, or press Enter.

Now let's try the new version of the macro. Select cell C10 in a blank work-sheet, enter *10/88*, and press Ctrl-d. The new macro operates just like the old one, except that instead of always beginning the six-month sequence of head-ings in cell B1, it begins the sequence in the cell you select before you run the macro. Your worksheet now looks like Figure 11-9.

Now you can appreciate why the R1C1 scheme is used in macro sheets: It's a more efficient and flexible means of controlling the relative vertical and hori-zontal movement of the active cell than the letter-number scheme.

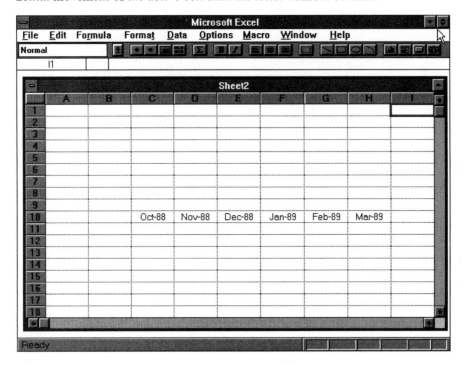

FIGURE 11-9. *The worksheet after the* Anydates *macro is run.*

 If the macro doesn't work, the most likely cause is a typo-graphical error in the SELECT function or the failure to enter a value in the active cell before running the macro.

Recording macros with relative referencing

Changing from fixed, or absolute, referencing to relative referencing after you've recorded a macro is a tedious process. You can save time by planning ahead. When you want to use relative referencing in a macro, simply choose the

Relative Record command from the Macro menu before you start recording. All the SELECT functions you subsequently record will use relative referencing.

 The first time you use the macro recorder in each Microsoft Excel session, you'll need to choose the Record command or the Set Recorder command before you can choose the Relative Record command.

After you choose Relative Record, the name of the command on the menu changes to Absolute Record (and vice versa), so that you can switch back and forth between fixed and relative modes as necessary while recording. When you choose the Relative/Absolute Record command while recording a macro, Excel doesn't record the command as part of your macro.

Deciding which referencing type to use

You can't always predict whether fixed or relative referencing will be more useful in a macro. Generally, however, you can make a decision by using the following guidelines:

- When you want the macro to enter data in, or perform operations on, a fixed worksheet range, use fixed referencing (the default mode).

- When you want to determine at the time you run the macro which cells in the worksheet are to be affected, use relative referencing.

CREATING MACROS THAT ASK FOR INPUT

The *Topdates* and *Anydates* macros require that you enter the beginning date in the series before you run the macro. Wouldn't it be nice to be able to enter the date while the macro is running?

Microsoft Excel provides a macro function that does just that. Excel's INPUT function prompts you to supply data that it can pass to other functions in the macro.

Using the INPUT Function

When Microsoft Excel encounters an INPUT function in a macro, it displays a simple dialog box containing a prompt, a text box, and OK and Cancel buttons. You design this box yourself by specifying arguments in the INPUT function.

The INPUT function has the following form:

=INPUT(*message_text,type_num,title_text,default,x-pos,y-pos*)

The first argument, *message_text*, specifies the prompt you want to display in the box. The second argument, *type_num*, controls the type of data the user can enter. You'll use only type 1 (numbers) in the examples in this book, but you could use type 2 to require that the user enter text, or type 8 to require that the user enter a cell reference. (For a list of other possible types of data, consult the Microsoft Excel documentation.) The remaining arguments control the title, the default response displayed in the text box (if any), and the horizontal and vertical position of the message box on the screen. The first argument, followed by a comma, is required; the other arguments are optional.

For example, the formula

```
=INPUT("Enter the account number:",1)
```

produces the dialog box in Figure 11-10. Entering text instead of a number in the dialog box generates an error message.

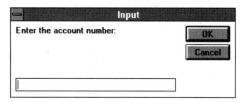

FIGURE 11-10. *An example of a dialog box produced by an INPUT function.*

Using the FORMULA Function

All the INPUT function does is display a dialog box and return in the cell containing the INPUT function the value that the user enters in the dialog box. To have Microsoft Excel enter that value in a cell in the worksheet, you must use the FORMULA function.

The FORMULA function has the following form:

```
=FORMULA(formula_text,reference)
```

The *formula_text* argument can be a formula in text form (that is, enclosed in quotation marks), a numeric constant, a logical value, or text. It can also be the address of a cell containing a value that you want to use. The *reference* argument tells Microsoft Excel where to put *formula_text*. If you don't supply a value for *reference*, the program enters *formula_text* in the active cell.

For example, to enter the value returned by a formula in cell D27 of the macro sheet in cell B6 of the worksheet, you use the following formula:

```
=FORMULA(D27,!B6)
```

The exclamation point that precedes the second cell address is necessary to tell Excel to enter the value in cell B6 in the active worksheet, rather than in the macro sheet. If you want the value to be entered in the active cell in the worksheet, you can simply omit the second argument in the FORMULA function.

Revising the *Anydates* Macro

Let's put the INPUT and FORMULA functions to work in our *DATES* macros. To add these functions, follow these steps:

1. Select the range B2:B3 in the *DATES* macro sheet.

2. Choose the Insert command from the Edit menu, select the Shift Cells Down option, and then click OK or press Enter.

3. Type the following formula cell B2:

```
=INPUT("Enter the starting month in MM/YY format:",1)
```

4. Type the following formula in cell B3:

```
=FORMULA(B2)
```

To test the edited macro, follow these steps:

1. Activate the worksheet. Delete any existing entries in row 10.

2. Select cell A10.

3. Run the *Anydates* macro by pressing Ctrl-d. The following dialog box appears:

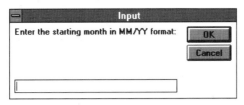

4. Type *April*, and then click OK or press Enter. An error message appears because you entered text in a dialog box that can accept only numeric values.

5. Click OK, or press Enter, to remove the error message.

6. Type *4/90* or *April 1990*, and click OK or press Enter. (As explained in Chapter 4, "Enhancing Your Worksheets," a month followed by a year is evaluated by Microsoft Excel as a date value, so *April 1990* is not considered a text entry.)

Your screen now looks like Figure 11-11. With the revised macro, you can enter a six-month series of headings anywhere in a worksheet.

	A	B	C	D	E	F	G	H	I
1									
2									
3									
4									
5									
6									
7									
8									
9									
10	Apr-90	May-90	Jun-90	Jul-90	Aug-90	Sep-90			
11									
12									
13									
14									
15									
16									
17									
18									

FIGURE 11-11. *The screen after the latest version of the* Anydates *macro is run.*

In the preceding example, you entered the INPUT function and the FORMULA function in separate cells. You can achieve the same result by combining the two functions in one formula, as shown in this example:

```
=FORMULA(INPUT("Enter the starting month in MM/YY format:",1))
```

Note that you do not enter an equal sign before the INPUT function when you use it within another function.

FIXING ERRORS IN MACROS

Error messages are very common when you're creating macros, but don't be concerned. Microsoft Excel provides some handy tools for isolating the source of the error so that you can correct the problem.

When Excel encounters a problem with a macro, it displays a dialog box similar to the one in Figure 11-12. In response, you can click Halt (to exit from the macro), Step (to continue with the macro one instruction at a time), Continue (to forge fearlessly ahead), or Goto (to go to the cell in the macro sheet that generated the error).

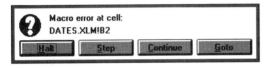

FIGURE 11-12. *The macro-error dialog box.*

When you see this dialog box, you already know you need to fix a problem, so neither continuing nor stepping through the remainder of the macro is generally a useful option. Occasionally, you might want to simply stop the macro, but usually Goto is the best choice. Examining the macro function that caused the problem is the first step toward fixing it.

If you can't identify the problem right away, you can rerun the macro in Step mode. Excel then carries out one instruction at a time, pausing after each instruction and displaying a dialog box like the one shown in Figure 11-13 so that you can view the results of the instruction.

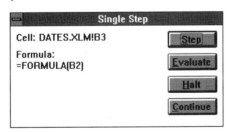

FIGURE 11-13. *The dialog box that appears after each instruction when a macro runs in Step mode.*

To see how Step mode works, follow these steps:

1. Choose the Run command from the Macro menu.

2. Select the *Anydates* macro.

3. Click the Step button. Excel evaluates the contents of cell B1 and displays the Single Step dialog box.

4. Click the Step button. The macro evaluates the contents of cell B2.

5. Click the Step button again. The macro prompts you for the starting month.

6. Enter any month and year, and then press Enter. The macro moves to cell B3.

7. Continue to click the Step button to move through the steps of the macro.

 When you locate a problem, you can exit from a macro that is in Step mode simply by clicking the Halt button in the Single Step dialog box.

Another useful function for tracking down errors in macros is the HALT function. This function has the following form:

=HALT()

You can insert a HALT function in a macro at a strategic location to cause the macro to stop. You can then examine the results produced by the macro up to that point. If everything is working correctly, you simply remove the HALT function and, if necessary, insert a new one later in the macro so that you can check the results of subsequent statements. This technique is especially useful when you are building a complex macro in stages and want to test each stage individually.

CONCLUSION

In this chapter, we have given you enough basic information to enable you to start creating and using macros. In Chapter 12, we introduce some advanced techniques that the more adventurous of you may want to use to automate often-performed tasks.

Chapter 12

More Advanced Macro Techniques

In Chapter 11, "Creating Macros," we merely
scratched the surface of Microsoft Excel's macro
capability. You may never need to go beyond
what you've already learned; but for those of you
who want to explore macros further, this chapter
provides a quick sampler of what Excel macros
can offer you. After creating a more complex
command macro, we'll take a quick look at
function macros before touching on a few
advanced concepts.

CREATING MORE COMPLEX COMMAND MACROS

Let's start by creating a macro that is more complicated than the ones you've seen so far. Suppose that one of your responsibilities is to provide a rolling three-month summary of sales by department. You want to record a Microsoft Excel macro with which you can produce this summary each month with a minimum number of keystrokes.

To follow along with this example, you need to create two worksheets: *SALESSUM*, which summarizes sales for the three previous months (March, April, and May in this example), and *NEWSALES*, which stores sales figures for the month just ended (June in this example).

Before you begin, close any open macro sheets. Then open a new worksheet, save it under the name *SALESSUM*, and enter the following data in the cells indicated:

Cell	Entry	Cell	Entry
A1	Department	C6	18800
A3	Furniture	C8	=SUM(C3:C6)
A4	Appliances	D1	May
A5	Audio	D3	33000
A6	Video	D4	32500
B1	March	D5	27000
B3	32000	D6	19200
B4	31000	D8	=SUM(D3:D6)
B5	24000	E1	Last 3 Months
B6	18000	E3	=SUM(B3:D3)
B8	=SUM(B3:B6)	E4	=SUM(B4:D4)
C1	April	E5	=SUM(B5:D5)
C3	33000	E6	=SUM(B6:D6)
C4	31500	E8	=SUM(E3:E6)
C5	26000		

Apply the $#,##0 format to the cells containing numbers.

Now open another new, blank worksheet, and then save it under the name *NEWSALES*. Copy the labels from A1:A6 of the *SALESSUM* worksheet to the same cells in *NEWSALES*, and then enter the data shown in the following table.

Cell	Entry
B1	June
B3	33600
B4	32800
B5	28500
B6	19300
B8	=SUM(B3:B6)

Apply the $#,##0 format to the same cells as in the *SALESSUM* worksheet.

Recording the Updating Macro

Because the *SALESSUM* worksheet is a three-month rolling summary, you need to update the worksheet by deleting the figures for March, entering the figures for June contained in the *NEWSALES* worksheet, and then creating new totals. To automate the updating procedure as fully as possible, you want the macro you're going to create to open the *SALESSUM* and *NEWSALES* worksheets. You must therefore save and close the *SALESSUM* and *NEWSALES* worksheets before you start the macro recorder.

 We recommend that you close all unrelated worksheets while you record or edit a macro. Otherwise, you might activate an unrelated worksheet, which could generate macro errors.

 In this example, the latest month's sales figures are stored in the NEWSALES worksheet, but in a real work situation, the worksheet would probably have a name such as 06SALE91 or SALE0691. For the macro to be able to find the worksheet with the latest sales figures, you would need to rename SALES0691 as NEWSALES before running the macro.

To create the sales-updating macro, check that all worksheets are closed, and then follow these steps:

1. Choose the Record Macro command from the File menu.

2. Type *Update* in the Name box, type *u* in the Key box, and then click OK or press Enter.

3. Open the *SALESSUM* worksheet.

4. Copy the entries in cells E1:E8 to cells F1:F8.

5. Select cells B1:B8.

6. Choose the Delete command from the Edit menu, select the Shift Cells Left option, and then click OK or press Enter.

7. Open the *NEWSALES* worksheet.

8. Copy the entries in cells B1:B8 of the *NEWSALES* worksheet to cells D1:D8 of the *SALESSUM* worksheet, overwriting the entries there.

9. Close the *NEWSALES* worksheet.

10. Choose the Stop Recorder command from the Macro menu.

11. Select the macro sheet, and save it under the name *UPDATE*.

To test the macro, you now need to enter sales figures for July in the *NEWSALES* worksheet, so save and close *SALESSUM*, open *NEWSALES*, and enter the following data:

Cell	Entry
B1	July
B3	35000
B4	34000
B5	30000
B6	20000

Now comes the acid test. Save and close *NEWSALES*, and then run the *Update* macro. Watch the July sales figures find their way into the summary. When the macro has done its work, your *SALESSUM* worksheet looks like Figure 12-1. Give yourself a pat on the back. You're on your way to mastering Microsoft Excel macros.

If you encounter the message shown in Figure 12-2 when you run the *Update* macro, one of the worksheets was open when you started the macro. Click Cancel, or press Esc, to halt the macro. Then save and close the worksheet, and try again.

FIGURE 12-1. *The three-month sales summary updated for July.*

FIGURE 12-2. *The message displayed when a macro tries to open a worksheet that is already open and has unsaved changes.*

If you click OK or press Enter in response to the Revert *message, you'll lose all the changes you've made to the worksheet since you last saved it. You cannot recover those changes.*

DESIGNING YOUR OWN FUNCTIONS

So far, we've concentrated on creating command macros. Now we'll show you the other type of Microsoft Excel macro: the function macro.

Like command macros, Excel function macros are stored in the columns of macro sheets, and their formulas are processed in sequence from top to bottom. The purpose of function macros is to perform calculations, not to carry out commands. For this reason, you cannot record function macros, and you cannot run them with shortcut keys.

Understanding Custom Functions

Like Microsoft Excel's built-in functions, custom functions consist of a name followed by a pair of parentheses, between which you supply the arguments Excel will use when calculating the function. Each custom function must contain the following elements, and the elements must occur in the sequence listed:

Element	Explanation
ARGUMENT function	You include one ARGUMENT function for each of the arguments to be supplied when you run the function macro. Generally, the first argument of an ARGUMENT function is a name enclosed in quotation marks. This name is then used by the formulas that follow.
Formula(s)	You can include one or more formulas to actually perform the calculations.
RETURN function	This function takes one argument: the address of the cell in the macro sheet that performs the final computation. The function returns the result of this cell to the worksheet.

In addition, you can include a RESULT function at the beginning of a macro to specify that the result of your function is to be a certain type of data. (You probably won't use the RESULT function until you have more experience with macros.)

Creating a Custom Function

To see the difference between command macros and function macros, let's create a typical function macro. Suppose you have to review the accuracy of the 1990 W-2 forms your company is about to send to its employees. You need a function that computes the amount of Social Security (FICA) taxes that should have been withheld for each employee. The function should accept the employee's total wages as an argument and return the appropriate amount of FICA withholding.

The tax to be withheld for 1990 is 7.65 percent of taxable wages. However, the maximum amount of 1990 wages subject to the tax is $51,300. If the employee's wages are greater than $51,300, you want to calculate 7.65 percent of $51,300. If the wages are less than or equal to $51,300, you want to calculate 7.65 percent of the total wages.

Before you open a new macro sheet and begin creating this custom function, take a minute to think about the calculation itself. If you name the cell containing the employee's earnings *WAGES*, you can use the following formula to calculate the 1990 FICA tax:

=IF(WAGES>51300,0.0765*51300,0.0765*WAGES)

You'll recognize the IF function from Chapter 2, "Using Formulas and Functions." In this formula, the IF function tests whether the wages are above $51,300 and calculates the FICA tax accordingly.

Now that you've worked out the formula, open a new macro sheet and save it under the name *FIN*. (You can use this macro sheet to store a library of custom financial functions.) The custom function you will create in this macro sheet has the three required elements: one ARGUMENT function, one formula, and the obligatory RETURN function.

To create the custom function that computes the amount of FICA tax, follow these steps:

1. Enter *FICA* in cell A1 as the macro name.

 We chose the name FICA *because it is short, yet descriptive. When naming macros, remember that brief names like* FICA *are preferable to long names like* Social_Security.

2. Enter the following functions in the specified cells of the macro sheet:

Cell	Function
A2	=ARGUMENT("WAGES")
A3	=IF(WAGES>51300,0.0765*51300,0.0765*WAGES)
A4	=RETURN(A3)

3. Select cell A1, and then choose the Define Name command from the Formula menu. A dialog box appears with the name *FICA* in the Name text box.

4. Choose the Function option in the Macro group.

5. Click OK, or press Enter.

You have defined the FICA function, which has one argument, *Wages*, which is passed to the formula that performs the calculation.

Using the FICA Custom Function

To test your latest creation, follow these steps:

1. Open a new, blank worksheet.

2. Enter the following formula in cell B1:

   ```
   =FIN.XLM!FICA(A1)
   ```

3. Enter *40000* in cell A1. Microsoft Excel returns a value of 3060 (7.65 percent of $40,000) in cell B1.

4. Enter *100000* in cell A1. Excel returns a value of 3924.45 (7.65 percent of $51,300) in cell B1.

  If you obtained different results or received an error message, check for typographical errors by comparing your macro with Figure 12-3. If you don't find any errors in the macro, check the name you assigned to the macro.

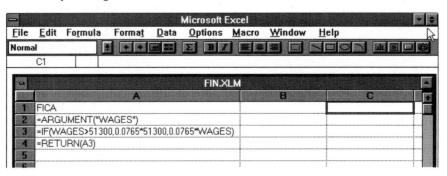

FIGURE 12-3. *A macro that computes Social Security tax.*

ADVANCED MACRO FEATURES

Microsoft Excel offers many macro features that are beyond the scope of this book. We will quickly review three advanced macro features here: using add-in macros (specifically the *Debug* macro), branching to *subroutines*, and creating custom dialog boxes. For information about more advanced features, see the Microsoft Excel documentation.

Using the Microsoft Excel Add-In Macros

Microsoft Excel includes a number of *add-in* macros, which are stored in the LIBRARY subdirectory. (You can use the LIBRARY subdirectory only if you elected to install the Macro Library when you ran the Excel Setup program.) Add-in macros work a little differently from ordinary macros. As they run, they appear to be part of the Excel program itself, rather than separate entities. You'll see an example of an add-in macro in a minute.

 The Microsoft Excel package also includes several useful "sample models." Most of the models are worksheets, but some are worksheet/macro sheet combinations. The models are useful, and they might inspire you to create similar templates of your own.

You can create your own add-in macros, but this process is complex and beyond the scope of this book. The purpose of this discussion is simply to familiarize you with some of the helpful tools provided with the program.

Microsoft Excel's add-in macros offer a variety of aids. For example, the *Add-In Functions* macro (ADDINFNS.XLA) adds six additional worksheet functions, and the *Worksheet Auditor* macro (AUDIT.XLA) helps you quickly find errors in worksheets. Another useful add-in macro is *Debug* (DEBUG.XLA), which we'll explore a little further as a good illustration of how you can customize Excel for specific purposes. The *Debug* macro is designed to save you time and frustration as you create macros.

Using the *Debug* macro

The *Debug* macro temporarily removes the Microsoft Excel menu bar and substitutes its own custom menu bar. To see how this part of the *Debug* macro works, follow these steps:

1. Open the DEBUG.XLA file (located in the LIBRARY subdirectory).

2. Select the Macro menu. Then notice that the *Debug* macro has altered this menu:

3. Open a macro sheet.

4. Choose the Debug command. The following menu bar and menu are displayed:

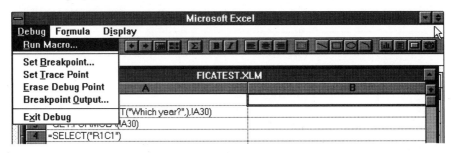

The *Debug* macro provides a quick means of specifying *tracepoints* and *breakpoints*, which you can use when developing your own macros. A tracepoint is a point at which your macro automatically shifts into single-step mode so that you can examine its operation. A breakpoint is a cell at which the macro displays a dialog box showing key pieces of information that you have specified beforehand. The dialog box lets you see whether the macro is producing the kind of results you expect.

When debugging a large macro, you will generally find it most efficient to concentrate on one part of the macro at a time. With the *Debug* macro, you can move tracepoints around with a few mouse clicks and set breakpoints equally easily. Then you can retest the macro by choosing the Run Macro command from the Debug menu.

To illustrate breakpoints, we inserted a breakpoint in a macro that uses named cells. We chose the Set Breakpoint command from the Debug menu and then chose the Breakpoint Output command. If you choose that command now, Excel displays a dialog box similar to the one in Figure 12-4. We specified in

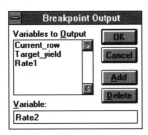

FIGURE 12-4. *The Breakpoint Output dialog box.*

this dialog box the particular information we wanted displayed in the Break-point dialog box when the macro reached the breakpoint cell. Figure 12-5 shows this dialog box, with the names of the cells on the left, and the values in the named cells at that point in the macro's operation on the right.

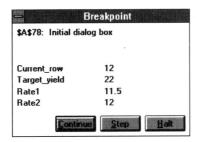

FIGURE 12-5. *The Breakpoint dialog box.*

To return to the Microsoft Excel default menu bar, choose the Exit Debug command from the Debug menu.

Creating Subroutines

You can design Microsoft Excel macros that run other macros. For example, if you want your main macro to run a macro that you've previously named *Newmacro*, you can use the function

```
=GOTO(Newmacro)
```

to transfer control to *Newmacro*. If you want the main macro to run *Newmacro* as a subroutine (that is, to have the main macro continue after *Newmacro* is done), use the function

```
=Newmacro()
```

instead of GOTO.

By using IF functions appropriately, you can even cause the main macro to branch to different macros, depending on the data. Figure 12-6 on the next page shows such a macro, which runs both command and function macros. Take some time to figure out how the macro works.

	A	B
	Microsoft Excel - FICATEST.XLM	
	File Edit Formula Format Data Options Macro Window Help	
	Normal	
	C1	
1	ficatest	
2	=FORMULA(INPUT("Which year?",),IA30)	
3	=GET.FORMULA(IA30)	
4	=SELECT("R1C1")	
5	=FORMULA("With wages of:")	
6	=FORMULA(INPUT("Enter wages:",),ID1)	
7	=IF(IA30=1990,GOTO(Lastyear),GOTO(Thisyear))	
8		
9	Lastyear	Thisyear
10	=SELECT("R3C1")	=SELECT("R3C1")
11	=FORMULA("1990 withholding should be:")	=FORMULA("1991 withholding should be:")
12	=SELECT("R3C4")	=SELECT("R3C4")
13	=Flca90(IA1)	=Flca91(IA1)
14	=FORMULA(A13)	=FORMULA(B13)
15	=RETURN()	=RETURN()
16		
17		
18	Flca90	Flca91
19	=ARGUMENT("WAGES")	=ARGUMENT("WAGES")
20	=IF(WAGES>51300,0.0765*51300,0.0765*WAGES)	=IF(WAGES>55200,0.0765*55200,0.0765*WAGE
21	=RETURN(A20)	=RETURN(B20)
22		

FIGURE 12-6. *A macro with conditional branching.*

Creating Custom Dialog Boxes

In Chapter 11, "Creating Macros," you learned how to create a macro that asks the user to enter a value. But what if you need the user to enter different types of data? You could create a long series of INPUT functions, but Microsoft Excel provides an easier method for interacting with the user. Excel's custom dialog box feature allows you to create your own dialog boxes, tailored to a specific situation. Although creating dialog boxes may seem like a highly technical process, the Dialog Editor program provided with Excel makes the process easier and much more intuitive.

If you chose to install the Dialog Editor when you first installed Excel and if you have not made any modifications to the standard Excel setup, the Dialog Editor icon (shown below) appears in the Microsoft Excel 3.0 group window:

Clicking the icon starts the program and displays an empty dialog box. You choose items from the Dialog Editor menus to create elements such as option and command buttons, which you can then position using the mouse.

A detailed discussion of the Dialog Editor is beyond the scope of this book. However, you can get an idea of how it works by looking at Figure 12-7. Here, a fairly complex dialog box is "under construction." From the visual image in Figure 12-7, the Dialog Editor will create specifications that you can copy into a macro sheet as part of a macro. When you run the macro from within Excel, the dialog box in Figure 12-8 appears on the screen.

You can also add new commands to the Excel menus, or you can design custom menus from scratch. For more information on these topics, consult the Microsoft Excel documentation.

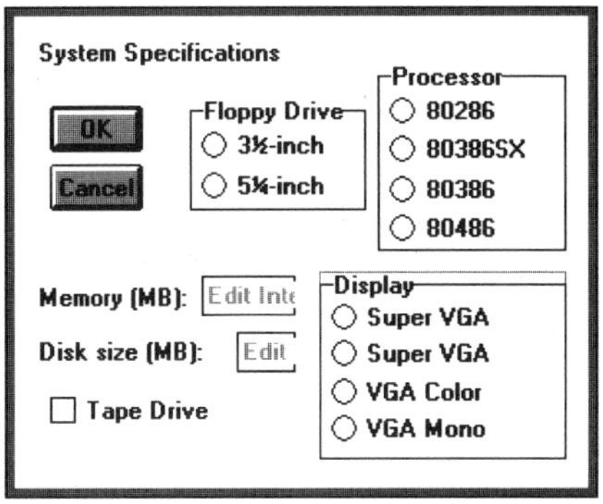

FIGURE 12-7. *A dialog box under construction in the Dialog Editor.*

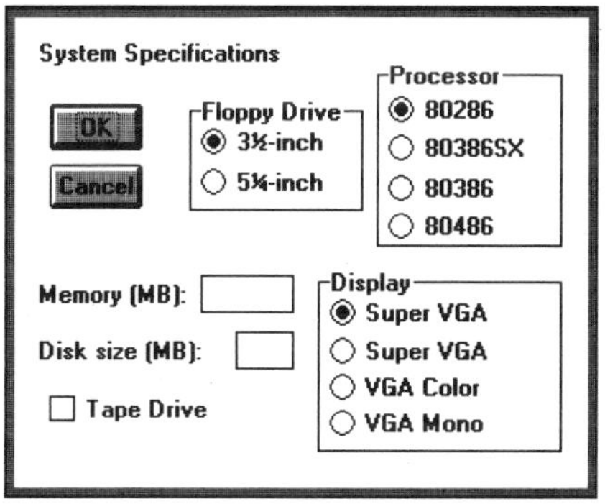

FIGURE 12-8. *The dialog box from Figure 12-7, as it is displayed in Excel.*

GETTING THE MOST FROM YOUR MACROS

At their simplest level, Microsoft Excel macros are easy to design and create. As you gain more experience, you'll likely create macros of increasing complexity. Here are a couple of tips for ways to avoid some of the pitfalls you might encounter.

Documenting Your Macros

Although Microsoft Excel uses English-like macro commands, you can lose your bearings when you try to follow macros you created some time ago. For that reason, be sure you document your macros as you write them. Figure 12-9 shows a macro with comments in the adjacent column. While running a macro, Excel ignores any entries that don't begin with an equal sign, so you can even intersperse comments within the macro itself.

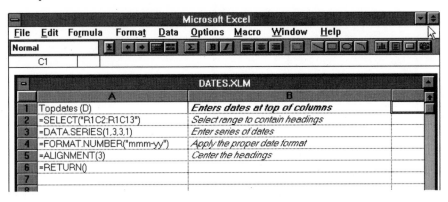

FIGURE 12-9. *A documented macro.*

Avoiding Overconfidence

Remember that simply because a macro runs without generating any error messages doesn't mean that it's error free. The errors that are hardest to detect, and thus the most dangerous, are logical errors. A macro with logical errors can run without a hitch and still not do what you want it to do.

No magic slate is available to wipe out logical errors, but you can take two precautions to skew the odds in your favor:

- Design complex macros in stages and test the stages individually before you bring them together.

■ Document your macros as you create them. Explaining your reasoning will alert you to possible logical errors. Documentation can also help eliminate logical errors when macros are revised.

GOING ON FROM HERE

We've really only scratched the surface where writing Microsoft Excel macros is concerned. As you will see if you run some of the samples provided with Excel, macros can do amazing things. You can even create macros that work as complete mini-applications that other people can use to perform specific tasks, even if they don't know much about Excel.

You don't have to stop here. With perseverance and a little ingenuity, you can continue learning about macros on your own. You might start by playing around with some of the macros you created in this section. For example, you might change the *Topdates* macro into one that extends across 24 columns. Or, using the *FICA* function macro as a starting point, you might design a macro that calculates your federal income-tax liability. By studying the tasks you perform on a daily, weekly, and monthly basis, you will probably find dozens of opportunities to increase your efficiency with macros. The power is there for the taking.

SECTION V

Appendixes

Appendix A

Installing Microsoft Excel

This appendix briefly reviews the procedure for installing Microsoft Excel. Before installing Excel, you must first install Microsoft Windows version 3. Consult the Microsoft Windows *User's Guide* for details on installing the Windows program.

To use Excel, you must run Windows in either Standard or 386 Enhanced mode. See the Microsoft Windows documentation for more information. Also see the Microsoft Excel *Getting Started* manual for details on the hardware required to run Excel.

When installing Excel, you will be asked to supply the drive letter of your hard disk (C or D, for example) and the name of the directory in which you want to install Microsoft Excel. The Setup program assumes that you'll use a directory called EXCEL, but you can specify a different directory.

If you've used Excel with earlier versions of Windows, you are accustomed to running the Excel Setup program from the DOS prompt. Microsoft Excel version 3 requires you to run Setup from *within* Windows. To install Excel, follow these steps:

1. Start Microsoft Windows.

2. Choose the Run command from Program Manager's File menu. The following dialog box appears.

3. Type the following in the Command Line text box:

   `a:setup`

4. Insert the Microsoft Excel for Windows Setup disk in drive A, and press Enter. In the User Information dialog box that appears, enter a user name and an organization name. Then click Continue, or press Enter.

5. Another dialog box asks you to verify the information you have entered. Click Change to go back to the previous dialog box and correct the information, or click Continue to proceed with installation. When you click Continue, the following dialog box appears:

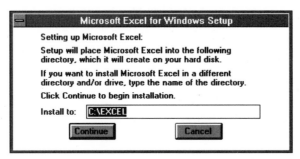

6. Press Enter to select the default C:\EXCEL directory, or enter the name of a different directory.

7. If you enter a directory name that does not presently exist on your hard disk, Excel displays a message stating that the directory does not exist and asking you to confirm that you want to create the directory. Click Yes. The Setup Options dialog box appears:

```
┌─────────────────────────────────────────────────────────┐
│ ─        Microsoft Excel Setup Options                    │
│ ☒ Microsoft Excel            ☒ Macro Library Files        │
│ ☒ Microsoft Excel Tutorial   ☒ Microsoft Excel Solver     │
│ ☒ Dialog Editor              ☒ Q+E  [ Select Drivers ]    │
│ ☒ Macro Translator                                        │
│ Space Required:   5,255K                                  │
│ Space Available:  21,496K         [ Setup ]  [ Cancel ]   │
└─────────────────────────────────────────────────────────┘
```

8. Provided that you have enough space on your hard disk, go ahead and click Setup, or press Enter, to install Microsoft Excel and its associated programs and data files.

By default, Excel and all its associated files are copied to your hard disk, taking up over 5 MB of disk space. The bottom-left corner of the Setup Options dialog box shows the total amount of disk space required for the selected programs and the amount of space available on the specified disk. Table A-1 describes the components of the Excel package.

Component	Description
Microsoft Excel	The Excel program itself.
Microsoft Excel Tutorial	A self-running program that teaches you how to use Excel.
Dialog Editor	A program that allows you to create custom dialog boxes by manipulating images on the screen (discussed in Chapter 12).
Macro Translator	A program that translates Lotus 1-2-3 macros into Excel macros (discussed in Appendix C).
Macro Library	Excel models and macros (described in Chapter 12).
Microsoft Excel Solver	A computational program that helps you find mathematically optimal solutions to complex problems.
Q+E	A database program that allows you to access files from Excel and a variety of database systems.

TABLE A-1. *Components of the Microsoft Excel package.*

If you proceed when the space available is less than the space required, the Setup program displays the following dialog box and prevents you from continuing:

When you see this message, you must decide how to proceed. You can do the following:

— Turn off options in the Setup Options dialog box until the space available is greater than the space required.

— Exit from the Setup program, delete non-Excel files from your hard disk to make room for Excel, and then run Setup again. (Note that you must install the Macro Library files to follow some of the examples in Chapter 12, ''More Advanced Macro Techniques.'')

9. After you complete the Setup Options dialog box and click Setup or press Enter, Excel displays a message asking if you want to turn on Excel's special Lotus 1-2-3 help features. (These features help you make the transition from Lotus 1-2-3 to Excel.) If you click Enable, you will be able to access Lotus 1-2-3 Help simply by pressing the slash (/) key.

10. The Setup program then displays a dialog box that advises you of the progress of the installation. At appropriate points, Setup instructs you to insert specific Excel disks. When Setup has finished, it displays a message that installation is complete. Click OK to close the message box.

You can then double-click the Microsoft Excel 3.0 icon in the Microsoft Excel 3.0 group (created during the installation process) to start Excel. The first time you run Excel, you are welcomed by a short preview of some of Excel's exciting new features. You can choose to continue or exit this preview.

The Excel screens appearing in this book display the tool bar near the top of the Microsoft Excel window. If you do not have a mouse installed, the tool bar doesn't appear on your screen.

The next time you want to start an Excel work session, simply open the Microsoft Excel 3.0 group window in Program Manager, and then double-click the Microsoft Excel 3.0 icon. You can also start Excel by typing *win excel* at the DOS prompt.

Appendix B

Using Microsoft Excel with Other Microsoft Windows Applications

This appendix's goal is to introduce ways in which you can maximize the benefits of working with Microsoft Windows. Using Microsoft Excel effectively with other Windows applications and using the Windows environment to switch quickly from one application to another will boost your productivity.

RUNNING MULTIPLE WINDOWS APPLICATIONS

You can start a Microsoft Windows application in two ways. The simplest way is to double-click the icon for the program in the Program Manager window, as explained in Chapter 1, "Getting Acquainted," and in Appendix A, "Installing Microsoft Excel." Or you can choose the Run command from the Program Manager File menu, as shown in Figure B-1 on the next page, and then enter the complete pathname (the drive, directory, and file name, separated by backslashes) for the program you want to run.

317

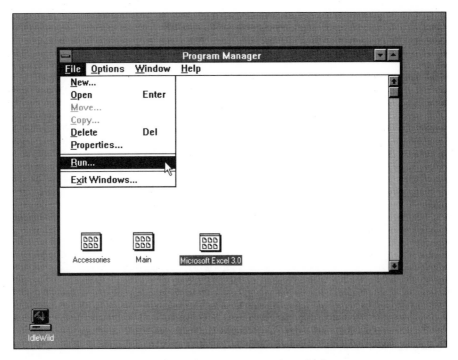

FIGURE B-1. *Starting Excel using the Run command on the Program Manager File menu.*

Having started one Windows application, you can start another one by using either of the two methods just described. To start a program whose icon is obscured by a window, simply uncover the icon by minimizing the window. (We'll show you how to minimize a window in a minute.)

ORGANIZING THE SCREEN

Obviously, the more screen space you devote to an application, the more data you can view on the screen. To expand an application window so that it fills the entire screen, click the Maximize button (in the top-right corner of the application window):

When an application is maximized, the Maximize button looks like this:

Clicking this button (the Restore button) restores the application window to its former size and position on the screen.

When several applications are displayed at one time, you can reduce clutter by shrinking some of them to icons at the bottom of the screen. Simply click the Minimize button (to the left of the Maximize/Restore button):

To use a minimized application, redisplay its window by double-clicking the appropriate icon.

SWITCHING BETWEEN OPEN APPLICATIONS

When you maximize an application window, other Windows applications you have started remain open. You can activate another open application and quickly switch between applications in one of three ways:

- Restore the maximized application to its former size and position, and then click the icon of the application you want to use.

- Press Alt-Esc to display the Windows Task Manager dialog box (shown in Figure B-2), and then double-click the name of the application you want to work with.

- If the application you want to activate has not been minimized and part of its window is showing on the screen, click that window.

FIGURE B-2. *The Windows Task Manager dialog box.*

Whichever method you choose, the activated application is then displayed in a window on top of the "pile" of windows on the screen.

SHARING DATA BETWEEN APPLICATIONS

One benefit of running multiple Microsoft Windows applications is that you can copy data between applications. For example, suppose you want to include the financial information shown in the Microsoft Excel worksheet in Figure B-3 in a letter you are writing with Microsoft Word for Windows.

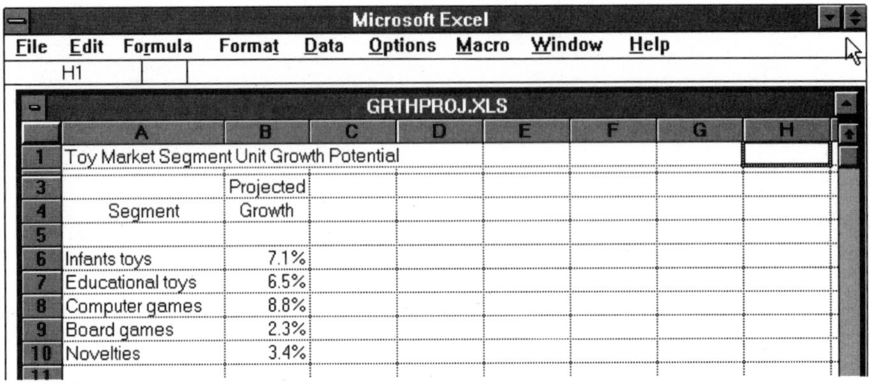

FIGURE B-3 *Worksheet data to be copied to Word for Windows.*

First, open the appropriate worksheet. (For this example, create the worksheet and enter the data shown in Figure B-3.) Then follow these steps:

1. Resize the Microsoft Excel application window (by dragging the title bar), and reposition it (by dragging the window borders).

2. Start the Word for Windows program (if it is not already running) by double-clicking the Word for Windows icon or by choosing the Run command from Program Manager's File menu.

3. Resize the Word for Windows application window so that your screen looks like the following screen. (Adjust the Excel window if necessary.)

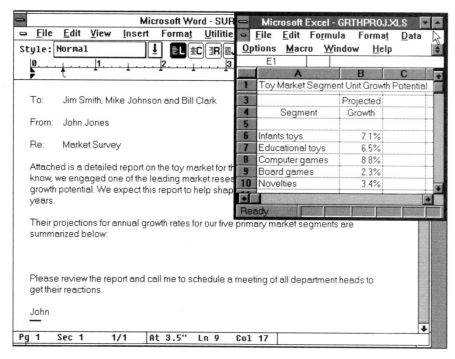

4. Select the Excel worksheet range you want to copy. (In this example, select A3:B10.)

5. Choose the Copy command from the Excel Edit menu to copy the data to the Windows Clipboard (the temporary holding place in your computer's memory).

6. Activate the Word for Windows window and move the cursor to the position in the document where you want to insert the worksheet data.

7. Choose the Paste command from the Word for Windows Edit menu to paste the data from the Clipboard into the Word document.

Your screen now looks like Figure B-4 on the next page. Word for Windows pastes the information into the document as a table, so the information is surrounded by gridlines.

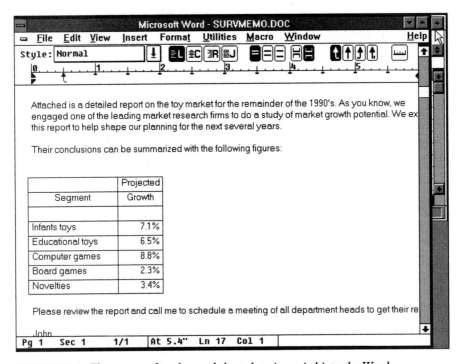

FIGURE B-4. *The screen after the worksheet data is copied into the Word for Windows document.*

Displaying the Excel worksheet and the Word for Windows document side by side makes it easy to quickly copy data from one to the other. However, if your computer's memory is limited, you may not be able to run two large applications simultaneously. In that case, follow these steps:

1. Select the Excel worksheet data you want to copy, and then copy the data to the Windows Clipboard.

2. Close Excel.

3. Start Word for Windows, open the document you want, and move the cursor to the position where you want to insert the worksheet data.

4. Paste the data from the Clipboard into the document.

With a little experimentation, you'll soon develop valuable techniques that will help you use Microsoft Windows to combine Microsoft Excel productively with other Windows applications.

Appendix C

Making the Transition from Lotus 1-2-3

This appendix will help experienced Lotus 1-2-3 users switch to Microsoft Excel version 3. You'll be pleased to know that you can use all your 1-2-3 data files in Microsoft Excel worksheets. In addition, Excel provides aids to ease the transition from Lotus 1-2-3 to Excel, including an online command cross-reference and a utility for translating 1-2-3 macros into Microsoft Excel macros.

WORKING WITH LOTUS 1-2-3 DATA FILES

Importing a Lotus 1-2-3 data file into Microsoft Excel couldn't be simpler—you choose the Open command from the File menu, select the correct drive and directory, type the name of the Lotus 1-2-3 file you want to import, and click OK or press Enter. You must include the appropriate filename extension (*.WKS* for version 1A, *.WK1* for versions 2 and 2.2, or *.WK3* for version 3) so that Excel doesn't look for data files in its own format.

 To list only the files with .WKS, .WK1, or .WK3 extensions, you can change the entry in the File Name box to ∗.wk?, *and then select the file you want to open from the Files list box.*

Generally, the file-opening process works quickly and smoothly. In the event that Excel has difficulty opening a Lotus 1-2-3 file, Excel displays a dialog box giving the address of the cell that caused the problem. (The dialog box is not pictured here because, despite our best efforts, we were unable to generate it—evidence that problems in importing 1-2-3 formulas are rare.)

Certain types of information do not carry over from 1-2-3 to Excel. For example, graphic pictures in 1-2-3 version 3 worksheets cannot be imported into Excel, and all Lotus 1-2-3 text and row formatting is lost. When you open an imported Lotus 1-2-3 worksheet in Excel, gridlines are turned off, and when you open an imported Lotus 1-2-3 Release 3 worksheet that contains linked formulas, Excel prompts you to specify the pathname of the supporting worksheet.

When you open a Lotus 1-2-3 file that contains a graph, Excel displays a dialog box asking whether you want to convert the graph as well as the data. If you click Yes, Excel creates a new chart for each Lotus 1-2-3 graph.

> *Although Lotus 1-2-3 data files generally can be loaded into Microsoft Excel without any problems, you may occasionally find that certain incompatibilities cause Microsoft Excel to change your data. For complete details on these incompatibilities, see the Microsoft Excel documentation.*

Saving Lotus 1-2-3 Files in Excel Format

Unless you anticipate that the Lotus 1-2-3 file you are importing into Excel will need to be exported back into Lotus 1-2-3 later, you should convert the file to a Microsoft Excel document. Choose the Save As command from the File menu, click the Options button to expand the Save As dialog box as shown in Figure C-1, and then select the Normal option. Excel applies its file format and extension to the data file. If Excel encounters a problem converting a cell formula, it attaches a note to the cell in the converted worksheet.

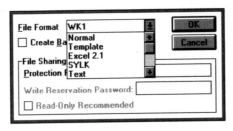

FIGURE C-1. *Using the Save As command to convert a Lotus 1-2-3 data file to a Microsoft Excel document.*

Saving Excel Files in Lotus 1-2-3 Format

If you need to export an Excel-format file to Lotus 1-2-3, you can save the file in any of the Lotus 1-2-3 formats (.*WKS*, .*WK1*, or .*WK3*). Simply choose the Save As command from the File menu, click the Options button, and specify the desired format, as we explained in Chapter 1, "Getting Acquainted."

Because Microsoft Excel has options and features not found in Lotus 1-2-3, some formatting and other attributes are lost when you save an Excel file in Lotus 1-2-3 format. For example, embedded graphics, font formatting, cell borders, and center alignment of numeric values don't carry over to Lotus 1-2-3 data files. In addition, references to rows beyond 8192 don't convert accurately to Lotus 1-2-3 Releases 2 and 3, and references to rows beyond 2048 don't convert accurately to Lotus 1-2-3 Release 1A.

When the worksheet being converted contains functions not offered by Lotus 1-2-3, Excel displays an alert box similar to the one shown in Figure C-2. The message identifies the problem cells, to help you correct the problem when you open the file in Lotus 1-2-3.

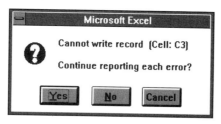

FIGURE C-2. *This alert box identifies cells containing Excel functions not offered by Lotus 1-2-3.*

LOTUS 1-2-3 COMMAND EQUIVALENTS

When you need to know how to carry out a familiar Lotus 1-2-3 command in Microsoft Excel, the answer is always close at hand. If you enabled Help for Lotus 1-2-3 when you installed Excel, you need only press the slash (/) key. (Appendix B, "Using Excel with Other Microsoft Windows Applications," gives more details.) If you didn't enable Help for Lotus 1-2-3, choose Lotus 1-2-3 from the Help menu. Excel displays the dialog box shown in Figure C-3 on the next page.

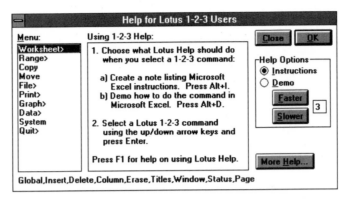

FIGURE C-3. *The Help For Lotus 1-2-3 Users dialog box.*

Next, select the appropriate Lotus 1-2-3 menu from the Menu list box, and move through the menus as you would if you were using Lotus 1-2-3. When a menu name is highlighted, commands on that menu appear at the bottom of the dialog box. You can also use the keyboard to move backward and forward through the menus, just as you can in Lotus 1-2-3. Pressing Esc takes you back to the previous menu. Pressing the first letter of a command name selects that command. If you are using a mouse, instructions on replicating the command in Microsoft Excel appear in a text box labeled To Perform Command In Microsoft Excel in the middle of the dialog box. Figure C-4 shows the instructions for replicating the Lotus 1-2-3 Range Protect command.

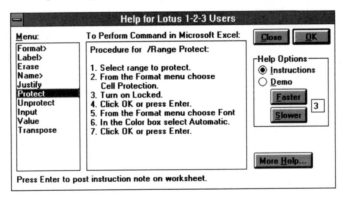

FIGURE C-4. *The Help instructions for replicating the Lotus 1-2-3 Range Protect command in Microsoft Excel.*

Reading the instructions in the text box may provide the quick reminder you need to get right back to work again. However, if you still feel a little shaky about your knowledge at this point, you can display the instructions in the worksheet itself. Select the Instructions option in the Help Options group to create a note in your worksheet that lists the steps you should take. Figure C-5 shows the worksheet note for the Lotus 1-2-3 Range Protect command.

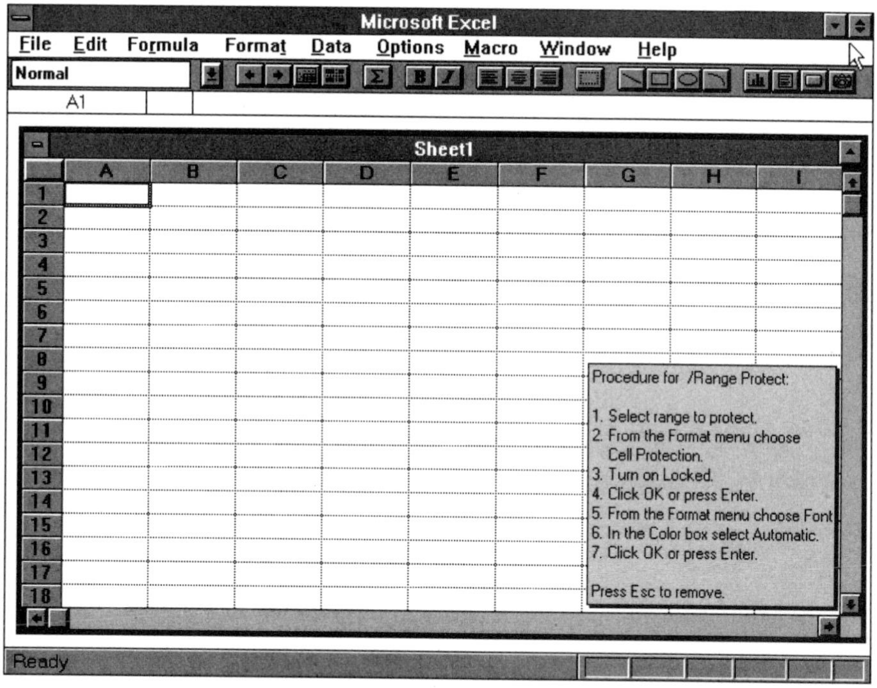

FIGURE C-5. *The Help instructions for the Lotus 1-2-3 Range Protect command, displayed in a worksheet.*

Alternatively, you can ask Excel Help to demonstrate how to create the equivalent Excel command. Be sure the Demo option in the Help Options group is selected, and then press Enter. Excel displays a dialog box that requests the information needed to carry out the command. The nature of the information requested varies depending on the particular command. The dialog box shown in Figure C-6 on the next page requests the information needed to carry out the Lotus 1-2-3 Worksheet Global Column-Width command.

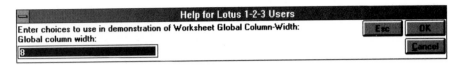

FIGURE C-6. *The dialog box that requests information needed to carry out the Lotus 1-2-3 Worksheet Global Column-Width command.*

Enter the required information (in this case, the desired column width), and press Enter. Excel then demonstrates the steps for performing that operation on your worksheet.

If you want to investigate the equivalent Excel command further before carrying it out, you can select the More Help button in the Help For Lotus 1-2-3 Users dialog box. Excel then moves you directly to its Help text file and displays information about the equivalent command.

Even if a Lotus 1-2-3 command doesn't have an exact equivalent in Microsoft Excel, the Help For Lotus 1-2-3 Users dialog box guides you to a solution. For example, Figure C-7 shows the dialog box for the Lotus 1-2-3 Data Distribution command. This command has no Microsoft Excel equivalent, but the dialog box advises that the CROSSTABS add-in macro, provided with Excel, does the same thing.

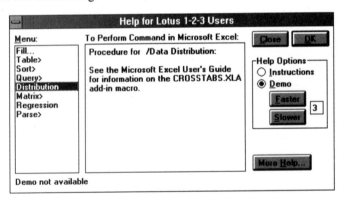

FIGURE C-7. *The Help For Lotus 1-2-3 dialog box for the Lotus 1-2-3 Data Distribution command.*

LOTUS 1-2-3 FUNCTION EQUIVALENTS

To find the Microsoft Excel equivalent of a specific Lotus 1-2-3 function, select the Switching From Lotus 1-2-3 topic from the Microsoft Excel Help index. Then select the Functions topic to display a list of Lotus 1-2-3 functions indexed to their closest Excel equivalents, as shown in Figure C-8. For additional information about any Microsoft Excel function, click the function name (or select the name with the arrow keys, and press Enter).

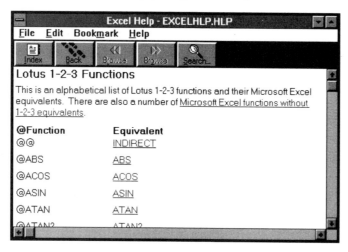

FIGURE C-8. *Lotus 1-2-3 functions and their equivalent Microsoft Excel functions, displayed in an Excel Help window.*

TRANSLATING LOTUS 1-2-3 MACROS

If you've been using Lotus 1-2-3 for a long time, you've undoubtedly made use of Lotus 1-2-3 macros. So you can preserve as much of your previous work as possible, Microsoft Excel includes the Macro Translation Assistant, a program that translates Lotus 1-2-3 macros into Microsoft Excel macros.

Macro translation is a complex process. Because of the radical differences between the Lotus 1-2-3 and Microsoft Excel macro languages, it is also an imperfect process. Most complex Lotus 1-2-3 macros generate errors as they are translated. You should think of Excel's Macro Translation Assistant as a helpful keystroke-saver, rather than as a fail-safe conversion device. For more information about macro translation, see the Microsoft Excel documentation or the Switching From Lotus 1-2-3 topic in Excel Help.

Index

Special Characters

\# (pound sign)
  display of 65
  as placeholder in numeric formats
    108
  sort order of 244
$ (dollar signs), display of 107
& (ampersand), sort order of 244
* (asterisk), use in searches 256
< (less than), as comparison
    operator 56, 257–58
<= (less than or equal to), as
    comparison operator 56
<> (not equal to), as comparison
    operator 56
= (equal sign), as comparison
    operator 56, 257–58
> (greater than), as comparison
    operator 56, 257–58
>= (greater than or equal to), as
    comparison operator 56
? (question mark), use in searches
    256
@ (''at'' sign), sort order of 244

A

add-in macros 300–1
addresses, cell 9, 42–43
  fixed 81–83
  relative 81–83
alert messages 53–54, 61–65
aligning data 113–15
Alignment buttons 114
Alignment command 113–18

amortization, formula for 60–61
ampersand (&), sort order of 244
AND criteria 259–60
Application Control menu 21
applications. *See also specific*
    applications
  sharing data between 144–45,
    320–22, 323–25
  using Excel with other 317–22
area charts 196–97
ARGUMENT function 298
arguments, in functions 44
Arrange Workgroup command
    148–50
arrows, in charts 187
ASCII format, saving data in 34
asterisk (*), use in searches 256
''at'' sign (@), sort order of 244
Attach Text command 188–90
Autosum button 47
AVERAGE function 54–55
axes
  definition of 187
  formatting 210–12
  labels for 189–90
  scaling 221–22

B

bar charts 195
bold type 118–20, 168
booting
  Excel 5–6
  Windows 4
Border command 122–26
borders 124, 215–16

CSV (comma-separated format),
saving in 34
custom function macros 297–300.
See also macros
Cut command 17, 76

D

data. *See also* cells
aligning 113–15
clearing 83–84
consolidating 152–53
entering and correcting 25–30,
91–92
exporting 144–45, 320–22
foreign formats for 33–34
importing 144–45, 320–22
moving and copying 74–78
via outlines 95–98
between programs 144–45,
320–22
between worksheets 136–37
positioning in cells 113–18
protecting from change 86–91
sharing between applications
320–22, 323–25
summarizing from multiple
worksheets 138–41, 152–53
transferring 136–37, 144–45,
320–22
databases
creating 233–42
and data forms 236–42, 265–66
dBASE program 34
definition of 232–33
fields
computed 235
definition of 232
input 237–39
Q+E program 313

databases *(continued)*
records
definition of 232
deleting 241–42, 267
editing 241
extracting 252–55
finding 239–41, 252–57,
264–65
selection criteria for (*see*
selection criteria)
sorting 242–49
wildcard characters in 256
data forms 236–42, 265–66
Data Interchange Format 34
Data menu 19
data series, changing plot order of
205–6
DATA.SERIES function 279
data-series markers 179, 187, 217–18
dates
display formats for 109–13
functions involving 67–68
in headers and footers 168
in worksheets 65–68
DATEVALUE function 68
DAY function 67
DAYS360 function 68
dBASE format, saving data in 34
debugging macros 291–92, 301–3,
306–7
Debug add-in macro 301–3
decimals, display of 108–9
Define Name command 68–69
deleting
cell names 71
cells 81
columns 80
database records 241–42, 267
data from cells 83–84

investments, assessing value of 58–60

italic type 118–20, 168

J

justifying text 117–18

K

keyboard. *See also specific keys*
  choosing menu commands with 14–15
  entering range in function with 46
  selecting
    cells with 10–12
    dialog-box options with 23–24
  status indicators 7
keys, for sorting 242

L

labels 164–67, 189–90
landscape orientation 170
language for macros 277–80
legends 187, 190
"less than or equal to" sign (<=), as comparison operator 56
"less than" sign (<), as comparison operator 56, 257–58
LIBRARY subdirectory 32, 300
line charts 195–96
linked worksheets 137–44
loans, amortizing 60–61
locking cells 87–88
logical functions 56–57
Lotus 1-2-3 format
  moving to Excel from 323–29
  saving data in 33–34

M

macro
  functions 278–80, 282–83
  language 277–80
  recorder 272–74
  sheets 282–83
Macro Library 313
Macro menu 19–20
macros
  add-in 300–3
  cell referencing in 285–87
  complex 294–97
  creating 272–77, 294–97
  and custom dialog boxes 304–5
  debugging 291–92, 301–3, 306–7
  design tips for 306–7
  documenting 306–7
  editing 280–81
  fixing errors in 291–92, 301–3, 306–7
  function 297–300
  input-requesting 287–91
  Lotus 1-2-3 329
  recorder range for 283
  recording 272–74
  running 274–75
  storing 283–85
  subroutines in 303–4
Macro Translation Assistant program 313, 329
margins 158, 169
markers, data-series 179, 187, 217–18
mathematical operations, order of precedence 41–42
MAX function 55
Maximize button 7, 8
memory, linked worksheets and 138
menu bar 7

S

saving
  charts 182–83
  in earlier Excel format 33
  in foreign format 33–34
  worksheets (*see* worksheets,
    saving)
Scale command 222
scatter diagrams 198–200
scroll
  arrows 12
  bars 8
  box 12, 13
Scroll Lock key 10
search criteria. *See* selection criteria
searching
  databases (*see* databases)
  for text 256–57
  with wildcard characters 256
SECOND function 67
Select Chart command 215–17
SELECT functions 287
selecting
  cells 10–12
  chart objects 187
  records (*see* databases, records;
    selection criteria)
selection criteria
  alternative 261–63
  AND 259–60
  combining 259–60
  comparison 257–58
  computed 263–64
  in data forms 265–66
  entering 250–51
  OR 261–63
  setting range 251–52
Select Visible Cells button 97–98
Series command 163–64, 247–48

SERIES function 227
Set Criteria command 251–52, 260,
  261
Set Database command 235–36
Set Extract command 252, 254–55
Set Page Break command 171–73
Set Preferred command 201
Set Print Area command 161
Set Print Titles command 164–67
Set Recorder command 283–85
Setup button 159
shading cells 125–26
Shift key 12
Short Menus 15
Solver program 313
sorting database records 242–49
Spacebar 12
starting
  Excel 5–6
  Windows 4
status bar 7
Step mode 291–92
Stop Recorder command 273, 276
subroutines, in macros 303–4
SUM functions 44–45, 47–49, 85
summarizing data 138–41, 152–53
SYLK format, saving data in 33

T

templates
  saving work as 33
  for worksheet formats 132–33
text. *See also* data
  in charts 188–92, 212–14
  entering and correcting 25–27,
    29–30
  formatting 113–15, 118–22, 168
  justifying 117–18

worksheets *(continued)*
  saving 31–34
    in other formats 144–45
    as templates 33, 132–33
  summarizing data from multiple
    138–41, 152–53
  using groups of (*see* workgroups;
    workspaces)
workspaces 150–51
  workgroups vs. 150
wrapping text 116–17, 118

X

X axis, labels 189–90
XY charts 198–200

Y

Y axis, labels 189–90
YEAR function 67

Z

Zoom button, print preview and 157

About the Author

Ralph Soucie is a C.P.A. who currently consults with businesses on Microsoft Excel and Great Plains accounting software. A long-time contributing editor to *PC World* magazine, Soucie has also contributed to *The Quantum PC Report* and *Connect* magazine. He lives and works in Lake Oswego, Oregon.

The manuscript for this book was prepared and submitted to Microsoft Press in electronic form. Text files were processed and formatted using Microsoft Word.

Principal word processor: Ted Cox
Principal proofreader: Jan Perkins
Principal typographer: Ruth Pettis
Interior text designer: Darcie S. Furlan
Cover designer: Rebecca Geisler and Leilani Fortune
Cover color separator: Rainier Color

Text composition by Microsoft Press in Times Roman with display type in Times Roman Bold, using the Magna composition system, the Newgen TurboPS high-resolution PostScript printer, and the Linotronic 300 laser imagesetter.

Printed on recycled paper stock.

RUNNING MICROSOFT® EXCEL, 2nd ed.

The Complete Reference to Microsoft Excel version 3 for Windows™

This book makes a perfect companion to *Getting Started with Microsoft Excel* by Ralph Soucie. With *Getting Started* you get a great hands-on introduction to Microsoft Excel. With RUNNING MICROSOFT EXCEL, you have a comprehensive reference that will be your primary source of information and advice.

Organized by work environment, this book covers all the basics of creating spreadsheets, charts, and graphics; developing and working with databases; and building macros. In addition, learn how you can use the new features of Microsoft Excel version 3 to increase your productivity.

- combine data from spreadsheets into a convenient summary sheet
- make a smooth transition from Lotus® 1-2-3® with the customized help system
- develop 3D charts in 24 styles and rotate them in any direction
- incorporate graphic objects into your spreadsheets
- use and share Microsoft Excel spreadsheets in a workgroup
- use the Solver command to perform "what if" calculations
- use the Toolbar™ to create charts and buttons

Turn to RUNNING MICROSOFT EXCEL for quick answers to all your spreadsheet, database, and charting questions and for in-depth information on scores of topics.

Available wherever computer books are sold. Or order directly from Microsoft Press.

NO POSTAGE
NECESSARY
IF MAILED
IN THE
UNITED STATES

BUSINESS REPLY MAIL

FIRST-CLASS MAIL   PERMIT NO. 74   LA VERGNE, TN

POSTAGE WILL BE PAID BY ADDRESSEE

MICROSOFT PRESS
P O BOX 7005
LA VERGNE TN 37086-9954